the ACTS 1:8 CHALLENGE

CHALLENGE

Empowering the CHURCH to Be on MISSION

Nate Adams

Leader Guide by
Art Criscoe & Alma Rivera

LifeWay Press®
Nashville, Tennessee

ISBN 0-6331-9614-2

Dewey Decimal Classification Number: 269.2
Subject Headings: EVANGELISTIC WORK/ CHURCH/ MISSIONS--STUDY

Unless otherwise noted, all Scripture quotations are taken from the Holman Christian Standard Bible®, © Copyright 2001 Holman Bible Publishers, Nashville, TN. Used by permission.

Scripture quotations identified GNT are taken from The Good News Bible © Broadman Press 1976. Used by permission.

Scripture quotations identified NIV are taken from the The New International Version © International Bible Publishers 1973, 1978, 1984. Used by permission.

Lottie Moon Christmas Offering®, Annie Armstrong Easter Offering®, Woman's Missionary Union®, WMU®, Women on Mission®, Acteens®, Girls in Action®, and Mission Friends® are registered trademarks of Woman's Missionary Union of the Southern Baptist Convention.

We believe that the Bible has God for its author; salvation for its end; and truth, without any mixture of error, for its matter and that all Scripture is totally true and trustworthy. The 2000 statement of *The Baptist Faith and Message* is our doctrinal guideline.

To order additional copies of this resource, WRITE to LifeWay Church Resources Customer Service; One LifeWay Plaza; Nashville, TN 37234-0113; FAX (615) 251-5933; PHONE (800) 458-2772; E-MAIL *customerservice@lifeway.com*; ORDER ONLINE at *www.lifeway.com*; or VISIT the LifeWay Christian Store serving you.

Printed in the United States of America

Leadership and Adult Publishing
LifeWay Church Resources
One LifeWay Plaza
Nashville, TN 37234-0175

Contents

The Author

Nate Adams is the vice-president of Mission Mobilization at the North American Mission Board (NAMB) of the Southern Baptist Convention. His group uses print and electronic communication, missions education, and volunteerism to help churches activate their members in both short- and long-term mission service. Adams's group coordinates ministries such as World Changers, Baptist Builders, Royal Ambassadors, and Mission Service Corps and publishes resources such as *On Mission* and *Go!* magazines.

Prior to joining NAMB in 1997, Adams served for 17 years at *Christianity Today*, Incorporated, most recently as its vice-president of publishing operations. From 1994 to 1997 Adams was also an ordained, bivocational church planter in Chicago's western suburbs.

Adams has written three books in additon to *The Acts 1:8 Challenge*, including *The Home Team: Spiritual Practices for a Winning Family* (Revell, 2004), and has published articles in numerous magazines, such as *Decision, Christianity Today*, and *Campus Life*. He has written a column for *New Man* magazine and regularly contributes to the NAMB's *On Mission* and *Go!* magazines.

Adams has a bachelor-of-arts degree in communication arts from Judson College in Elgin, Illinois, and a master-of-science degree in management and the development of human resources from National-Louis University in Evanston, Illinois. He and his wife, Beth, and their three sons are members of Sugarloaf Community Church in Suwanee, Georgia.

The leader guide and the teaching tools were written by Art Criscoe and Alma Rivera. Dr. Criscoe, a full-time writer, is retired from LifeWay Christian Resources of the Southern Baptist Convention in Nashville, Tennessee. Dr. Rivera, a hematologist and an oncologist in San Juan, Puerto Rico, is the education director for the Puerto Rico/Virgin Islands Southern Baptist Association and the discipleship director for Calvary Baptist Church in San Juan.

Preface

Commitment to missions has always been a defining characteristic of Southern Baptists. Praying for lost peoples, sending devoted missionaries, and sacrificially giving so that the gospel can spread to new frontiers—these are the humble hallmarks of congregations large and small. By cooperating with other believers, every Southern Baptist can make a worldwide impact, and every church can be a worldwide mission center.

Although that missions commitment has not changed in the 21st century, it requires fresh vision and strategies. Churches today still need inspiration to care about the lost world and information to effectively pray and give. But with unprecedented wealth, mobility, and opportunities, today's churches also need to step up to new levels of involvement. New generations, in particular, need a fresh vision of God's mission to the world that is relevant and inspiring.

In the last words of the risen Lord Jesus before He ascended to heaven, we find a powerful challenge from which we can launch an exploration not only of missions but also of mission action. Acts 1:8 provides a biblical paradigm for how the Spirit-filled, Spirit-led New Testament church is to fulfill God's mission on earth until Jesus returns: " 'You will receive power when the Holy Spirit has come upon you, and you will be My witnesses in Jerusalem, in all Judea and Samaria, and to the ends of the earth' " (Acts 1:8).

This study will help believers understand Jesus' Acts 1:8 challenge and discover biblical principles the New Testament churches used to reach their mission fields. By personalizing these principles in a modern-day mission strategy, a local church can respond to Jesus' challenge by becoming actively involved in God's history-long, worldwide mission.

The local church, as a worldwide mission center, can formulate a comprehensive mission strategy that simultaneously reaches out to its community (Jerusalem), state or region (Judea), continent (Samaria), and world (ends of the earth). Over the years Southern Baptist churches have gathered into local associations and state conventions and have cooperated to establish and work through the International Mission Board and the North American Mission Board. Providentially, churches organized and networked to carry out Jesus' fourfold Acts 1:8 challenge.

In essence, Jesus' Acts 1:8 challenge calls for each local church to—
* acknowledge and accept its Great Commission responsibility to reach its Jerusalem, Judea, Samaria, and ends of the earth;
* embrace a comprehensive, integrated missions strategy that sends people, resources, and prayer to each mission field;
* work cooperatively with its association, state convention, and national agencies to maximize its impact.

Embracing its responsibility and devoting itself to God's worldwide mission strengthens a church and helps it fulfill its role in God's redemptive plan.

Jesus' Acts 1:8 challenge also calls for each denominational partner to focus on the local church as the primary channel through which God's redemptive purposes flow. The International Mission Board, the North American Mission Board, state conventions, and local associations exist to serve churches as they fulfill the Great Commission. Each denominational partner seeks to help churches form strategies and access resources to reach the mission field in which it specializes. Each entity can help your church know and assist the missionaries who work in your Acts 1:8 mission fields.

This study is part of a coordinated effort to communicate Jesus' Acts 1:8 challenge to local churches. The International Mission Board, the North American Mission Board, state conventions, and local associations are speaking with one voice—the voice of Jesus' last words on earth—to challenge individual believers and local churches to embrace their worldwide mission responsibility. As you explore the implications of Jesus' challenge, look for ways you and your church can become Jesus' witnesses in your community, your state or region, your continent, and your world. Complete the learning activities you will find in each chapter to apply the concepts you are learning to your church's mission. After you have completed your study, use the contact information on page 142 to discover ways you can take action.

After two thousand years Jesus' Acts 1:8 challenge still invites today's church to join Him in His redemptive mission until He returns. May this study awaken and activate your church to truly be the body of Christ on mission.

Chapter 1

Famous Last Words:
Jesus' Acts 1:8 Challenge

YOUR MISSION

After completing this chapter, you will be able to—

• identify God's purpose for humanity;
• explain the meaning of Jesus' last words to His followers;
• identify God's purpose for Israel;
• identify God's purpose for the church;
• commit to become more involved in telling others about Jesus.

Imagine for a moment that you are conversing with a young man from a remote, undeveloped part of the world who has just come to North America as an exchange student. He has a basic education and speaks English but has no knowledge of Christianity or the church. When you invite him to church, he asks you to define what a church is and to explain its purpose.

How would you answer? _____

_____

_____

Maybe most of your explanation focused on the experiences and activities that happen within your church's walls or among the fellowship of Christians who worship, grow, and serve there. That is what *going to church* means for many Christians.

Group Session 1

1. Greet participants, make introductions, and lead in prayer. Make sure everyone has a copy of the book.
2. Show cel 1 and overview the study. Call attention to the word *mission* in the titles of the three main divisions of the book. Explain the difference between *mission* and *missions*: Mission refers to the "total redemptive purpose of God to establish His kingdom." *Missions* refers to the "activity of the church to proclaim and to demonstrate the kingdom of God to the world."[a] Missions is the church's work to accomplish God's mission.

How much of your definition of church and your explanation of its purpose was devoted to ways your church is on mission to the world?

None	I mentioned it.	A big part of my explanation

The fact that God charges each local church to be on mission to the world is the focus of this study. You may have chosen your church because of the pastor's gifted preaching, the warm welcome you experienced, your family connections there, or any number of other reasons. You may continue to attend your church because you are growing and learning, because of the quality children's or youth program, or because of close friendships. All of these factors can be wonderful benefits of church membership. But if all you have discovered about your church is what happens on the inside, you have missed the major reason your church exists: to take the gospel to the entire world.

Rate your church as a worldwide mission center, taking the gospel to your community, to the ends of the earth, and everywhere in between.

Not doing much	Doing a little	Doing a great job

Spend a few minutes praying that your church will have a greater heart for missions. Ask God to use this study to strengthen your church's missionary outreach.

The church is the body of Jesus Christ, and its assignment is to continue Jesus' work. Christ's unique mission was to pay for the sins of fallen humankind and to offer a pathway of forgiveness and reconciliation with God. Yet after Jesus accomplished that mission on the cross and God raised Him from the dead, Jesus continued to appear to His followers for 40 days. Not only was He proving to them that He was really alive, but He was also giving them clear directions on how to continue His mission.

Jesus' Last Words Are His First Priority

Several Web sites record the last words of famous people. According to one site, writer Oscar Wilde's final words before he died in 1900 were "Either that wallpaper goes, or I do." Actor Douglas Fairbanks Sr.'s last words in 1939 were "I've never felt better." And in 1864 General John Sedgwick, a Union commander during the Civil War, was reported to have been killed immediately after saying, "They couldn't hit

3. Ask, Who is the mission's Founder? Where are the mission's fields? Who are the mission's followers?
4. Show cel 2 and ask a member to read aloud Jesus' Acts 1:8 challenge. Point out the four mission fields Jesus identified and state that Jesus' challenge still applies to believers and churches today. Show cel 3 and present the goals for this course. Lead the group to pray aloud the prayer on the cel.
5. Refer to "Your Mission" for chapter 1 on page 7 and state that this session will examine God's redemptive mission throughout history and His purpose for churches today.

an elephant at this dist——." Perhaps the most revealing quotation was the final words of Mexican revolutionary Pancho Villa, who just before his death in 1923 said, "Don't let it end like this. Tell them I said something."[1]

Unlike these men, who could not choose the times of their deaths or predict which words would be their last, Jesus very purposefully and memorably chose His final words on earth (see Acts 1:7-8.)

> " 'It is not for you to know times or periods that the Father has set by His own authority. But you will receive power when the Holy Spirit has come upon you, and you will be My witnesses in Jerusalem, in all Judea and Samaria, and to the ends of the earth.' " **Acts 1:7-8**

Learn the background of Jesus' commission by reading Acts 1:1-8 in your Bible and answering the following questions.

What was the length of Christ's ministry on earth between His resurrection and His ascension (see v. 3)? _____

What was the main thing Jesus taught to His disciples between His resurrection and His ascension (see v. 3)?

_____

Why did Jesus instruct His disciples to wait in Jerusalem (see v. 4)?

_____

What was the gift promised to the disciples (see v. 4)? _____

Why do you think God does not give us specific information about the times or dates He sets (see v. 7)?

_____

What promise did Jesus give the disciples in verse 8? _____

_____

What is a witness (see v. 8)? _____

What are we to witness about (see v. 8)? _____

Where are disciples to witness (see v. 8)? _____

9

6. Call for responses to the activity on page 7. Distribute copies of your church bulletin or newsletter and ask members to identify evidence that your church focuses on taking the gospel to the entire world.

7. Ask volunteers to read the following Scriptures, which record the last words of several biblical figures: Genesis 50:24 (Joseph); Judges 16:28 (Samson); 1 Kings 2:2-3 (David); 2 Timothy 4:6-8 (Paul). Ask members to turn to Acts 1:8 and point out that these are Jesus' last words. Ask a volunteer to read Acts 1:1-8.

Jesus' words were in part a response to His disciples' question: " 'Lord, at this time are You restoring the kingdom to Israel?' " (Acts 1:6). It's as if Jesus heard in His followers' last question their persistent nearsightedness. They were still seeing the kingdom of God as something temporal, national, and political, even though Acts 1:3 tells us that throughout the 40 days following Jesus' resurrection He had spoken specifically to them "about the kingdom of God." The disciples, focused on the present and on Israel, still struggled to see in terms of eternity and the non-Jewish peoples of the world. They still needed help seeing how big God's vision and love for the world are and how far-reaching the kingdom of God is.

So Jesus left them—and us—with a very clear picture of how the kingdom of God would come and, amazingly, what our role would be in that kingdom. He said that God's kingdom—His rule in our lives and around the world—would come when the miracle of His Holy Spirit came on us. God's own presence and power would dwell within us, and we would be His witnesses. Our personal stories of His grace would radiate throughout the world and welcome people into His kingdom.

Use a separate sheet of paper to write your personal story of God's grace in your life. Plan to share your story with a member of your family. Ask God to give you the opportunity this week to share your story with someone who is not a Christian.

As you learned at the time you were saved, Jesus' disciples were discovering that entering the kingdom of God begins with a personal relationship with Jesus, the King. Their Jewish ancestry was significant because the King, the promised Messiah, had come to and through the Jewish nation. But the kingdom of God was no longer to be limited to the people of Israel. The gates to the kingdom of God were about to be thrown wide open so that all who believed the good news about Jesus' resurrection and accepted Him as Savior and Lord could enter.

Furthermore, Jesus' disciples would soon learn that their mission would be to invite individuals from every people group in the entire world to become subjects of the kingdom Jesus came to establish—the kingdom of God. What the disciples saw as exclusive (restoring the kingdom to Israel) Jesus now intended to be inclusive (restoring the peoples of the world to a right relationship with God). Instead of hoarding the blessings and power of knowing Jesus the King, they were to spill out into the highways and byways of life and invite all who would believe to let King Jesus reign in their lives as well. Their worldwide mission would be to serve the kingdom of God by reclaiming all people who had been separated from Him by sin.

With Jesus' last words on earth ringing in their ears, the disciples watched Him miraculously ascend into heaven. Because Jesus had appeared to them numerous times over the past 40 days, perhaps this dramatic departure signaled to them that Jesus would not continue to appear to them in bodily form. Amazed and perhaps

8. Call for responses to the activities on page 9. Call attention to and display on a marker board the principles in verse 8: (1) Our power comes from the Holy Spirit. (2) Our presence is as witnesses. (3) Our challenge is the world.[b]
9. Ask: What is the difference between the terms *exclusive* and *inclusive*? How does Jesus' thinking about the kingdom of God differ from that of His disciples (see p. 10)? What are some ways we tend to be exclusive in our churches today? How can we become more inclusive?

still a little perplexed, the disciples simply followed Jesus' earlier instructions. They returned to Jerusalem "to wait for the Father's promise" (Acts 1:4).

Read Acts 1:12-26. What was the disciples' main activity during this waiting time?

_____

During the 10 days following Jesus' ascension into the clouds, the Bible says the disciples "were continually united in prayer" (Acts 1:14), and it also implies that they were searching the Scriptures for instruction. In Acts 1:20 Peter referred to Psalm 109:8 as their scriptural direction for selecting Matthias to replace the apostolic position vacated by Judas Iscariot.

> "Let his dwelling become desolate;
> let no one live in it; and
> Let someone else take his position." **Acts 1:20**

If the disciples were indeed praying and searching the Scriptures for direction as they obediently waited, they would have been able to find a historical and scriptural pattern that beautifully set the stage for the Day of Pentecost and the coming of the Holy Spirit. It would not be surprising if, during those 10 days, they also reflected on Scripture that was not yet formally recorded—the words and actions of Jesus they had heard and observed during their time with Him.

In those Scriptures and in Jesus' life, the first-century believers could have discovered what God's people often had such difficulty grasping: God is moving throughout history and all over the world with the missionary purpose of seeking and saving the lost, forming for Himself one people from all people groups who would faithfully trust and worship Him. From the garden of Eden, to the ark of Noah, to the covenant with Abraham, and to the nation of Israel, God demonstrated that He is a seeking, loving God. Then He sent Jesus, the "radiance of His glory, the exact expression of His nature" (Heb. 1:3). Passionately speaking of lost sheep, lost coins, and lost sons, Jesus had openly declared His own purpose when He said, " 'The Son of Man has come to seek and to save the lost' " (Luke 19:10).

If you and I spent 10 days praying, searching the Scriptures, and seeking to discern God's direction for the future, what would we discover? As passionate followers of Jesus Christ, longing for His return and desiring to honor Him with our local fellowship of believers, what would we learn about the kingdom of God from His viewpoint? What would we discover about our role in bringing the kingdom to pass " 'on earth as it is in heaven' " (Matt. 6:10)?

Jesus' last words on earth demonstrate God's heart for the world, and they are consistent with God's revealed purpose throughout the Old Testament. By examining what the Bible says about God's ongoing mission throughout history, we will learn the primary purpose of His church today.

11

10. Call attention to the term *people group* on page 10. State that this term refers to a group of people who share a common identity such as language, race, religion, heritage, and socioeconomics. Say, "From the viewpoint of evangelization, this is the largest possible group within which the Gospel can spread without encountering barriers to understanding or acceptance."ᶜ Summarize that Jesus' Acts 1:8 challenge is for us to go to every people group in the world.
11. Ask volunteers to share their responses to the activity on page 10.

Jesus' Last Words Continue God's Old Testament Purpose

The mission for which God established the church finds its roots in the very nature of God Himself. It spans all of history and is significant to all humanity. That mission begins with God's glory.

God's Glory Radiating

Before the beginning of time there was only God. Perfect and complete, the Father, Son, and Holy Spirit existed alone as the Godhead. Unlimited by time or space, independent and needing nothing, Holy God was simply glorious. Many have tried to describe God's greatness and majesty. But all of the great hymns, poems, books, and paintings—in fact, all of humankind's best efforts throughout all of history—cannot begin to describe God's glory. We simply cannot fathom it.

In John 17, just before His crucifixion, Jesus prayed to His Heavenly Father:

> *"I have glorified You on the earth*
> *by completing the work You gave Me to do.*
> *Now, Father, glorify Me in Your presence*
> *with that glory I had with You before the world existed."* **John 17:4-5**

Jesus was referring to eternity past, before creation, when only the eternal Father, Son, and Holy Spirit existed. Triune God's matchless glory radiated from His very presence. Only God can speak of eternity past, before the universe existed.

Then God created. The first seven words of Genesis are packed with wonder and grandeur. From His own imagination and initiative God chose to create both time ("In the beginning God …") and space ("… created the heavens …"). So glorious is our God that He stands outside that which most people, including many famous philosophers, consider ultimate: time and space. He spoke them into being.

God's physical creation radiates a natural, complex glory (see Ps. 19:1-2). Throughout Genesis 1 God proclaimed each part of His creation good, but when He created humans, He described His creation as very good (see Gen. 1:31). Because people are the crowning touch of God's creation, we have a special role in reflecting His glory.

God's Creation Reflecting

When we consider God's glory and the vast universe He created, we can join the psalmist David in marveling at the role God gave us in reflecting His glory and bringing honor to His name (see Ps. 8:3-5). Yet when God created us "in His own image" (Gen. 1:27), He gave us not only a phenomenal blessing but also a serious responsibility: to voluntarily obey and worship.

12. State that Jesus' last words continue God's redemptive purpose throughout history and that we will trace that purpose in the Old and New Testaments. Refer to cel 4 as you present the sections in "Jesus' Last Words Continue God's Old Testament Purpose."
13. Summarize the section "God's Glory Radiating." Read the poem "The Creation" by James Weldon Johnson, which captures the marvel of creation and the grandeur of humanity.

God's nonhuman creation reflects His glory without making a choice, but we humans bear the miraculous responsibility of God's image. Therefore, our ability to reflect God's glory depends on our Godlike, spiritual decision to worship Him.

How important is this to God? When God gave His people the Ten Commandments through Moses, the first four dealt specifically with humankind's relationship to God (see Ex. 20:3-11). All four focus on worship—not giving it to anyone or anything else, not misusing God's holy name, and setting aside at least one day each week for focused worship. In the second commandment God even describes Himself as a jealous God. In Isaiah God said to His people, " 'I will not give My glory to another' " (Isa. 48:11).

> "When I observe your heavens,
>   the work of Your fingers,
>   the moon and the stars, which
>   You set in place,
> what is man that You
>   remember him,
>   the son of man that You look
>   after him?
> You made him little less
>   than God
> and crowned him with glory
>   and honor." **Psalm 8:3-5**

What are some ways to express our worship of God?

God-pleasing worship does not take place only in ceremonies or church services designed for that purpose. The apostle Paul wrote, "By the mercies of God, I urge you to present your bodies as a living sacrifice, holy and pleasing to God; this is your spiritual worship" (Rom. 12:1). Worshiping God means acknowledging His great worth. We express worship by knowing Him, loving Him, and obeying Him—reflecting His image purely in our thoughts, words, and actions. Worship is something we do with our entire beings and our entire lives.

Underline a sentence in the following paragraph that identifies God's purpose for humanity.

Our lives are not primarily about us; they are primarily about God. We cannot overestimate the worship He deserves, and we should not underestimate each worshiper's value to God. We were designed to worship God for now and eternity (see Ps. 113:1-2). Hundreds of Bible verses emphasize that God is God and that we are His worshipers, His faithful people, the sheep of His pasture (see Ps. 100:3). We are never more pleasing to God and never more complete in fulfilling our created purpose than when we engage in true spiritual worship of our great, worthy God.

God's People Rebelling

Very early in the Bible we discover why worship of the true and living God is so precious: throughout history it is rarely chosen.

Genesis 3 recounts the serpent's attack on the worship of God. Worship, for those made in God's image, should be a natural response to His glory. Notice that

13

14. Ask two volunteers to read Psalm 8 and Psalm 19:1-6. Ask: How do creation and the natural world reflect God's glory? How do people reflect His glory? What is special about people reflecting His glory? Present the ideas in the section "God's Creation Reflecting."

15. Ask: What is worship? What are some ways we express our worship? State that our purpose is to worship God for now and eternity.

each time the writer referred to God, he wrote, "Lord God" but that each time the serpent spoke, he simply said, "God." Through this subtle, sinister twisting of words, the serpent planted in Eve's mind the idea that God does not have to be Lord God. God could be God, and Eve could be Eve without being a worshiper.

Eve bought the lie, and her willing husband, Adam, tragically made it a two-for-one sale. Sin and selfishness entered the world, and humanity's nature was corrupted. This event, known as the fall, is devastating and demoralizing from humanity's point of view. The pinnacle of God's creation, those who walked and talked with God in paradise and who were made managers over a perfect world, sold out their position and posterity, exchanging blessing for curse, life for death. The necessity of redemption for each human was established.

But humankind's rebellion and separation from God are even more tragic from a cosmic perspective. God was not separated from something as comparatively trivial as a star or a galaxy. He was separated from His own likeness. Humanity—the unique, created reflection of His character and the object of His love—was stolen, not just by a renegade angel in the form of a reptile but also by the creation's own spiritual choice. In that moment the bridge of right relationship to God over which worship flowed was replaced by a huge chasm of sin.

We can only imagine God's agony when Adam and Eve—and later you and I—chose to pull away from His hand, gleefully jumping into the arms of sin. But although God is hurt by our sin, He is not surprised by it. And He is anything but helpless in pursuing the children, the worshipers, who have pulled away from His loving hand. Immediately in Genesis 3 we see God walking in the garden, knowing that His created image in humanity had been tarnished.

Because God is holy, He had to bring judgment on the sin that entered paradise. However, He immediately spoke of an offspring that would come from woman, who would one day crush the source of sin and death (see Gen. 3:15). God's mission to redeem fallen humankind is first mentioned in Genesis 3, but Revelation 13:8 describes Jesus as the Lamb who was slaughtered "from the foundation of the world." God's amazing revelation is that He created us knowing that He would need to redeem us.

Genesis 3–11 paints a bleak picture of humankind wallowing in the muck and mire of sin, though there are occasional bright spots on the canvas of early history.

Read the following verses and match them with examples of people who loved and obeyed God during this period of history.

___ 1. Genesis 4:4   a. Noah
___ 2. Genesis 4:25   b. Enoch
___ 3. Genesis 5:24   c. Abel
___ 4. Genesis 6:9   d. Seth

14

16. Ask each member to team with a partner and to write a one-sentence summary of Genesis 3. Call for responses. Summarize the section "God's People Rebelling."
17. Ask members to turn to Genesis 12:1-3. Call for responses to the activity on page 15. Summarize the section "God's Love Reaching."

By Genesis 6 the entire world was deeply engulfed in wickedness. God had short-ened the span of a person's life (see Gen. 6:3), and He expressed a readiness to wipe humankind, as well as animals and birds, from the face of the earth (see Gen. 6:5-6). Only Noah and his family found favor with God, and they were spared from God's great flood of judgment.

It is notable that when Noah and his family gratefully exited the ark, they worshiped with an obedient blood sacrifice (see Gen. 8:20). A clean start from a single family, however, could not solve humankind's sin problem. As Noah and his family repopulated the earth, the inescapable sin problem persisted. Instead of spreading over all the earth as God had instructed Noah, people began to congre-gate, building a monument to their own greatness rather than God's. As a result, God confounded their self-serving efforts on the tower of Babel by giving them multiple languages (see Gen. 11:1-9). Though they were still one human race, the fallen children of Adam separated into distinct people groups, or nations. And like lost sheep unwilling to follow their shepherd, they begrudgingly began to wander the earth. Again people fell short of God's glory and of their purpose as His worshipers.

God's Love Reaching

After God had watched generation after generation and people after people disregard their Creator, His initiative with Abram in Genesis 12:1-3 is remarkable. In His sovereign timing God began the next phase of His mission to reclaim His fallen creation.

Scripture records nothing about Abram's goodness, merit, or special standing prior to God's call. God chose Abram not because Abram was special but because God is special. He is a perfect, holy, glorious God whose love for His lost people is active and relentless. His long-term, worldwide plan to return the wandering peoples of the world to a right relationship and right worship continued as it had begun with Adam and Noah: with one man and one family.

Read Genesis 12:1-3. Underline God's seven promises. Circle God's promise about what Abram would be to other peoples.

> "The LORD said to Abram:
> 'Go out from your land,
> your relatives,
> and your father's house
> to the land that I will show you.
> I will make you into a
>   great nation,
> I will bless you,
> I will make your name great,
> and you will be a blessing.
> I will bless those who bless you,
> I will curse those who treat you
>   with contempt,
> and all the peoples on earth
> will be blessed through you.' "
> **Genesis 12:1-3**

When God first told Abram to leave his home and go to a new place, He made it clear that He was going to do wonderful things both for and through Abram. God promised that Abram would become the father of a great people, that he would be famous, and that he would be a blessing to all the families of the earth. Abram's response to God is noteworthy: Abram believed the Lord (see Gen. 15:6).

15

18. State, God called Abraham to be a channel of blessing to others. Slowly read the following stanza of a hymn and ask members to respond silently to the four questions:

Is your life a channel of blessing?
Is the love of God flowing thro' you?
Are you telling the lost of the Savior?
Are you ready His service to do?

Remarkably, Abram responded to God's initiative as humankind was designed to respond to God. He believed. He trusted. He obeyed. God acted in love, and Abram responded in faith. Throughout Abram's life God repeated and reinforced His promises to Abram (see Gen. 18:18; 22:18; 26:4), offering breadcrumbs of reassurance along a lifelong journey of faith. God gave him a new name, Abraham, which denoted the change in his relationship with God (see Gen. 17:5). And though Abraham was flawed by sin, he steadfastly believed God, obeyed God, followed God, and worshiped God over the course of his life.

Because of this love-faith relationship, Abraham was able to obey when God unexpectedly asked him to take his son, Isaac, to the mountain. More than one child trusted his father on that excursion! As Abraham trusted God and Isaac trusted Abraham, they had a wonderful, life-changing experience together. Hundreds of years before Jesus would die on a cross for their sin, Abraham and Isaac saw a picture of that miraculous provision. And their family tree, recorded in Genesis 22:20-24, continues to remind us of God's provision today.

In addition to blessing Abraham's family, God promised to bless all families of the earth. By restoring a pathway of right relationship back to Him, God extended His unmerited favor to all who would respond to Him as Abraham did—in faith.

God's blessing on Abraham extended to a family, a people, and ultimately the lost people groups of the world. It shouldn't surprise us that God's initial call to Abram required that he leave his home and go to a place where God would make him a blessing to others. And it shouldn't surprise us that God's promise to bless all peoples through Abraham was guaranteed solely by God's commitment and ability to do so and not by Abraham's. When God entered a covenant with Abraham in Genesis 15, only God (in the form of a "smoking fire pot and a flaming torch," according to Gen. 15:17) passed through the split animal carcasses, signifying the seriousness of the oath being made. Humankind had repeatedly proved incapable of finding or working its way back to God. In His covenant with Abraham, God was clearly demonstrating that human effort had never been His plan.

God's People Revealing

In his lifetime Abraham saw only glimpses and foreshadows of the blessings God had promised him. Yet, as Hebrews 11:8-10 reminds us, Abraham was able to look beyond his own life with faith's eyes to see God's history-long, worldwide purposes. God was blessing a family, but He was also forming a new people for His purposes. Eventually, this new people, the Hebrews, became the nation of Israel. So He repeated His promise to Abraham's son, Isaac (see Gen. 26:1-5); He wrestled with Abraham's conniving grandson, Jacob (see Gen. 32:22-32); and He protected Abraham's self-assured great-grandson, Joseph (see Gen. 45:4-8; 50:19-21). God was superintending His purposes through that frail, often dysfunctional family.

19. Ask: What is one way you can be a channel of blessing to your family? To your community? To your country? To your world? Read the chorus as a prayer:

Make me a channel of blessing today,
Make me a channel of blessing, I pray;
My life possessing, my service blessing,
Make me a channel of blessing today.[d]

Only about 70 descendants of Israel (Jacob's new name since Gen. 32:28) moved to Egypt during the great famine that reunited them with Joseph. But in the four hundred years that followed, Egypt served as a secure womb in which the Hebrews were nurtured and eventually grew into the nation of Israel. Scholars estimate that between two and three million Hebrews participated in the exodus from Egypt. Through the pain of slavery and the dramatic exodus, God gave birth to the new chosen people He had promised Abraham. When God brought Moses and the Hebrews to Mount Sinai, He clearly announced to them their purpose in His overall plan.

Read Exodus 19:3-8 and underline God's promise that the people of Israel would be His kingdom of priests.

What was a priest's main duty? _____

What do you think God meant by "kingdom of priests"?

_____

> "Moses went up the mountain to God, and the LORD called to him from the mountain: 'This is what you must say to the house of Jacob, and explain to the Israelites: You have seen what I did to the Egyptians and how I carried you on eagles' wings and brought you to Me. Now if you will listen to Me and carefully keep My covenant, you will be My own possession out of all the peoples, although all the earth is Mine, and you will be My kingdom of priests and My holy nation.' " **Exodus 19:3-8**

The new people of Israel had splendid moments in their history. In the promised land the Israelites' conquests under Joshua's leadership demonstrated God's power and provision (see Josh. 6–12), as did the heroics of judges like Deborah (see Judg. 4–5), Gideon (see Judg. 6–8), and Samson (see Judg. 13–16). The kingdom united under the warrior-king David (see 2 Sam.) and the time of blessing and prosperity under the wise king Solomon (see 1 Kings 1–11) gave glimpses of how a holy people ordained by God could display His glory for the other people groups of the world. Even during very difficult times, miracles through prophets like Elijah (see 1 Kings 17–19) and Elisha (see 2 Kings 2–8) showed those who worshiped no god or other gods that the true and living God was powerfully and gloriously working in and through the Hebrew people.

In the following paragraph underline a sentence that identifies God's purpose for Israel.

Throughout the Old Testament we frequently read about God's desire to display His glory through the Hebrew people (see Isa. 49:3) and for Israel to declare that glory among the other peoples. God wanted the many godless peoples to be drawn to the one godly people. Isaiah said Israel would be a witness: " 'So you will summon a nation you do not know, and nations who do not know you will run to you. For the LORD your God, even the Holy One of Israel, has glorified you' " (Isa. 55:5).

17

20. Stretch a cord across the room to serve as a display line as you introduce the sections "God's People Revealing" and "God's People Resisting." Use clothespins or tape to mount small placards with the following names: *Abraham, Isaac, Jacob, Joseph, Moses/the Exodus, Joshua, Judges, David, Solomon, Elijah and Elisha, Psalms, Prophets*. The display line is not intended to show chronology, so use equal spacing between the placards. Ask previously enlisted members to explain how their assigned characters or topics carried forth God's redemptive plan.

Many times the Book of Psalms reminds us that the glory of God is reflected in His creation and that the pinnacle of creation, His people, are to reflect His glory to unbelieving peoples. The psalmist frequently urged Israel to praise God and sing of Him among other peoples (see Ps. 57:9) or to make known to others what He had done (see Ps. 105:1-2). Faithful Israelites like David (see Ps. 72:18-19), Habakkuk (see Hab. 2:14), and Isaiah (see Isa. 60:1-3; 66:18-19) recognized that the Hebrew people had a unique purpose: to reflect God's glory to the other peoples of the world.

The early years of King Solomon's reign certainly gave Israel the picture of a glorious, united kingdom—one that would establish Israel's expectations of an earthly kingdom for hundreds of years to come. But during the declining years of Israel, under the often disobedient kings who succeeded Solomon, God, through His prophets, began to speak of a coming Messiah. The people of Israel tended to view the salvation referred to in Scriptures like Psalm 69:35, Isaiah 25:9, and Jeremiah 42:11 as salvation from their political or military enemies. Prophecies such as Isaiah 53, speaking of the Messiah as a Servant who would suffer and die, were often overlooked or ignored. But these were God's announcements that His complete revelation through Israel would come at "the completion of the time" (Gal. 4:4), when God Himself would be born of a virgin (see Isa. 7:14) in Bethlehem (see Mic. 5:2).

God's People Resisting

Even as a sometimes mighty nation bearing God's name and reputation, Israel was still a group of sinful humans. Consequently, Israel's brief moments of triumph as the holy people of God were far eclipsed by a history of frustration and failure.

The Hebrews were scarcely out of Egypt when they impatiently turned their worship to a golden calf (see Ex. 32). To their disgrace this transgression occurred while Moses was on Mount Sinai receiving the law from the true and living God, the One who had miraculously demonstrated His power and glory and rescued them from slavery. Not long afterward, 10 of the 12 spies who were sent into the promised land led the Hebrews to fear the large men of Canaan instead of revering and trusting their capable Deliverer (see Num. 13–14). Then, wandering in the desert for 40 years, God's chosen people failed test after test. By complaining and resisting God's leadership, they forfeited a generation of opportunities to reflect God's glory and accomplish His purposes (see Num. 13:20-23; Deut. 8:2-5).

Even as a new generation prepared to follow Joshua into the promised land, God predicted that they would " 'soon commit adultery with the foreign gods of the land they are entering' " (Deut. 31:16). He said to Moses and Joshua, " 'I know what they are prone to do, even before I bring them into the land I swore [to give to them]' " (Deut. 31:21). And though Israel experienced many great victories in the promised land and sporadically obeyed the leaders God provided, the Old Testament clearly portrays the people's unwillingness to fulfill their purpose as His faithful instrument to reach the non-Jewish peoples. The Book of Judges describes a pattern that Israel unfortunately repeated: "The Israelites did what was evil in the LORD's sight. They worshiped the Baals and abandoned the LORD, the God of their fathers, who had brought them out of Egypt" (Judg. 2:11).

Judges and then kings and prophets repeatedly led the Hebrews out of calamity into repentance and restored relationship, only to watch it spiral through disobedience and idolatry back into calamity. God had fulfilled His promise to make a special people from Abraham's descendants, giving them the land He had promised while driving out the wicked people of Canaan. Ironically, God would next allow wicked peoples like Assyria and Babylon to bring a similar expelling judgment on Israel.

In 722 B.C. the 10 tribes of the northern kingdom of Israel were conquered by Assyria; most Israelites were deported. Over the years the region was colonized by various peoples, including Syrians and Babylonians, and the resulting mixed population was the origin of the Samaritans. The southern kingdom of Judah prevailed a while longer, but in 586 B.C. even the stronghold of Jerusalem fell to the Babylonians. These events are especially significant in light of Jesus' eventual challenge in Acts 1:8 to go to both Judea (the area of the southern kingdom) and Samaria (the area of the northern kingdom). As the remaining remnant of God's people from the southern kingdom was deported from the promised land to Babylon, they must have wondered if God's purpose for their nation had come to an end (see Isa. 26:18).

Yet even during these disappointing times God communicated messages of hope for His people and love and concern for the peoples to whom Israel should have been a beacon. Read Isaiah 49:6-7.

The prophet Jonah's call to go to Ninevah gives a classic example of God's concern for the peoples of the world in spite of the weakness and lack of vision of His chosen people and prophets. Even in the closing verse of Jonah, God was still coaxing the reluctant prophet to see the world—even the sinful, non-Jewish world— as He sees it: " 'Should I not care about the great city of Nineveh, which has more than 120,000 people who cannot distinguish between their right and their left?' " (Jonah 4:11).

After decades of Babylonian captivity, the remainder of God's discouraged and depleted people returned to Jerusalem with Ezra and Nehemiah (see Ezra 1-6; Neh. 1-6). God had again provided a thread of redemption and leaders around whom to rally His humbled remnant.

Throughout much of the Old Testament, Israel failed to live up to its appointed role as God's set-apart people and its missionary

> " 'It is not enough for you
> to be My servant
> raising up the tribes of Jacob
> and restoring the protected
> ones of Israel.
> I will also make you a light
> for the nations,
> to be My salvation to the ends
> of the earth.'
> This is what the LORD,
> the Redeemer of Israel,
> his Holy One says
> to one who is despised,
> to one abhorred by people,
> to a servant of rulers:
> 'Kings will see and stand up,
> and princes will bow down,
> because of the Lord, who is
> faithful,
> the Holy One of Israel—
> and He has chosen you.' "
> **Isaiah 49:6-7**

role as God's people; however, God's plan for Israel to be a channel of blessing and redemption to the world had not changed (see Ezek. 36:19-21). His long-term plan for fulfilling His missionary purpose through Israel had not yet been revealed. Through Israel God would bring the world a Savior who would establish a new covenant with God's people, revealing a new chapter in His worldwide, history-long mission to the world.

In the previous section, "God's People Resisting," underline at least five specific examples in which the people sinned and failed to be God's holy nation of priests.

Jesus' Last Words Communicate God's New Testament Purpose

God's Son Restoring

Jesus is the center of history and the center of God's redemptive plan. Throughout Isael's history, no one had been able to complete the mission of restoring the lost peoples of the world to their Creator. Yet those who were faithful had always looked forward to a time when God would break the cycle of rebellion that plagued His chosen people.

> "The Word became flesh and took up residence among us. We observed His glory, the glory as the One and Only Son from the Father, full of grace and truth." **John 1:14**

God sent Jesus at a time when hope seemed very dim. More than four hundred years had passed since a prophet had spoken to Israel. Since that time the people of God had been conquered, occupied, and oppressed. Those who knew God's promises through His prophets had assurance of a coming Messiah, but even those few were expecting Him to come as a military leader, not a Suffering Servant. Yet even though God's plan was a mystery (see Eph. 1:9-10) that was not understood until after Jesus' resurrection, the Bible states that Jesus came at just the right time to accomplish His purpose (see Gal. 4:4-5).

God's plan of attack on sin and Satan was not to send a human leader to try and reform the people, disciplining them to live by God's law in their own strength. Instead, He sent the only solution to humanity's sin problem: Jesus, God Himself made human (see John 1:14).

Consider what it meant for Jesus to be God's glory in human form. Jesus showed us not only God's glory but also what God's glory should look like in a person. He gave us a picture of the power, wisdom, purpose, and fellowship with the Father that was ours before sin stole us away from Him. Through miracles, on the mount of transfiguration (see Matt. 17:1-13), and through His resurrection (see Matt. 28:1-7), Jesus proved that God's glory, which predates the universe, was in Him (see Heb. 1:1-3).

20

21. State that Jesus' last words also communicate God's New Testament purpose. Refer to cel 5 as you present the sections in "Jesus' Last Words Communicate God's New Testament Purpose."
22. Summarize the section "God's Son Restoring."

That glory had come to earth " 'to seek and to save the lost' " (Luke 19:10). In the incarnation God Himself became human, taking up residence with humankind, invading the world of sin, and setting its captives free. What a miracle! What an amazing turn of events! Yet the Bible tells us, "He was destined before the foundation of the world, but was revealed at the end of the times for you who through Him are believers in God, who raised Him from the dead and gave Him glory, so that your faith and hope are in God" (1 Pet. 1:20-21).

Throughout history Jesus had been God's plan for restoring His fallen creation. In hindsight Paul and other New Testament writers were able to recognize and clarify the prophetic hints about Jesus that were there all along. For example, in Galatians 3:16 Paul wrote, "The promises were spoken to Abraham and to his seed. He does not say 'and to seeds,' as though referring to many, but 'and to your seed,' referring to one, who is Christ." This idea is beautifully expressed many times in the New Testament but never more majestically than in the first chapter of Colossians:

> *He is the image of the invisible God,*
> *the firstborn over all creation;*
> *because by Him everything was created,*
> *in heaven and on earth, the visible and the invisible,*
> *whether thrones or dominions or rulers or authorities—*
> *all things have been created through Him and for Him.*
> *He is before all things, and by Him all things hold together.*
> *He is also the head of the body, the church;*
> *He is the beginning, the firstborn from the dead,*
> *so that He might come to have first place in everything.*
> *For God was pleased to have all His fullness dwell in Him,*
> *and through Him to reconcile everything to Himself*
> *by making peace through the blood of His cross—*
> *whether things on earth or things in heaven.*
> *And you were once alienated and hostile in mind because of your evil actions.*
> *But now He has reconciled you by His physical body through His death,*
> *to present you holy, faultless, and blameless before Him.* **Colossians 1:15-22**

Jesus' stated mission was first to the Jewish people (see Matt. 10:5-6; 15:24; John 1:11), but clearly His long-range mission included all peoples.

State how the following passages show that Jesus' mission included all peoples.

Mark 7:24-30: _____

23. Call attention to Colossians 1:15-22 on page 21. Ask members to draw a line under statements that tell who Jesus is and to draw a circle around statements that tell what Jesus did. Then discuss the statements as members identify them.
24. Call for responses to the activity on pages 21–22.

Luke 4:16-19: _____

Luke 4:25-27: _____

Luke 7:1-10: _____

During His early ministry Jesus was already looking ahead to the day when His Great Commission to His church would include all peoples (see Matt. 28:19), even the Gentiles, or non-Jewish people groups (see Acts 26:17-18).

Before continuing His mission of inviting the Hebrews and the Gentile peoples of the world into a right relationship with Him, God had to do what only He could do. He laid down His perfect life to atone for the sin that separates us from Him. To seek us and save us from sin, to break the Devil's power over us, to bring us eternal life, to give us renewed access to God, to restore our fallen race from worthless sinners to worshiping saints—Jesus died to accomplish all this.

> "Since by the one man's trespass, death reigned through that one man, how much more will those who receive the overflow of grace and the gift of righteousness reign in life through the one man, Jesus Christ. So then, as through one trespass there is condemnation for everyone, so also through one righteous act there is life-giving justification for everyone."
> **Romans 5:17-18**

Read Romans 5:17-18. Humbly thank God for the unspeakable gift of His Son, who died to bring you into a relationship with the Father. If you've never trusted Christ as your personal Savior, do so now. Pray a prayer like this one: "Dear God, I know that I'm a sinner, and I'm sorry. I confess to You my sins and my need for salvation. I know that You love me and that Jesus came to earth and suffered on the cross for my sins. I now turn away from my sins and place my faith and trust in Jesus as my Savior and Lord. Thank You for saving me. From this day forward I will live my life for You." Share your decision with your family, pastor, and church.

God's Church Receiving

Under the old covenant the Hebrews demonstrated that sin-sick humanity cannot earn right standing with God. And without that right standing, Israel could not be the light for other peoples that God had challenged them to be. God lovingly provided leader after leader, prophet after prophet, and judgment after judgment. He repeatedly demonstrated that what His people needed, He alone could provide.

Then He sent Jesus. While on earth, Jesus made it clear that His coming meant God's mission plan to the world was moving to its next phase:

> Jesus said to them, "Have you never read the Scriptures:
> The stone that the builders rejected has become the cornerstone.
> This came from the Lord and is wonderful in our eyes?

25. In summarizing the section "God's Church Receiving," write the following Scripture references on a line across a marker board: Genesis 12:1-3; Exodus 19:3-8; Matthew 21:42-44. Beneath the references write, *Abraham, Israel, Church*. Using a long strip of colored cloth or paper, connect the three references, letting the cloth or paper hang down between each one. Point out that in these three passages God first commissioned Abraham to be a blessing to the world, the commission was extended to the nation Israel, and then the commission was given to the church. Point out that this is a key concept in understanding the Bible.

Therefore I tell you, the kingdom of God will be taken away from you and given to a nation producing its fruit. Whoever falls on this stone will be broken to pieces; but on whomever it falls, it will grind him to powder!" **Matthew 21:42-44**

To whom does the word "nation" refer in this passage? _____

When Israel stumbled in its assignment to be on mission with Him, God raised up the church, a new kind of nation united not by race or ethnicity but by God's Spirit. Jesus said that He would build His church (see Matt. 16:18) and that it would be built from the living stones (see 1 Pet. 2:5) of His own disciples. If we stopped there, we would have to wonder how the church could hope to be any more successful in God's mission than the people of Israel. Jesus paid the penalty for our sins and conquered sin and death by His resurrection power. But until Jesus returns, the church still lives in a fallen world, and its members still struggle with the sinful nature they inherited from Adam. How can the church be a brighter light to the peoples of the world than Israel was before Christ?

The answer came on the day of Pentecost, 50 days after Jesus' resurrection and 10 days after He had ascended into heaven. Pentecost, an Old Testament celebration marking the end of the barley harvest, would that year become the birth date of Jesus' church, the body through which He would continue His mission on earth. Pentecost became the day when the early church received an amazing gift that empowered them for the worldwide mission.

Jesus' followers were waiting together in Jerusalem as Jesus had instructed. Suddenly the sound of a mighty wind filled the house, and flaming tongues rested on each person (see Acts 2:1-4). In the Bible, fire consistently symbolizes God's presence. God appeared as fire to Moses, both in the burning bush (see Ex. 3:1-3) and on Mount Sinai (see Ex. 19:18). God answered Elijah with fire (see 1 Kings 18:38) and used a fiery coal to cleanse Isaiah's lips, preparing him to proclaim God's message (see Isa. 6:6).

By sending the Holy Spirit in the form of fiery tongues, God demonstrated that His presence was coming in a significant, unprecedented way. No longer would God's presence with them be temporary or reserved for special leaders on special occasions. As Jesus had promised more than once (see John 14—16), God's Spirit would come to stay, providing all the power the church needed to fulfill Jesus' Great Commission.

Jesus said, " 'I assure you: The one who believes in Me will also do the works that I do. And he will do even greater works than these, because I am going to the Father' " (John 14:12). God

> "When the day of Pentecost had arrived, they were all together in one place. Suddenly a sound like that of a violent rushing wind came from heaven, and it filled the whole house where they were staying. And tongues, like flames of fire that were divided, appeared to them and rested on each one of them. Then they were all filled with the Holy Spirit and began to speak in different languages, as the Spirit gave them ability for speech." **Acts 2:1-4**

23

26. Explain that the Day of Pentecost, also called the feast of weeks, the feast of harvest, and the day of firstfruits, was an annual Jewish festival that was celebrated 50 days after the Passover.ᵉ Point out the parallel between the feast and the ingathering of the firstfruits of believers after Peter's sermon. Explain that Holy Spirit came to provide power and presence for the church's missions task.

has provided to His church the same power Jesus demonstrated when He was on earth. Because today's church has the incredible resource of Spirit-filled Christians, its influence can spread throughout history and all over the world as people come to faith in Christ.

In addition to the power God provided the church, He gave each believer the amazing gift of His presence. Thus, we are Spirit-filled witnesses because we are Spirit-filled temples. Paul wrote to the Corinthians who were professing Christ with their mouths but often not honoring Him with their behavior: "Do you not know that your body is a sanctuary of the Holy Spirit who is in you, whom you have from God? You are not your own, for you were bought at a price; therefore glorify God in your body" (1 Cor. 6:19-20). Paul later wrote to the Corinthians that we carry the treasure of the Holy Spirit in clay jars (see 2 Cor. 4:7). Although our physical bodies are frail, the glorious Spirit of God in a human vessel yielded to the lordship of Christ is the instrument God uses to radiate His glory and draw others to Himself: "God, who said, 'Light shall shine out of darkness'—He has shone in our hearts to give the light of the knowledge of God's glory in the face of Jesus Christ" (2 Cor. 4:6).

Before believers can truly radiate God's light and love to others, they must receive the fullness and power of the Holy Spirit. God makes His Spirit available to us when we place our faith in Christ, but sometimes we don't completely yield to His Spirit. Without the power of the Holy Spirit flowing through us, we are more like the striving and often failing nation of Israel than the empowered, radiant church of Jesus.

God's restored glory, along with a renewed desire to return that glory to God, should be evident in the life of a sincere Christian. Because we are new creations reflecting His image (see 2 Cor. 5:17), everything we do should be for God's glory (see 1 Cor. 10:31). The purpose of the Christian life is "that in everything God may be glorified through Jesus Christ. To Him belong the glory and the power forever and ever" (1 Pet. 4:11). We must receive in order to radiate.

God's Church Radiating

In Matthew 24:14 Jesus revealed that because the church's mission assignment is of limited duration, it must be carried out with urgency. The work of salvation is complete (see Heb. 10:12-14), but the work of proclamation remains (see Rom. 10:14-15), and it is the church's primary mission (see Acts 13:44-49), just as salvation was Jesus' primary mission (see Luke 19:10). When history ends, God's mission will be complete (see 1 Thess. 4:16-18).

" 'This good news of the kingdom will be proclaimed in all the world as a testimony to all nations. And then the end will come.' " **Matthew 24:14**

In the following paragraph underline a sentence that identifies God's purpose for the church.

24

27. Introduce the section "God's Church Radiating" by emphasizing the urgency of the church's mission assignment. Form five small groups and give each group a set of Scripture references: (1) Matthew 10:5-15; Mark 13:9-13; Luke 9:1-6; (2) Matthew 9:37-38; Luke 10:1-16; (3) John 3:13-19; John 4:34-38; (4) Acts 26:12-18; Romans 13:12-14; (5) 1 Thessalonians 1:8-10; 1 Peter 2:4-10. State that these are significant New Testament missionary texts. Ask the groups to discover the central truths of the passages and to identify an application for believers or churches today. After group work, call for responses.

Until the completion of the mission, the church has a tremendous privilege and responsibility. God's mystery of salvation through Christ has been revealed (see Eph. 3:8-12), and the final stage in His redemptive plan is for Spirit-filled believers to carry the good news of salvation through Jesus to the ends of the earth. God's plan was at work through Abraham; Israel; and His Son, Jesus. Now God looks to the church to continue seeking those who are lost, telling them the good news about salvation through Jesus. The church fulfills its role as it gathers worshipers from the peoples of the world as if it were collecting treasure to present to its beloved King. Those eternally alive worshipers were designed to give God the glory that is due Him.

The Great Commission to take the gospel throughout the world is so important that it is repeated at least five times in Scripture.

Read Matthew 28:19-20; Mark 16:15; Luke 24:46-48; John 20:21; and Acts 1:8. Stop and pray that the lost peoples of the world will trust Jesus as Savior and Lord, that Christians and churches will become more involved in telling others about Jesus, and that you will obey Jesus' command to share the good news.

The Great Commission is given to every follower of Jesus, not just to pastors, missionaries, or full-time Christian workers. Regardless of what we are doing in our lives and in our churches, the Great Commission reminds us of God's redemptive goal throughout history. We have a great opportunity to join Him on this mission.

How do we join Him? How does a local church go about fulfilling its Great Commission assignment in its own Jerusalem, Judea, Samaria, and ends of the earth? The remaining five chapters of this study will help answer that question. First we must understand the mission task God revealed to the early church.

In the Acts 1:8 statement of the Great Commission, God called local churches to have worldwide missions involvement. New Testament churches had a radiating influence on the community, distant parts of the world, and many places in between.

The early churches did not have identical master plans for reaching the world in neat concentric circles. But the healthy churches featured in the New Testament seriously and sacrificially accepted the Great Commission. Their people shared their resources and cooperated in evangelistic and missionary endeavors. They sent their strongest leaders and teachers over barriers that separated the lost world from the gospel message. Devoted Christians were bold, passionate witnesses of Jesus' resurrection and of the way to the salvation God had provided.

The early churches therefore had a radiating, permeating influence that quickly spread throughout the world, whether it was initiated through persecution, as in the Jerusalem church (see Acts 8:1-3), or through specific missionary assignments, as in the Antioch church (see Acts 13:1-3). Instead of retreating within their walls

28. Assign the five Great Commission texts to the same small groups: (1) Matthew 28:18-20; (2) Mark 16:15; (3) Luke 24:46-49; (4) John 20:21; (5) Acts 1:8. Ask each group to study its assigned passage and to answer the following questions: What is the command given? On what authority is the command given? What is the scope or extent of the command? What is the reassurance given?[f]

until they could grow stronger or get more organized, the churches urgently and systematically shared the good news everywhere. And as Christians went about their daily lives and travels, they consistently sought to extend that influence. From its beginning, when the church is turned inside out, the world is turned upside down.

Today every local church has a Jerusalem, Judea, Samaria, and world responsibility. The church has received the gift, the news, the secret, and the treasure of the gospel. Not to share the good news is unthinkable. And while the words *local* and *world* may at first seem paradoxical, they represent the unique post-Pentecost, Spirit-filled missions task of the New Testament church. Local churches can have worldwide influence!

In the mission of the church, history and God's plan for the world come full circle. The glory of God is again reflected in His people, and the people of God join Him in radiating that glory to the world. Local churches are God's instruments for revealing His mercy and forgiveness to the lost. The Holy Spirit's presence in a believer's life gives the believer great potential, not only as a worshiper who reflects God's glory but also as a witness who radiates God's glory.

God's Redeemed Responding

Thousands of years ago God scattered fallen humankind, confounding their language so that they couldn't cooperate for sinful, self-aggrandizing purposes (see Gen. 11:1-9). As the many peoples of the human race populated the earth, entire cultures were isolated from God. As generation after generation passed, God chose to reveal Himself in multiple ways, including nature, a family, a nation, leaders, prophets, and His Word. When the right time came (see Rom. 5:6; Gal. 4:4-5), God fully revealed Himself through Jesus, whose death on the cross continues to provide redemption for those who call on Him for salvation.

How significant, then, that after Jesus commissioned His church and returned to heaven, the first miraculous sign of the Holy Spirit's coming was the ability of the Jerusalem believers to speak in different languages (see Acts 2:4). God did not choose to miraculously restore humankind to one common language. Instead, by miraculously equipping those believers with the languages of the international community in Jerusalem, God demonstrated that the church's commission was to go and seek all lost peoples of the world to share the news of salvation.

> "All the nations You have made
> will come and bow down before
>   You, Lord,
> and will honor your name.
> For you are great and
>   perform wonders;
> You alone are God." **Psalm 86:9-10**

Today God is gathering a people to Himself who will cooperate for the noblest, most God-honoring purpose: gathering people from around the world to worship the Lord God and serve Him forever (see Ps. 86:9-10). By giving us a clear vision of His love and purpose for His world, God invites us to join Him on mission. And one day God's history-long, worldwide mission through His people will finally be fulfilled:

29. Summarize the section "God's Redeemed Responding."
30. Ask someone to read 2 Corinthians 5:18-20. State that God has assigned us His ministry of reconciliation and that we are His ambassadors. Read Revelation 7:9-10, the fulfillment of God's history-long, worldwide mission.
31. Ask a previously enlisted member to summarize "Jesus' Last Words Challenge Churches to Their Purpose Today."
32. Show cel 6 and read the definition of *missionary*. Emphasize that each believer and each church is to obey God's call to be a missionary to those who need to know Jesus.

"After this I looked, and there was a vast multitude from every nation, tribe, people and language, which no one could number, standing before the throne and before the Lamb. They were robed in white with palm branches in their hands. And they cried out in a loud voice: Salvation belongs to our God, who is seated on the throne, and to the Lamb!" (Rev. 7:9-10).

Of course, before that glorious time of continuous worship, judgment will come. Jesus said, " 'When the Son of Man comes in His glory, and all the angels with Him, then He will sit on the throne of His glory. All the nations will be gathered before Him, and He will separate them one from another, just as a shepherd separates the sheep from the goats' " (Matt. 25:31-32). An untold number of people will not have accepted God's revelation and invitation and will refuse to worship God forever. Tragically, they will spend eternity separated from God in a place "prepared for the Devil and his angels!" (Matt. 25:41).

God will also hold his church accountable (see Rom. 14:9-12; 2 Cor. 5:9-11), and a large part of that accountability will relate to our obedience in carrying out the Great Commission He gave us to take the gospel to the ends of the earth. However, neither fear nor guilt is the motivation a maturing Christian needs to join God in His mission to the world. Our desire to be on mission with God flows from our restored relationship with Him—a relationship characterized by love and worship.

Jesus' mission to the world emanated from a love relationship with His Father. Jesus, knowing God's supreme value and worthiness, knowing it is not right for the created not to worship the Creator, left His heavenly throne to gather wayward worshipers back to God.

Read Philippians 2:5-11. Check some of the things Jesus did from His love for the Father. ❏ Emptied Himself ❏ Took the form of a slave ❏ Stayed in heaven ❏ Came to earth ❏ Died on a cross ❏ Became obedient ❏ Replaced His Father

This passage says that Jesus left God's presence to reclaim God's people. Likewise, the longer we are in God's presence in our personal worship, the more we recognize that His glory merits more worship than we alone can bring. In order to magnify the worship God receives, we go to those who do not yet know Him, inviting them to join us in worshiping Him. Our passion for God fuels our compassion for humankind.

An unmistakable connection exists between the worship of God and the mission of God. God's glory is infinitely valuable, and He merits the pure, faithful reflection of His creation's worship: "We all, with unveiled faces, are reflecting the glory of the Lord and are being transformed into the same image from glory to glory; this is from the Lord who is the Spirit" (2 Cor. 3:18).

God deserves nothing less than the praise and adoration of every nation, tribe, and people. And this is exactly what He will receive for eternity. In the meantime,

27

33. As a review, read this statement about the mission's Founder: God's history-long, worldwide mission is to redeem and reclaim the sin-enslaved peoples of the earth. Through the family of Abraham, the nation of Israel, Jesus, and the church, God has revealed Himself and restored relationships with those who come to Him in faith. One day the mission will end, but the fruit of the mission—eternal worshipers who reflect God's glory—will live forever. Remind members who the mission's Founder is. Call for responses to the first activity on page 30.

His people, empowered by the Holy Spirit, are responsible for carrying out His redemptive mission to the world: "Everything is from God, who reconciled us to Himself through Christ and gave us the ministry of reconciliation: that is, in Christ, God was reconciling the world to Himself, not counting their trespasses against them, and He has committed the message of reconciliation to us. Therefore, we are ambassadors for Christ; certain that God is appealing through us, we plead on Christ's behalf, 'Be reconciled to God' " (2 Cor. 5:18-20).

Jesus' Last Words Challenge Churches to Their Purpose Today

I have an unusual pair of eyes: my right eye is nearsighted, and my left eye is farsighted. For years I didn't know that my vision needed correction because each eye compensated for the other. When I was reading, my right eye was on duty, and when I was driving or watching a movie, my left eye did most of the work. Because my eyes weren't working together in the messages they sent to my brain, my nearsighted right eye began dominating what my brain saw, while my distance vision became fuzzier. Gradually, my left eye was giving up.

The same thing can happen to our spiritual vision. When we focus primarily on that which is close to us in distance or in time, we can lose perspective on the whole world and on all of history. It is easy for a church to become nearsighted if it focuses only on the activities and programs inside its walls. Every church is challenged to maintain God's vision of the relationships He desires for the individuals and peoples who do not know Him. The busy world of a local church can be wonderful. But God also wants a local church that is busy in the world.

With the powerful Holy Spirit dwelling in us, our lives can touch both eternity and the entire world. Time and space are no longer limitations for a follower of Christ! When we help usher people into the kingdom of God through the doorway of Jesus, we participate in God's mission, which spans the entire scope of history. And when we participate with our church and other churches in multiplying that witness, no place on earth is beyond our reach.

The next chapters will help you and your church see your world through the lens of Jesus' famous last words recorded in Acts 1:8. This world is beyond your church's walls and beyond the trivial pursuits that sometimes govern our personal lives. We will look at that world—Jerusalem, Judea, Samaria, and the ends of the earth—through the eyes of 1st-century churches and 21st-century churches.

When Jesus referred to Jerusalem, Judea, Samaria, and the ends of the earth, His followers would have pictured very specific places and would have had strong feelings about what it meant to be witnesses there. The same can be true for our

34. Show cel 2 again and lead the group in reading Acts 1:8 in unison. Distribute three-by-five-inch cards. Challenge members to write the verse on their cards and to memorize it this week.
35. Call attention to the teaching posters on the walls. Ask volunteers to read selected posters and to explain the statements.
36. Point out that missionaries through the centuries crossed numerous barriers to tell others about Jesus. However, by the 18th century the churches in England and America were lethargic about propagating the gospel. God

churches today as we discover our own contemporary mission fields and obey God's call to be a missionary in the area to which He leads us. A missionary is simply someone who, in response to God's call and gifting, leaves his or her comfort zone and crosses cultural, geographic, or other barriers to proclaim the gospel and live out a Christian witness in obedience to the Great Commission.

As the first-century churches responded to Jesus' Acts 1:8 challenge to be Spirit-filled witnesses in all of the places Jesus named, the peoples of the world began to hear the message of salvation. Some rejected it, as some do today. But many accepted the message and became sincere, eternal worshipers of the God who

A CHURCH ON MISSION

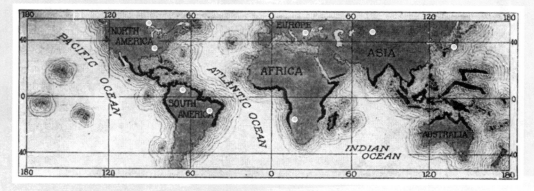

Churches around the country are embracing their call to missions. One such church is Faith Baptist Church in Bartlett, Tennessee. "If you attend this church, you'd better be prepared to go on a mission trip," says George Silar, an associate pastor at Faith Baptist. "One of the main reasons we exist is to be on mission."

Faith Baptist Church in Bartlett, Tennessee, actively goes on mission to each of its four Acts 1:8 mission fields.

The church has traveled on mission trips to many countries, including Romania, Brazil, Japan, Russia, Canada, and Venezuela, and has adopted missionaries in Namibia, South Africa. The church annually gives to the Annie Armstrong Easter Offering®; the Lottie Moon Christmas Offering®; local and statewide Christian agencies, such as the Tennessee Baptist Children's Home; and disaster relief.

"One of the church's goals is to enlist a missions leader for every Sunday school class," Silar says. The church also supplies missions opportunities for nearly all ages. Middle-school students participate in local mission projects, while high-school and college students help with World Changers and take international mission trips.

Silar stresses that missions is about the heart of the people. He states, "Being a mission-minded Christian will result in an impact on the world."[2]

used a Baptist pastor named William Carey as a catalyst to get churches involved in missions. Carey eventually went to India and served for 41 years until his death in 1834. He is known today as the father of modern missions. State that the group has the opportunity to hear Carey describe his work. At this point a member you have previously enlisted should come forward and deliver the dramatic monologue on page 147.

37. Close by praying that members will realize God's love for the world and will embrace Jesus' Acts 1:8 challenge to reach their ends of the earth, their Samaria, their Judea, and their Jerusalem with the good news.

had been pursuing them since the garden of Eden. In today's world many lost, potential worshipers still wait to hear the message.

We will intentionally begin by looking at the ends of the earth before focusing our vision on Samaria, Judea, and Jerusalem, because these are not sequential but simultaneous mission fields. The early church went to all of these areas very quickly and with a great sense of urgency. Not only are the resources and opportunities of today's churches larger, but the urgency is also greater. We approach a time when it is more and more possible for all peoples of the world to hear the gospel and to join the throng of worshipers who will give praise to God for all eternity.

Review chapter 1. Then explain how Jesus' last words in Acts 1:8—

reflect Jesus' first priority: _____

_____

continue God's Old Testament purpose: _____

_____

communicate God's New Testament purpose: _____

_____

challenge the church to its purpose today: _____

_____

Ask God to help you and your church become more involved in telling others about Jesus.

Write Acts 1:8 on a card. Keep the card with you and memorize the verse this week.

——

[1]"The Last Words Spoken by Famous People at Death, or Shortly Before," *Brain Candy* [online], [cited 26 January 2004]. Available from the Internet: *http://www.corsinet.com/braincandy/dying.html*.
[2]Appreciation is expressed to Shawn Hendricks, International Mission Board, for providing this account.

Answers to matching activity on page 14: 1. c, 2. d, 3. b, 4. a

[a]Avery T. Willis Jr., *The Biblical Basis of Missions* (Nashville: Convention Press, 1979), 11.
[b]Paul Borthwick, *Six Dangerous Questions to Transform Your View of the World* (Downers Grove, IL: InterVarsity Press, 1996), 25.
[c]A. Scott Moreau, ed., *Evangelical Dictionary of World Missions* (Grand Rapids: Baker Books, 2000), 745.
[d]Harper G. Smyth, "Make Me a Channel of Blessing," *Baptist Hymnal* (Nashville: Convention Press, 1991), 564.
[e]Larry Walker, *Holman Bible Dictionary*, ed. Trent C. Butler (Nashville: Holman Bible Publishers, 1991), 488.
[f]The idea for this activity came from William J. Larkin Jr. and Joel F. Willams, eds., *Mission in the New Testament: An Evangelical Approach* (Maryknoll, NY: Orbis Books, 1998), 46.

Chapter 2

A New Worldview:
Your Church's Ends of the Earth

YOUR MISSION

After completing this chapter, you will be able to—

• identify the Holy Spirit's role in missions;

• summarize mission principles the early churches followed to reach the ends of the earth with the gospel;

• apply these principles to modern-day churches' efforts to reach the ends of the earth;

• summarize believers' responsibility to carry the gospel to the ends of the earth;

• commit to pray for the people at the ends of the earth.

My friend Bob really enjoys yard work. He's especially proud of his high-powered leaf blower. One autumn day Bob was having difficulty moving his fallen leaves where he wanted them to go. The wind was blowing in a different direction, so just as he got the leaves where he wanted them, a gust of wind would blow them back.

Finally Bob's wife, Phyllis, went outside and suggested, "Why don't you work with the wind instead of against it?" Bob considered her idea and took a minute to form a new plan for moving the leaves to a different spot. He soon discovered that although he was moving the leaves farther, the job was 10 times easier! In fact, he simply had to stir up the leaves and let the more powerful wind at his back do the rest. Bob was so delighted with his newfound power and effectiveness that he not only finished his yard in record time but also cleaned up his neighbors' yards.

Group Session 2

1. Read "Your Mission" for chapter 2 on page 31. Distribute copies of study sheet 1, "How Can They Hear?" Divide members into two groups and lead them to read the Scriptures responsively. That is, the groups should alternate reading, with one group reading together the passages in plain type and the other group reading together the passages in bold type. After the responsive reading, ask a member to lead in prayer.

Working with the Wind

Bob's experience illustrates what the Holy Spirit does to empower believers for the mission. Trusting in their own abilities, the Israelites in Old Testament times and Jesus' disciples before Pentecost were often like individual leaf blowers: they had limited fuel and a tendency to determine their own direction. If not for the gift of the indwelling Holy Spirit, Jesus' disciples would have had little hope of effectively carrying out God's mission. But with the powerful wind of the Holy Spirit behind them, even reaching the ends of the earth was not too great a mission or task. The same is true for individual believers today.

" 'You will receive power when the Holy Spirit has come upon you, and you will be My witnesses in Jerusalem, in all Judea and Samaria, and to the ends of the earth.' " **Acts 1:8**

In chapters 2–5 we will examine the mission fields that Jesus assigned in Acts 1:8. But first we must recognize the source of our ability to reach those mission fields. Our effectiveness in reaching our own ends of the earth—and our own Samaria, Judea, and Jerusalem—completely depends on the power of the Holy Spirit. Because the Great Commission is a supernatural task of supernatural proportions, it requires supernatural power (see Eph. 6:10-20).

Read Ephesians 6:10-20 from two translations. In your own words summarize the main teaching of this passage.

_____

_____

_____

Through the centuries many believers have been persecuted and put to death for their faith. In recent years a number of missionaries have been murdered. How do these facts illustrate and underscore the truths of Ephesians 6:10-20?

_____

_____

The Book of Acts records that the Holy Spirit was bestowed on the early church in miraculous, demonstrative ways. And the power available to believers today is just as great as it was in the first century. Let's look at ways the Holy Spirit directed and empowered early churches and our churches today.

2. Share that 119 million Christians were martyred during the 20th century.[a] Call for responses to the activities on page 32. State that we are engaged in spiritual warfare. As Paul requested, we must pray that the Holy Spirit will give us direction and boldness in our witness.

As you read each Scripture, match the reference with the Holy Spirit's activity.

___ 1. Acts 2:1-13   a. Carried Philip away to Azotus.

___ 2. Acts 2:14:42   b. Filled Stephen, enabling him to see God's glory
                                    as he was martyred.

___ 3. Acts 7:54-60

___ 4. Acts 8:4-8   c. Filled Saul and empowered him to proclaim Christ.

___ 5. Acts 8:26-38   d. Filled the early believers and enabled them to speak
                                    in different languages.

___ 6. Acts 8:39-40

___ 7. Acts 9:1-20   e. Directed Paul's missionary travels in Europe.

___ 8. Acts 10:1-33   f. Emboldened Peter to speak the truth about Jesus,
                                  and three thousand people were saved.

___ 9. Acts 16:6-10

g. Directed Philip to witness to an Ethiopian official.

h. Directed Peter to go to Cornelius to announce
     the good news to the Gentiles.

i. Empowered Philip to preach in Samaria and perform signs.

What do these passages teach us about the importance of sensitivity and obedience to the Holy Spirit?

The Holy Spirit calls out missionaries. The Book of Acts describes the early believers who participated in God's redemptive mission as having joyful boldness and supernatural effectiveness. The individual "leaf blowers" were working, but the Holy Spirit always directed, encouraged, and provided power.

As the Holy Spirit guided the early church, His activity at first seemed much like the rushing wind or fiery tongues that announced His arrival in the upper room—powerful, unstoppable, and, sometimes unpredictable (see Acts 2:1-13). When the Holy Spirit filled Peter, his message drew thousands to faith in Christ (see Acts 2:14-42). Yet when the Holy Spirit filled Stephen, his message led to Stephen's death as the first Christian martyr (see Acts 7:54-60). The Holy Spirit led Philip to Samaria, where He empowered great miracles and many believed (see Acts 8:4-8), but then directed Philip to an individual divine appointment with an Ethiopian eunuch (see Acts 8:26-38) before whisking him away to Azotus (see Acts 8:39-40).

God chose the reluctant Peter as an unlikely missionary to Cornelius, the first Gentile convert (see Acts 10:1-33). But then He made the startling selection of the persecutor Saul as the apostle whose primary ministry would be to the Gentiles (see Acts 9:1-20). Paul, always attuned to the Spirit's leadership, was planning to turn east and head toward Asia when the Holy Spirit intervened and directed him to turn west toward Europe instead (see Acts 16:6-10). Observing all this, the early believers surely must have wondered where the Holy Spirit would lead them next.

3. Show cel 7 and identify ways the Holy Spirit directed and empowered the early churches. Form four small groups and assign each group a New Testament figure: Peter (see Acts 2:14-42; 10:1-33), Stephen (see Acts 7:54-60), Philip (see Acts 8:4-8,26-40), Paul (see Acts 9:1-20; 16:6-10). Ask each group to discover and report on ways the Holy Spirit guided and empowered these early witnessses. Call for reports. Conclude by emphasizing that the Holy Spirit also directs and empowers churches in the same ways today.

The early churches and their missionaries remind us that sensitivity and obedience to the Holy Spirit are essential and are far more important than our plans. Redeeming the lost peoples of the world is God's mission, and we simply join Him in that mission. We must hold our strategies or intuitions loosely as we watch for evidence of the Holy Spirit's leadership.

The Holy Spirit communicates God's heart. The Holy Spirit is a perfect witness who hears Jesus' voice and communicates his will. Jesus explained the role of the Holy Spirit to His disciples shortly before His death and resurrection: " 'When the Spirit of truth comes, He will guide you into all the truth. For He will not speak on His own, but He will speak whatever He hears. He will also declare to you what is to come. He will glorify Me, because He will take from what is Mine and declare it to you. Everything the Father has is Mine. This is why I told you that He takes from what is Mine and will declare it to you' " (John 16:13-15).

> "As they were ministering to the Lord and fasting, the Holy Spirit said, 'Set apart for Me Barnabas and Saul for the work that I have called them to.' Then, after they had fasted, prayed, and laid hands on them, they sent them off." **Acts 13:2-3**

The Holy Spirit leads churches where He is already at work. Luke wrote that Jesus gave "orders through the Holy Spirit to the apostles whom He had chosen" (Acts 1:2). The Holy Spirit is specifically named, not only as the One who called Barnabas and Saul as missionaries from the church at Antioch (see Acts 13:2-3) but also as the One who sent them out (see Acts 13:4). The Holy Spirit is mentioned more than 60 times in the Book of Acts, so it is clear that He was the One who was directing the mission activity of the early church and that He led early believers to those already being drawn to faith in Christ. The witnesses were effective only where the Witness was already present.

The Holy Spirit carries out God's plan. As spontaneous and unpredictable as the Holy Spirit's New Testament activity may have seemed, there was a pattern to the Spirit's leadership. The Holy Spirit exhibited a missionary intentionality that still inspires and instructs churches today. Over the years that spanned the New Testament record and the miles that spanned its churches' missions activity, believers continued to be surprised and amazed by the Spirit's leadership, but they also began to ask strategic questions:

- Who needs the good news?
- Who will go to them?
- What unique barriers exist?
- Where do they live?
- Who will help and support?
- How will we bridge the barriers?
- How can new disciples and new churches join us in the mission?

God's intentional plan to pursue the lost peoples of the world became clearer to the early churches as the Holy Spirit led believers to participate in His mission. Believers today can also learn more of God's mission perspective as we live the adventure of a modern-day witness. In addition, we can benefit from the New

Testament and centuries of Christian history, which show us the way God started with one church and a few hundred Spirit-filled believers and modeled His plan for every local church and every Spirit-filled believer. Because the New Testament record gives us accurate hindsight and a comprehensive missions perspective, we can learn from God's Word many things that the early churches learned by experience.

This chapter will focus on a church's mission responsibility to spread the good news to the ends of the earth. Subsequent chapters will progressively narrow the focus to Samaria, Judea, and Jerusalem, viewing them as mission fields both for the early churches and for churches today.

Fill in the blanks to identify the Holy Spirit's role in missions.
The Holy Spirit calls out _____.
The Holy Spirit communicates God's _____.
The Holy Spirit leads churches where He is already _____ _____.
The Holy Spirit carries out God's _____.

The Early Churches' Ends of the Earth

As vast as the world seems to us today, we can only imagine how incredible Jesus' Acts 1:8 challenge to go to the ends of the earth seemed to the early churches. Relative to the world's population, there were few believers in the first century. The consensus is that the world contained between two hundred million and three hundred million people at the time of Christ. According to 1 Corinthians 15:6, the number of people who had seen the risen Christ when He gave the Great Commission numbered about five hundred. Acts 1:15 says that 120 people waited in the upper room after Jesus' ascension. Numerically speaking, the early church's task can be compared to one small or medium-sized church today that decides to take the gospel to the entire population of the United States—except this vast number of people is spread around the entire globe! Furthermore, in biblical times those millions of people were divided into hundreds of different languages and cultures, bordered by oceans and mountains, and sometimes ruled by hostile governments.

Imagine how encouraging the day of Pentecost must have been to the early believers. When the Holy Spirit first came on the believers in Jerusalem, He gave them the miraculous ability to speak in languages they had not learned. A great barrier to the spread of the gospel was lifted! Immediately, they were able to communicate with Jews visiting in Jerusalem from "every nation under heaven" (Acts 2:5).

More than a dozen different locations and nationalities are specifically named in Acts 2:9-11. The gospel would be carried as far as those places—more than 1,500 miles—within the first 60 years of the church's existence. About three thousand people became followers of Christ after Paul's first sermon. Presumably, they shared

35

4. Tell members to imagine that they belong to a church with 120 members that Jesus has commanded to spread the gospel throughout the United States. No other churches exist in the country, and your church has no organization, building, or money. Brainstorm strategies to carry out Jesus' command. Explain that the task faced by the early church was much more difficult because of limited transportation and communication. State that apart from the Holy Spirit's miraculous empowering, the rapid spread of the gospel would have been impossible.

with others, and soon the good news reached their homelands. In one day God demonstrated that faithful believers, empowered by the Holy Spirit, would indeed carry the message of Christ to the ends of the earth.

This event stands in contrast to the tower of Babel, where God first confused self-aggrandizing humans by giving them different languages. That judgment not only scattered people around the world but also birthed people groups. Though at Babel God judged humankind's sinful, selfish cooperation, He continued to express His love for rebellious humanity and His intent that worshipers from those peoples would one day gather at His throne. At Pentecost the Holy Spirit demonstrated that in addition to empowering the church to cross the barriers of language and culture, He would allow redeemed humankind to help build His kingdom. Soon the young church of Jews and Jewish converts in Jerusalem would be astonished to learn that God intended to reach out not only to Jews of all languages and locations but also to the Gentiles, or non-Jewish people groups, who inhabited the rest of the world.

What timeless principles can we learn from New Testament churches that became Jesus' witnesses to the ends of the earth? Examine the chart on page 37 and preview the ends-of-the-earth principles we will study in this chapter. You will discover parallel principles for the other three mission fields in subsequent chapters.

Notice the headings along the left side of the chart. Whether we are discussing the ends of the earth, Samaria, Judea, or Jerusalem, all of the mission principles we will examine in this study fit into the following broad mission concepts.

- **Calling.** God calls His witnesses to join Him in His redemptive mission.
- **Cultures.** God calls witnesses to go to specific groups of people who share common characteristics.
- **Church planting.** When people believe and receive the gospel message, they gather into fellowships with other believers.
- **Cooperation.** Because no single church can take the gospel to an entire mission field alone, cooperation with other churches is essential and rewarding.
- **Challenges.** Each Acts 1:8 mission field holds huge challenges that churches must overcome to effectively take the gospel to lost people.

Keep these five overarching mission concepts in mind as you study the following mission principles from the early church's ends of the earth.

The Calling Principle from the Ends of the Earth

God calls Christians to the world in ways that are both incidental and intentional. Acts 8 and Acts 13 present two ways God dispersed His young church.

Read Acts 8:1-8. What happened to the church when persecution broke out?

_____

5. Read Acts 2:5-13. Say, Assume that you were a visitor to Jerusalem who observed the events at Pentecost. Ask, How would you have described what you saw and heard to your friends and neighbors when you returned home?
6. Direct attention to the chart on page 37 and explain that chapters 2–5 examine biblical principles for carrying out Jesus' Acts 1:8 challenge to the ends of the earth, Samaria, Judea, and Jerusalem. Show cel 8 as you explain the five mission concepts on page 36. Point out how the five mission concepts relate to the principles on the chart.

PRINCIPLES FROM THE MISSION'S FIELDS

Mission Concepts	Ends of the Earth	Samaria	Judea	Jerusalem
Calling	STARTING God calls Christians to the world in ways that are both incidental and intentional.			
Cultures	PEOPLE GROUPS God's mission to the world includes all people groups.			
Church Planting	MOVEMENTS When the gospel is successfully planted, new churches grow and multiply.			
Cooperation	GIVING Taking the gospel to the world is costly.			
Challenges	RULERS Many kingdoms oppose God's kingdom, but God has sovereign authority over all.			

7. Draw attention to the framework of the Acts 1:8 visual that you prepared in advance and attached to the wall (see p. 144 for instructions for making the visual). Plan to add to the same visual in the remaining sessions.

What did the believers do as they were uprooted and fled to other areas?

_____

After Stephen's martyrdom in Acts 8, the mass persecution of the church resulted in the believers' scattering beyond Jerusalem. Some dispersion of the gospel message had probably already occurred as the international Jews who were converted at Pentecost returned to their homelands. Travelers and traders who came through Jerusalem may also have carried the gospel message abroad. But for many converts who had chosen to stay in Jerusalem, Stephen's martyrdom made it clear that the Holy Spirit was leading them to carry the good news beyond their current location.

Incidental scattering came through the course of regular life events, whether the events were bad, as in the case of persecution, or good, as in the case of the converts' returning home after Pentecost. This pattern was consistent with Jesus' Great Commission in Matthew 28:18-20.

Read Matthew 28:18-20 from two translations. Jesus' word "go" in verse 19, a verb in the continuous present tense, could also be expressed "as you are going." List three actions the early believers were to take as they were going to different places.
1. _____ 2. _____ 3. _____

An important vehicle in God's plan for delivering the gospel to the ends of the earth is the normal traffic of believers' lives. Jerusalem in particular and the promised land in general, for most of world history, have been hubs of religious pilgrimage and commercial trade. It was no accident that Jesus and then the Holy Spirit chose this location as the launching pad for God's redemptive world mission.

In Acts 13 the dispersion of believers appears much more intentional than incidental (although both methods are intentional for God). As the Antioch church went about its God-given purposes—proclaiming His word, teaching, ministering, worshiping—the Holy Spirit revealed the church's missions purpose. And the first tangible expression of that purpose was sending two gifted leaders to distant lands with the gospel.

Read Acts 13–14. In what way was Paul's first missionary journey intentional?

_____

How does the trip in Acts 13–14 illustrate the fact that the command in Acts 1:8 is to be implemented simultaneously in all four mission fields rather than sequentially?

_____

8. Add to the Acts 1:8 visual a placard with the calling principle, *God calls Christians to the world in ways that are both incidental and intentional.* Explain the concepts of incidental and intentional witnessing. Call for responses to the activities on pages 36 and 38. Ask members to find other examples in Acts of both incidental and intentional witnessing, such as Acts 3:1-10; 16:13-34; 17:1-4.

The fact that Barnabas and Saul went directly to the international mission field illustrates that Jesus' Acts 1:8 challenge is not sequential but simultaneous. Neither all of Antioch nor all of Syria had to be evangelized before the Antioch church sent missionaries abroad.

In the experiences and examples of both the Jerusalem and Antioch churches, we see that the local church is to be a launching pad for missionaries and mission trips. Recall the definition of *missionary* from chapter 1: a missionary is someone who, in response to God's call and gifting, leaves his or her comfort zone and crosses cultural, geographic, or other barriers to proclaim the gospel and live out a Christian witness in obedience to the Great Commission. The Holy Spirit works in the lives of local church members, teaching them their missions purpose and calling out faithful witnesses for missionary service. Some receive a vocational call that may last for years; others, a volunteer call for short-term assignments.

The *scattering* of witnesses from the Jerusalem church shows us that a local church's missionary purpose can be fulfilled *wherever witnesses go*. The *sending* of witnesses from the Antioch church shows us that a church's missionary purpose can be fulfilled *when witnesses go wherever*. Jesus promised that the Holy Spirit is at work at the ends of the earth, no matter how the other witnesses get there.

Define the two ways early believers were called into the world.
The sending of witnesses: ❏ Incidental   ❏ Intentional
The scattering of witnesses: ❏ Incidental   ❏ Intentional

Read Acts 14:26-28. What is the value of reports from mission trips and from missionaries?

_____

The New Testament gives accounts of missionaries who returned to their home churches to inform and inspire them with news of the Holy Spirit's activity at the ends of the earth. The Holy Spirit probably used these reports to call others into missionary service, to motivate those who stayed home to support missionary endeavors abroad, and to encourage them to be on-mission witnesses in their own circles of influence.

> "From there they sailed back to Antioch where they had been entrusted to the grace of God for the work they had completed. After they arrived and gathered the church together, they reported everything God had done with them, and that He had opened the door of faith to the Gentiles. And they spent a considerable time with the disciples." **Acts 14:26-28**

The Cultures Principle from the Ends of the Earth
God's mission to the world includes all people groups. Early in the Book of Matthew, Jesus stated that His own redemptive mission had a specific sequence. Jesus the Messiah came through the family of Abraham and David, and His disciples

9. Show cel 6 with the definition of *missionary,* which you used in session 1. Point out that whether someone goes to the ends of the earth as a vocational missionary or a short-term volunteer, the Holy Spirit is at work to send and empower witnesses.
10. Add to the Acts 1:8 visual a placard with the cultures principle, *God's mission to the world includes all people groups.* Summarize this section and call for responses to the two activities on page 40.

> " 'This good news of the kingdom will be proclaimed in all the world as a testimony to all nations. And then the end will come.' " **Matthew 24:14**

were to go first to the " 'lost sheep of the house of Israel' " (Matt. 10:6). However, in Matthew 24:14 Jesus made it clear that His ultimate plan had a much larger scope: the good news was to be proclaimed in all the world and to all people groups. The all-inclusive nature of the mission was not just about places; it was about people: "When Jesus gave us the Great Commission, the terminology he used was 'panta ta ethne' which literally means all the peoples of the world. Every people group deserves the opportunity to hear, understand and respond to the Gospel in their own language and cultural context."[1]

Someone said, "No one deserves to hear the gospel twice until everyone has heard it once." How is this statement an indictment of U.S. churches and Christians?

_____

_____

In the Bible the word *nations* is best understood as *ethnolinguistic people groups*. Virtually every country, regardless of geographic boundaries, includes multiple groups, families, or clans who share a common identity. Factors such as language, race, religion, heritage, and socioeconomics help define a distinct people group or its subgroups.

The first-century Christian missionaries benefited from fairly widespread common languages such as Greek, Hebrew, and Aramaic, as well as a stable Roman government that provided common law and customs. Nevertheless, they quickly learned that the farther from home they traveled, the more often their mission would cross language and culture barriers.

The multiple languages spoken at Pentecost (see Acts 2:1-13) remind us that even the Jewish people were composed of many different language groups. And Paul's experience in Athens (see Acts 17:16-34) indicates that even those speaking a common language may have come from many different cultures and belief systems. Throughout the international missionary journeys of Acts 13–28, Paul and other missionaries adapted to different cultures and occasionally spoke different languages in order to navigate their circumstances and credibly deliver the good news about Jesus.

Read Acts 21:33-40; 22:1-2 from two translations. How did Paul's ability to speak both Greek and Aramaic come to his rescue as he was about to be mobbed?

_____

11. Relate that God called Adoniram (pron. *add-uh-NIGH-rum*) Judson (1788–1850) and his wife, Ann Hasseltine Judson, to go to the ends of the earth with the gospel. As the first missionaries from America, they labored under great hardships in Burma (now Myanmar). State that we have the opportunity to hear Judson describe his work. The previously assigned member should come forward and present the dramatic monologue on page 148.

The pervasiveness of the Greek language and the Roman system of roads gave the New Testament churches the capability to spread the gospel rapidly. Paul's documented journeys across the Roman Empire covered more than 20,000 miles.[2] Why were the first churches and missionaries so passionate about carrying the gospel message to all peoples? And why should today's churches and missionaries be equally passionate about delivering the gospel to people groups that are hard to reach? Each lost soul in each people group—even at the ends of the earth—has value as a potential worshiper of God.

God deserves nothing less than the praise and adoration of every tribe, tongue, and people (see Ps. 86:9-10). When we realize that all we have to offer God is our adoration, we will long to express our worship adequately. As we hear the voices of every people joining ours in praise, we will rejoice in the presence of the treasures we helped bring to the throne of our great, worthy Redeemer.

The Church-Planting Principle from the Ends of the Earth
When the gospel is successfully planted, new churches grow and multiply.
As the first-century witnesses sought out the lost at the ends of the earth, what did the Holy Spirit lead them to do?

Read Acts 14:21-23. List three priorities of the first international missions team.

1. _____   2. _____   3. _____

What does Acts 14:23 imply about the importance of a local church?

_____

_____

Activities on the New Testament mission fields included teaching, healing, debating, encouraging, praying, writing, and performing miracles. But it is evident that the Holy Spirit's primary objective was to make disciples of Jesus. This would be accomplished as witnesses, in the power of the Holy Spirit, proclaimed the gospel and gathered believers into local churches. As disciples in a local congregation awaiting Jesus' return, they were to worship, fellowship, spiritually mature, and serve. And they were to accept Jesus' Acts 1:8 challenge and join the Holy Spirit and other churches as His witnesses in their own Jerusalem, Judea, Samaria, and ends of the earth.

> "After they had evangelized that town and made many disciples, they returned to Lystra, to Iconium, and to Antioch, strengthening the hearts of the disciples by encouraging them to continue in the faith, and by telling them, 'It is necessary to pass through many troubles on our way into the kingdom of God.' When they had appointed elders in every church and prayed with fasting, they committed them to the Lord in whom they had believed."
> **Acts 14:21-23**

41

12. Add to the Acts 1:8 visual a placard with the church-planting principle, *When the gospel is successfully planted, new churches grow and multiply*. Call for responses to the activities on page 41.

Of course, many churches in the first century were small. For example, Paul referred to Aquila and Priscilla as believers who had a church meeting in their home (see 1 Cor. 16:19). With the advantages of mobility and flexibility, however, these young churches were able to assimilate new believers quickly and to multiply rapidly by adding new converts. By the middle of the second century, flourishing churches had been planted in nearly all of the provinces between Syria, where the Holy Spirit called Barnabas and Saul from the Antioch church, and Rome.[3]

Sadly, the church-planting movements in early church history are relatively unfamiliar to American churches today but increasingly common on international mission fields. One missionary in an unevangelized region of Asia recently reported that 3 small churches with 85 mostly elderly Christians had grown to 550 churches with 55,000 believers in just four years. Erich Bridges writes:

> Similar reports come from almost every region of the world. What's going on? A phenomenon called church-planting movements. It is a "rapid and exponential increase of indigenous churches planting churches" within a people group, city, region or country.
>
> Church-planting movements have common characteristics: They begin through the work of missionaries or other outsiders but soon become indigenous and self-reproducing. They increase exponentially, since new churches quickly plant churches themselves. The movements emerge from prayer and build their foundations upon the Word of God.
>
> They also thrive with lay leaders and don't depend upon professional clergy or buildings for growth. They don't wilt under persecution: New believers learn to expect it, endure it and, if necessary, die under it.[4]

The priorities the Holy Spirit gave the New Testament witnesses are still the priorities of today's missionary endeavors:
1. Proclaim the gospel message.
2. Make disciples of those who believe.
3. Organize the disciples into a healthy local church that joins you on mission.

The Cooperation Principle from the Ends of the Earth

Taking the gospel to the world is costly. While in Corinth, Paul supported himself by working as a tentmaker (see Acts 18:1-4). Yet Paul also argued in a letter to the Corinthians that those whose lives are dedicated to proclaiming the gospel deserve the financial support of the churches that commissioned them or that benefit from their ministry (see 1 Cor. 9:3-6,13-14). The latter is most often the case in missions efforts to the ends of the earth, where new churches are often unable to support the missionary who plants the gospel or helps establish a new church.

42

13. Point out the three priorities the Holy Spirit gave the New Testament witnesses (p. 42).
14. Add to the Acts 1:8 visual a placard with the cooperation principle, *Taking the gospel to the world is costly.* Using the same four small groups that were formed in step 3, assign the groups the following passages: (1) Acts 2:45; 4:36-37; (2) Acts 11:27-30; (3) 2 Corinthians 8:1-15; (4) 2 Corinthians 9:1-15. Ask each group to identify the occasion, the need, and the response in each case and to explain how the passage illustrates the cooperation principle.

The reality of missions, especially at the ends of the earth, is that spanning distances, spanning cultural barriers, and overcoming opposition to the gospel all take time, and time costs money.

There is no better investment than helping move a missionary family to the mission field and providing them food, shelter, and necessities while they build relationships and plant the gospel message. This support is the best way to " 'collect for yourselves treasures in heaven' " (Matt. 6:20), as Jesus urged us to do. Jesus also said that our hearts will naturally follow our treasure (see Matt. 6:21). Knowing that God's heart is in redeeming a lost world, we can be sure that placing our treasure and our hearts in His mission is the soundest investment we can make. Southern Baptists are blessed to have a unified giving plan called the Cooperative Program, through which churches can invest in missions causes throughout the world.

First-century churches were more than generous in their giving; they gave sacrificially. In Acts 2:45 the Jerusalem believers sold their possessions and property, distributing the proceeds to meet one another's needs. Acts 4:36-37 records that Barnabas sold a field and laid the money at the apostles' feet. And one of Saul's first leadership assignments in Acts 11:27-30 was to deliver a famine-relief offering from the Antioch church to believers in Judea.

Some of the greatest Scriptures on stewardship come from Paul's letters in which he coordinated an offering collection among several churches. Their generous cooperation enabled them to do far more together than what they could have done individually.

Read 2 Corinthians 8:1-5. List two factors indicating that the Macedonians' giving was sacrificial.

1. _____

2. _____

> "We want you to know, brothers, about the grace of God granted to the churches of Macedonia: during a severe testing by affliction, their abundance of joy and their deep poverty overflowed into the wealth of their generosity. I testify that, on their own, according to their ability and beyond their ability, they begged us insistently for the privilege of sharing in this ministry to the saints, and not just as we had hoped. Instead, they gave themselves especially to the Lord, then to us by God's will." **2 Corinthians 8:1-5**

Although these churches were severely tested and impoverished, they begged for the privilege of participating in this offering! Paul said this kind of sacrificial giving came from the grace of God, and it came after they had first given themselves to the Lord.

Some offerings described in the New Testament were directed to other believers or other churches. Some were to relieve suffering, and some were to support missionary efforts. All were given sacrificially, benefiting the kingdom of God and furthering its advance.

This is the kind of sacrificial giving required to reach the ends of the earth with the gospel. Giving for the advance of the kingdom doesn't ask, "Will we be paid back?" or "Will we benefit in return?" It doesn't purchase greater blessings for the church but greater influence for the gospel message. A church's missions giving is similar to an individual's tithe: it acknowledges that all wealth and blessing come from God and that the consumption of those blessings should not precede their sacrificial dedication to the purposes of God's worldwide redemptive plan.

The Challenges Principle from the Ends of the Earth

Many kingdoms oppose God's kingdom, but God has sovereign authority over all. As the early witnesses took the gospel to the ends of the earth, they encountered many political, religious, racial, and economic authorities and forces. Sometimes these forces worked in the favor of the mission, such as when Philip shared the gospel with an important Ethiopian official (see Acts 8:26-38), when Barnabas and Saul found a favorable reception with the proconsul Sergius Paulus on the island of Cyprus (see Acts 13:4-12), or when Paul invoked his Roman citizenship to preserve his life (see Acts 16:12-40; 22:24-29; 25:11-12).

More often, however, human authorities opposed the gospel and its witnesses. Peter and John encountered this opposition by the Jewish leaders in Jerusalem.

Read Acts 4:23-31. List the adversaries to Jesus and the gospel.

_____   _____   _____

_____   _____   _____

What was the main thing the disciples prayed for? _____

Referring to Psalm 2:1-2, the apostles acknowledged that the kings of the earth naturally resist the lordship of the true King. Their prayer's list of opponents includes groups such as Gentiles, kings, rulers, and the people of Israel; they also specifically named the rulers Herod and Pontius Pilate. These earthly authorities are described as assembling in united defiance of Jesus, the Messiah-King.

Yet the apostles' focus in this Acts 4 prayer was not on earthly authorities, whose strong intimidation would intensify to become punishment and persecution. Instead, the apostles focused on their anointed King Jesus and on God's sovereign hand that guarantees His mission plan. Recognizing their privileged role in that plan, they prayed not for safety or escape but for boldness and power in the name of Jesus, who had suffered infinitely more on their behalf.

From that point forward the first-century witnesses would face stronger opposition and more severe persecution. Sometimes the opposition came from Jewish

15. Add to the Acts 1:8 visual a placard with the challenges principle, *Many kingdoms oppose God's kingdom, but God has sovereign authority over all.* Have a member read Acts 4:23-31. Call for responses to the related activity on page 44.

rulers who feared losing their religious authority. Sometimes governmental rulers who feared losing their civic authority opposed the message.

Match each Scripture with the way people in each city opposed the gospel.

___ 1. Acts 16:16-24   a. A riot swept up Paul's companions in Ephesus.
___ 2. Acts 17:1-9   b. Some Athenians ridiculed Paul in the Areopagus.
___ 3. Acts 17:16-34   c. A slave's owners in Philippi seized Paul and Silas,
___ 4. Acts 18:1-11   and chief magistrates had them beaten.
___ 5. Acts 19:21-41   d. Jews in Corinth rejected Paul.
                        e. A mob attacked Paul and Silas in Thessalonica and
                           dragged them before city officials.

In one notable instance in Ephesus (see Acts 19:21-41), local businessmen and merchants who feared losing economic power if people stopped worshiping the local goddess, Artemis, became the opposition. Ephesus is one of several large, political cities that played strategic roles in the early church's mission to the ends of the earth. Most of these urban areas were very difficult places to sow the seed of the gospel. In the city of Corinth Paul found the Jewish people particularly hostile to the good news. Acts 18:6 states that when the Jews "resisted and blasphemed," Paul grew so angry that he "shook out his clothes and told them, 'Your blood is on your own heads! I am clean. From now on I will go to the Gentiles.' "

Paul must have been frustrated and discouraged, having just come from the idol-filled city of Athens, where the intellectual elite rejected Jesus' resurrection (see Acts 17:16-17). Now the Corinthian religious establishment opposed the truth of the gospel. Although cities were the homes of many adversaries, in Corinth the Lord reassured Paul of his calling to these great cities (see Acts 18:9-10).

To this day the world's rulers do not easily relinquish power. Many value the servitude of the world's lost peoples and often fear the freedom that the gospel brings. Sometimes God brings earthly authorities to immediate judgment, as in the case of wicked Herod Agrippa in Acts 12:21-23, or to submission, as in the case of the Philippian magistrates in Acts 16:35-39. Other times earthly authorities' opposition to the gospel seems to go unchecked. Even in these cases the Holy Spirit continues to sovereignly accomplish Jesus' mission through His bold witnesses, irrespective of human authorities.

Like the early witnesses, today's churches are wise to consider the reality of earthly authorities as they carry the gospel to the ends of the earth. But they can do so with the same confidence displayed in the apostles' prayer in Acts 4, knowing that God's mission will prevail regardless of opposition and seeking boldness and power rather than relief or escape.

45

16. Ask volunteers to summarize the Scripture passages in the activity on page 45 that show ways people in the first century opposed the gospel. Answers: 1. c, 2. e, 3. b, 4. d, 5. a.

Your Church's Ends of the Earth

For early Christians the ends of the earth were practically everywhere. Every city, region, and nation was full of people who had not yet heard that Jesus had risen from the dead, offering eternal life to all who would place their trust in Him.

Two thousand years later, even in remote parts of the world, many have heard the gospel. Thousands of churches have been faithful to send missionaries, to evangelize people groups, and to start new congregations. However, today's ends of the earth still represent a daunting assignment. Consider the following examples.

- China has 1.3 billion people, 1.2 billion of whom do not believe in Jesus. Most of them have never heard the gospel. While 93 percent are Han Chinese, there are also approximately 495 minority people groups. Beijing is one of the world's most unreached cities, with a population of 18 million, only 2.4 percent of whom are thought to be Christians.[5]

- Indonesia's nearly 220 million people make up the largest Muslim country in the world. They inhabit 4,000 of the 17,000 islands in the Indonesian archipelago—stretching 4,000 miles across the Indian Ocean. One island, Sumatra, is the home of 52 known unreached people groups consisting of 25 million people. Of those 52 people groups, 48 have no indigenous churches, and 34 of them have no known gospel workers.[6]

- Eighty million Bengali Hindus inhabit India and Bangladesh. As one of the world's largest people groups, they have enormous cultural influence throughout the subcontinent. Yet two centuries after British Baptist missionary William Carey pioneered the modern missions movement in Bengal, evangelical Bengali believers still number only in the thousands, not in the millions.[7]

- In addition to the mass lostness described in the previous examples, the ends of the earth present the challenges of many people groups who are scattered or difficult for churches to reach. For example, the Tuareg (TWA-reg) people, estimated to number between 500,000 and 3 million, live in a wide range of countries that includes Algeria, Libya, Mali, Niger, and Burkina Faso. Their nomadic lifestyle makes them a difficult people on whom to gather statistics and even more difficult to reach with the gospel.[8]

- Approximately two-thirds of the world's people do not communicate through reading or writing but orally.[9]

In spite of these challenges, today's church is breathtakingly close to delivering the gospel to the whole world. International missionaries now engage more than 1,500 of the 5,000 Last Frontier people groups, adding almost 200 per year. The term *Last Frontier* refers to groups that have few evangelical Christians and little or no access to the gospel. Just as the good news spread from the Jerusalem church, it can now spread among those peoples—from one Christian and one church.

17. Ask five members to read the statistics on page 46 that characterize our ends of the earth.
18. As you discuss modern-day applications of each principle in "Your Church's Ends of the Earth," refer to the five placards that you have already added to the Acts 1:8 visual.
19. Refer to the placard with the calling principle, *God calls Christians to the world in ways that are both incidental and intentional.* Help members apply this principle to the callings of Christians today. Ask members how they responded to the activities on page 47.

The principles that guided 1st-century churches to the ends of the earth also guide 21st-century churches. Let's consider general ways to apply those principles today.

The Calling Principle at Today's Ends of the Earth
God calls Christians to the world in ways that are both incidental and intentional. A church today that responds to Jesus' Acts 1:8 challenge remains sensitive to the Holy Spirit when He calls missionaries from that local body. Those missionaries may be called to go as witnesses to a specific mission field or to be witnesses as they go, traveling or moving because of their vocation.

Identify each call as intentional or incidental: Diane and Thomas are a married couple who feel that God is calling them to reach Hindus with the gospel.   ❏ Intentional   ❏ Incidental   Mitch finds many opportunities to witness as he goes to the gym and the grocery store.   ❏ Intentional   ❏ Incidental

Think about the normal travel and traffic patterns of your life—how you spend your time, where you work, and the places you go. Use the scale below to evaluate how well you share the gospel during the everyday patterns of your life. 1 = not at all; 3 = occasionally; 5 = consistently.

I share the gospel—

With my friends	1	2	3	4	5	While shopping	1	2	3	4	5
With my neighbors	1	2	3	4	5	At sporting events	1	2	3	4	5
At work	1	2	3	4	5	At social events	1	2	3	4	5
At church	1	2	3	4	5	On vacation	1	2	3	4	5
At the gym	1	2	3	4	5						

The Cultures Principle at Today's Ends of the Earth
God's mission to the world includes all people groups. Many people groups today have little or no access to the gospel because churches have not yet sufficiently overcome barriers to the good news. Today there are only about 192 countries in the world[11] but at least 11,000 documented people groups.[10] The International Mission Board of the Southern Baptist Convention classifies a little more than half of these (almost 6,500) as unreached people groups, meaning that the number of evangelical Christians among that group totals less than 2 percent of the population. Those 6,500 unreached people groups have a combined population of around 3.4 billion—roughly 54 percent of the world's population. And among those 3.4 billion are approximately 1.5 billion people in 5,000 Last Frontier people groups.[12]

Whether a church sends missionaries from its own body or supports those who have been called from other church bodies, it can partner with those missionaries in

47

20. In dealing with the cultures principle, *God's mission to the world includes all people groups,* review the definition of *people group* from session 1 (see leader guidance, bottom of p. 11). Call attention to the definitions of *Last Frontier* at the bottom of page 46 and *unreached people group* at the bottom of page 47. Call for responses to the activity at the top of page 48.

reaching specific people groups. Many churches adopt one or more people groups for focused prayer, developing personal relationships with the missionaries who seek to reach those people groups.

Today the pervasiveness of the English language and tools like radio, the Internet, and modern transportation systems also give today's churches unprecedented opportunities to reach the ends of the earth.

List ways the following tools can help churches spread the gospel.
❑ High-speed transportation: _____
❑ Widespread use of English language: _____
❑ Financial resources: _____
❑ Books: _____
❑ Postal services: _____
❑ Radio: _____
❑ Telephone: _____
❑ Television and film: _____
❑ Internet: _____

Go back and check each item your church uses to spread the gospel internationally.

The Church-Planting Principle at Today's Ends of the Earth

When the gospel is successfully planted, new churches grow and multiply. Churches with a heart for reaching the ends of the earth frequently provide training in evangelism, church-planting principles, and the missionary use of education and technology. When their members go on short-term mission trips, they are more effective and helpful to the missionaries on the field.

Indicate how your church has been involved in church planting at the ends of the earth.
❑ Provided training
❑ Provided financial support
❑ Sent members on short-term mission trips
❑ Partnered with missionaries on the field

The Cooperation Principle at Today's Ends of the Earth

Taking the gospel to the world is costly. Providing finances and other key resources for missions is a biblical principle that every church can follow. For example, the Southern Baptists' unified giving plan, the Cooperative Program, and the Lottie Moon Christmas Offering® for international missions enable the International Mission Board of the Southern Baptist Convention to place more than five thousand missionaries in strategic locations at the ends of the earth. These mission-

48

21. Refer to the placard with the church-planting principle, *When the gospel is successfully planted, new churches grow and multiply.* Point out ways churches today can support church planting.
22. As you introduce the cooperation principle, *Taking the gospel to the world is costly,* ask members to identify ways believers and churches can support world missions financially.

aries also provide the infrastructure for churches to be personally involved in international missions. Many churches today, however, are not sacrificially supporting God's worldwide mission. As a result, hundreds of missionaries who have answered the Holy Spirit's call cannot be assigned to the mission field. There has never been a more critical time for churches to sacrificially give to God's worldwide mission.

A CHURCH ON MISSION

First Baptist Church in Concord. Tennessee. reaches the Mapuche people by planting churches like this one in Llanko Pullu. Chile.

Reaching lost people who have the least chance to hear the gospel characterizes ends-of-the-earth missions at First Baptist Church in Concord, Tennessee. Church members have built relationships with International Mission Board missionaries to expand their ministries. In Chile volunteers partner with missionaries to reach the Mapuche people by planting churches. Working alongside international missionaries, church members teach English, distribute gospel materials, and reach out to North African immigrants in Madrid, Spain. Volunteers in upper Southeast Asia partner with missionaries to reach the Tai Lue people.

First Baptist also works with the International Mission Board to reach peoples who have no missionaries. The church has taken responsibility for a city of 250,000 in East Asia. "In essence our church is the missionary to the city," says Phil Nelson, associate pastor, missions. The church is also beginning work in Turkey and Iraq, while continuing relationships in Vietnam and Nicaragua.

Even when church members are not overseas, the world is on their hearts. A weekly prayer group lifts up missionaries and lost peoples. At an annual missions and evangelism expo, the congregation interacts with missionaries and explores missions opportunities. Discipleship groups at the church offer missions training.

The church's next goal is to involve all Sunday School classes in effective Acts 1:8 outreach to support local, national, and international missions efforts.[13]

What are some ways your church gives to world missions?

The Challenges Principle at Today's Ends of the Earth

Many kingdoms oppose God's kingdom, but God has sovereign authority over all. As today's churches send missionaries and participate in missions projects, they still face the resistance of rulers and authorities. World governments change rapidly, and many are hostile to Christian missions efforts. On the other hand, government changes have also brought unprecedented access to people groups who were long isolated from the gospel message. International travel, communication, and commerce often allow more opportunities for on-mission believers than are available to career missionaries.

Although America's reputation for decadence and capitalism creates barriers to penetrating some countries and people groups, America's reputation for wealth, education, technology, democracy, and Christian compassion often opens doors. Nowhere is this more evident than in the great cities of the world, where international business and technology enable on-mission Christians to crisscross the world.

What are some forms of opposition to the spread of the gospel at the ends of the earth today?

Today's churches must always remember that the mission is God's and that the Holy Spirit's power and direction are indispensable to the missions task. Each church has the responsibility and joy to discern where the Holy Spirit is calling it to join Him in reaching the ends of the earth.

How Far Will We Go?

The example of the first-century churches makes it clear that no place and no people group are beyond the reach of Jesus' Great Commission. How far will your church go to proclaim the gospel?

Today the Holy Spirit continues to speak to the church from God's worldwide, history-long perspective. Without that breadth of vision for all the peoples of the world, today's churches are unlikely to go beyond their own Jerusalems. In fact, they are unlikely to go beyond their own walls.

This study begins with the ends of the earth rather than Jerusalem for several important reasons. First, the Holy Spirit immediately led the first-century churches

23. Ask members to give examples of opposition to the spread of the gospel today. Discuss implications of the challenges principle, *Many kingdoms oppose God's kingdom, but God has sovereign authority over all.*
24. Ask a volunteer to quote last week's memory verse, Acts 1:8.
25. Show cel 9 of Matthew 28:19-20. Lead the group to read the verse in unison. Challenge members to memorize the verses before the next session.
26. Ask volunteers to read the teaching posters on the walls and to comment on their meanings.

to the ends of the earth. All of Jerusalem, Judea, and Samaria did not have to be evangelized before the Holy Spirit scattered and deliberately sent witnesses abroad. Today, as in the New Testament, a church's ends of the earth, Samaria, Judea, and Jerusalem are to be reached simultaneously.

A second important reason we began with the ends of the earth is that international missions gives us the broadest view of the world's lostness and of God's heart for all peoples everywhere. This perspective can be compared to a view of the world from outer space. From beyond the earth's atmosphere we can see continents, natural barriers, and even weather patterns. Similarly, God's mission to the ends of the earth helps us see large principles like those detailed in this chapter.

But as our space shuttle descends toward the Samaria part of our mission field, we can more clearly see additional biblical principles. As the ends of the earth show us the breadth of lostness in the world, Samaria shows us the depth of lostness that characterizes our own North American culture. The principles we've observed in this chapter are also true of the Samaria mission field, but chapter 3 will also teach us additional principles about our Samaria as we continue to examine ways the Holy Spirit first worked through His churches.

Review the chart on page 37. Note how each mission principle relates to a broad mission concept. Now without referring to the chart, summarize each ends-of-the-earth mission principle in your own words.

Calling principle: _____

_____

Cultures principle: _____

_____

Church-planting principle: _____

_____

Cooperation principle: _____

_____

Challenges principle: _____

27. Distribute copies of study sheet 2, "Evangelism and Missions." If time does not permit members to complete it during the session, ask them to do so at home and to bring it with them to the next session.

28. State: Rick Warren shares three ways to shift from local thinking to global thinking: (1) Begin praying for specific countries. (2) Read and watch the news with Great Commission eyes. (3) Go on a short-term missions project to another country.[b] Display these three actions on a large sheet of paper that you have prepared in advance. Challenge members to adopt these three actions.

Complete this sentence: Believers have a responsibility to carry the gospel to the ends of the earth because—

_____

_____

_____

Pray that all churches today will have a greater vision and will work harder to carry the gospel to the ends of the earth. Commit to pray each day that the gospel will reach the ends of the earth.

Recite Acts 1:8 from memory. Write Matthew 28:19-20 on a card. Keep the card with you and memorize the verses this week. Read it along with Acts 1:8 at least once each day during this study.

____

[1] Jerry Rankin, "34 billion unreached. Where do we start?" *BP News* [online] 8 December 2003 [cited 28 January 2004]. Available from the Internet: *http://www.bpnews.net/bpnews.asp?ID=17224*.

[2] James Pritchard, ed., *The Harper Atlas of the Bible* (New York: Harper and Row, 1987), 172.

[3] Tim Dowley et al., *Eerdman's Handbook to the History of Christianity* (Grand Rapids: Wm. B. Eerdman's Publishing Company, 1977), 65.

[4] Erich Bridges, "Erich Bridges: Church-planting movements started in the Book of Acts," *Pastors.com* [online] 20 August 2003 [cited 29 January 2004]. Available from the Internet: *http://www.pastors.com/article.asp?ArtID=4068*.

[5] International Mission Board, "What information should my church know?" *International Missions Emphasis 2003: Follow God's Purpose*, 18–19.

[6] Rankin, "34 billion reached."

[7] Erich Bridges, "Acts of God," *The Commission* (January 2002), 42–48.

[8] Sue Sprenkle, "Day of prayer and fasting for world evangelization: The Tuareg," *The Commission* January 2003, 6–11.

[9] Tex Sample, *Ministry in an Oral Culture—Living with Will Rogers, Uncle Remus, and Minnie Pearl* (Louisville: Westminster/John Knox Press, 1994), 6.

[10] "Independent States in the World," *U.S. State Department* [online], 27 February 2004 [cited 25 March 2004]. Available from the Internet: *http://www.state.gov/s/inr/rls/4250pf.htm*.

[11] People Groups [online] *http://peoplegroups.org/Downloads.aspx*.

[12] International Mission Board, "Your gifts changing the world," *International Missions Emphasis 2003: Follow God's Purpose*, 4. Research Team Statistics, North American Mission Board of the Southern Baptist Convention.

[13] Appreciation is expressed to Manda Roten, International Mission Board, for providing this account.

Answers to matching activity on page 33: 1. d, 2. f, 3. b, 4. i, 5. g, 6. a, 7. c, 8. h, 9. e
Answers to matching activity on page 45: 1. c, 2. e, 3. b, 4. d, 5. a

29. Call for responses to the first activity on page 52.
30. Close by praying that members and your church as a whole will use every opportunity to reach the ends of the earth for Christ.

[a] James and Marti Hefley, *By Their Blood: Christian Martyrs of the 20th Century*, 2nd edition (Grand Rapids: Baker Books,1996), 11.
[b] Rick Warren, *The Purpose-Driven Life* (Grand Rapids: Zondervan, 2002), 300–330.

Chapter 3

The Lost Continent:
Your Church's Samaria

YOUR MISSION

After completing this chapter, you will be able to—

• identify mission principles the early churches followed to reach Samaria with the gospel;

• apply these principles to modern-day churches' efforts to reach their Samarias;

• characterize North America as a modern-day Samaria;

• summarize believers' responsibility to carry the gospel to Samaria;

• commit to pray for the people of North America.

Growing up as a pastor's son, I was consistently taught that missions is important and that all people need Jesus. I invited my closest friends to church, especially to revival services. One year at one of those services, I was awarded a new Bible for filling up a pew with friends.

But out on the edge of town lived a family I would never have even thought about inviting to our church. I'll call them the Thirsty family. Ralph Thirsty was my age, but he was much smaller and thinner than I. He had an older sister and four younger brothers and sisters.

The Thirsty kids began attending our church regularly on Sunday mornings and even more consistently on Sunday evenings. Although it was probably two miles from their house to our church, the six kids regularly walked that distance without their parents. I have a feeling they were already pretty dirty when they left home, but by the time they trudged two miles in the summer heat, the Thirsty kids were usually soiled and smelly. They were obviously quite poor, judging by the worn, out-of-style clothes they wore.

Group Session 3

1. Write the word *Atlantis* on a marker board. Ask, What do you know about Atlantis? Write members' responses beneath the word. Possible answers include *lost continent, myth, Greek gods, strong race, movie.* Point out that the only known references to the mythic kingdom are in the writings of Plato in the fourth century B.C. Circle the words *lost continent* and state that this session is about a real lost continent: North America. Call attention to the title of chapter 3.

Though I'm ashamed to admit it now, I didn't like seeing the pack of Thirsty kids coming. One reason was their appearance and smell, and another was my general discomfort with their poverty. I didn't like imagining what their home life was like. But even more shameful to me now is the disdain I had for Ralph Thirsty because he was smart and because he soaked up Bible lessons like a sponge. When we had Bible drills or played games that depended on Bible knowledge, Ralph was quite competitive—even with me, the preacher's son. Our church's teachers lavished attention on him, and Ralph and the other Thirsty kids blossomed under their care.

The Thirsty family was not like anyone else in our church, and Ralph Thirsty was not like me or my friends. Our children's teachers had to make concerted efforts to reach out to the Thirsty kids. Today I'm sorry I didn't make the same effort.

Thirsty for the Gospel

The prejudices I had against the Thirsty family don't begin to approximate those that a devout Jew would have had for the Samaritan people in Jesus' day. Yet in His Acts 1:8 challenge, Jesus specifically listed Samaria as a key place the Holy Spirit would work through His faithful witnesses.

Read Matthew 4:24-25 and Mark 3:7-8. List the places beyond Jerusalem and Judea from which people came to hear Jesus.

_____

Jesus did not choose Samaria as a random example in His memorable final words on earth (see Acts 1:8). He could have named Galilee (see Mark 3:7-8), Syria (see Matt. 4:24), Decapolis (see Matt. 4:25), Tyre and Sidon (see Mark 3:7-8), or any number of other nearby regions. But Jesus knew that Samaria was a significant place and that the Samaritans were significant people. And I believe He knew that His future followers would come to understand not only the literal nature of first-century Samaria but also its symbolic meaning for missions today.

In this chapter we will descend from our imaginary space shuttle's perspective in outer space to view the large but specific region of Samaria. We will try to understand Samaria's Old Testament origins and history, and we will examine the approach that Jesus, the Holy Spirit, and His other witnesses took with Samaria. We will discover that the implications of the Samaria mission field for today's on-mission churches are not only geographic but also cultural, ethnic, and religious. The early witnesses who understood Samaria's history found the Samaritans as thirsty for

> " 'You will receive power when the Holy Spirit has come upon you, and you will be My witnesses in Jerusalem, in all Judea and Samaria, and to the ends of the earth.' " **Acts 1:8**

54

2. Read "Your Mission" for chapter 3 on page 53. Ask a member to lead in prayer.
3. If members were assigned to complete study sheet 2 at home, ask volunteers to share their responses.

the gospel as the woman at the well whom Jesus had offered living water (see John 4). If we learn from the Bible what those early witnesses learned by experience, we will find the families of our Samaria to be Thirsty families as well.

The Early Churches' Samaria

As overwhelmed as the early churches may have felt by Jesus' assignment to be witnesses to the ends of the earth, His mention of Samaria must have aroused an entirely different set of emotions. At first Jesus' followers assumed that the good news about the Messiah was only for Jewish people. Jews regarded Samaria, the region north of Jerusalem and Judea, as a place without devoted Jews. The despised Samaritans were the descendants of the northern tribes of Israel whom Assyria had conquered several hundred years earlier. After generations of intermarriage and compromise, the Samaritans represented both mixed race and mixed religion.

Read Ezra 4:1-5. When the Jews returned from exile and began rebuilding the temple, what did the Samaritans propose to do?

_____

What was the Jews' response? _____

_____

What did the Samaritans then attempt to do? _____

_____

Read Nehemiah 2:10; 4:6-9. When Nehemiah set out to rebuild the walls around Jerusalem, what did Sanballat, a Samaritan, and those with him do?

_____

When Nehemiah led a small Jewish remnant back from the Babylonian captivity in 444 B.C., the Samaritans sought to participate in rebuilding the temple in Jerusalem (see Ezra 4:1-5). When refused, Sanballat of Samaria became a serious hindrance to Nehemiah and the Jews (see Neh. 2:10,19; 4:6-9). Because of God's command not to mix with the other peoples, Nehemiah expelled Sanballat's son-in-law, Manasseh (who was also the grandson of the Jewish high priest) from Jerusalem. Manasseh

55

4. Ask two members to read Matthew 4:24-25 and Mark 3:7-8. Refer to the activity on page 54. Write on a marker board the places mentioned in the passages. Display a large map of the holy land in the time of Christ and locate each area on the map. Then locate Samaria and point out that Jesus chose to name this place in His Acts 1:8 challenge rather than the other places.

5. Explain who the Samaritans were. Ask two volunteers to read Ezra 4:1-5 and Nehemiah 2:10; 4:6-9. Call for responses to the activities on page 55.

left with a large group of dissident Jews and settled in Samaria, where Sanballat built an alternative temple on Mount Gerizim. From that time forward a deep religious rift divided the Jewish remnant in Judea and the rebel sect in Samaria.

Read each Scripture and match the reference with the correct statement.

___ 1. Matthew 10:5-6	a.	Jesus told the parable of the Good Samaritan.
___ 2. Luke 9:51-53	b.	Jesus talked with a Samaritan woman.
___ 3. Luke 9:54-56	c.	A Samaritan village did not welcome Jesus.
___ 4. Luke 10:25-37	d.	Jesus had to go through Samaria.
___ 5. Luke 17:11-19	e.	Jesus commanded His disciples not to enter any Samaritan town.
___ 6. John 4:1-4		
___ 7. John 4:5-26	f.	A Samaritan thanked Jesus for healing.
___ 8. John 4:39-42	g.	James and John wanted to destroy a Samaritan village.
___ 9. John 8:48	h.	The Jews called Jesus a Samaritan.
	i.	Many Samaritans believed in Jesus.

Understanding the history of Jews and Samaritans, Jesus' disciples must have been baffled when He deliberately chose to go through Samaria (see John 4:4). Jews usually walked around Samaria when traveling between Judea and Galilee. But Jesus even stayed there a couple of days, teaching a sinful Samaritan woman and her village about true worship of the true God (see John 4:23-24,40). Surely Jesus' listeners were also puzzled when He made the Good Samaritan the hero of his famous parable (see Luke 10:25-37). Every Jewish person who heard it must have been annoyed when Jesus depicted the priest and the Levite as calloused cowards and presented a loathed Samaritan as the one who truly understood the concept "Love your neighbor."

In fact, when Jesus' Jewish enemies really wanted to discredit and insult Him, they called Him demon-possessed and a Samaritan (see John 8:48). They were not suggesting Jesus was literally from Samaria. Jews labeled anyone they perceived to be a dissident against the Jewish religious establishment as a Samaritan. Just as being accused of demon-possession was the worst spiritual judgment, being called a Samaritan was the worst racial slur.

In spite of Jesus' wonderful encounter with the Samaritan woman (see John 4:1-26) and the many Samaritans who believed in Him (see John 4:39-42), Jesus and His disciples were not welcome in another Samaritan village because they were on their way to Jerusalem (see Luke 9:51-53). They found a place to stay but not before James and John hotly proposed calling down fire from heaven to consume the Samaritans who had rejected them (see Luke 9:54-55). Clearly, a couple of positive encounters had not erased centuries of racial and religious hatred that separated Jews and Samaritans.

6. Ask volunteers to read the Scriptures listed in the activity on page 56 and to give the answers (1. e, 2. c, 3. b, 4. a, 5. f, 6. d, 7. b, 8. i, 9. h).

Jesus' disciples may have felt that they were getting mixed signals from Jesus about the Samaritans. Just after commissioning His 12 disciples, Jesus sent them out with these instructions: " 'Don't take the road leading to other nations, and don't enter any Samaritan town. Instead, go to the lost sheep of the house of Israel' " (Matt. 10:5-6). Yet when Jesus healed the 10 lepers in a village between Galilee and Samaria (see Luke 17:11-19), He noted that the one who returned to give thanks was a Samaritan. While commending this man's faith, Jesus also asked rhetorically: " 'Were not 10 cleansed? Where are the nine? Didn't any return to give glory to God except this foreigner?' " (Luke 17:17-18).

Jesus did not wish to withhold the good news from the Samaritans. Rather, His mission promised priority to the Jewish people but not continued exclusivity. The kingdom of God and salvation through Jesus were first revealed to the Jews but were then offered also to the Samaritans and the Gentiles of the entire world. Jesus' inclusion of the Samaritans in His Acts 1:8 challenge may have puzzled the disciples at first, but soon they would learn what Peter later declared: " 'In truth, I understand that God doesn't show favoritism, but in every nation the person who fears Him and does righteousness is acceptable to Him' " (Acts 10:34-35).

The Samaritan woman, the people from her town, the thankful leper, and the Good Samaritan of Jesus' parable all foreshadow the new favor Jesus would confer on Samaritans in His Acts 1:8 challenge. Even these impure, rebellious people who had mingled with the world and walked away from their religious heritage would hear, through the Holy Spirit and His witnesses, of Jesus and salvation. Surprisingly, the Jewish witnesses would find many Samaritans to be thirsty and thankful for the gospel and even more willing to accept God's righteousness than many Jews were.

For most readers of this book, the Samaria of the 21st century can be seen as our own diverse nation and the North American continent. As in the Samaria of Jesus' day, our religious heritage has given way to a predominantly secular, pagan, and even idolatrous culture. Ethnically and religiously diverse, the peoples of North America are often as deeply cynical of Christians as Samaritans were of Jews.

Examine the chart on page 58 for an overview of biblical principles related to Samaria. Notice again that the key mission concepts of calling, cultures, church planting, cooperation, and challenges operate in the Samaria mission field.

The Calling Principle from Samaria

God calls Christians to personalize the gospel for the diverse peoples in and near their homeland. In the previous chapter we saw that God calls Christians to the ends of the earth in ways that are both incidental (wherever you go, the Spirit calls you to witness) and intentional (go wherever the Spirit calls you to witness). These patterns also apply to first-century Samaria. Stephen's martyrdom scattered the Jerusalem Christians throughout Judea and Samaria (see Acts 8:1) to the diverse peoples in and near their

7. Read the paragraph on page 57 that begins, "For most readers of this book. ..." State that as we examine the principles that New Testament believers followed in reaching their Samaria, we will learn how our churches can use these principles to reach our Samaria today.

8. Refer to the Acts 1:8 visual you began last week. Under *Samaria* add a placard with the calling principle, *God calls Christians to personalize the gospel for the diverse peoples in and near their homeland.* Use the chart on page 58 as a guide for attaching the placards to the wall during this session.

PRINCIPLES FROM THE MISSION'S FIELDS

Mission Concepts	Ends of the Earth	Samaria	Judea	Jerusalem
Calling	STARTING God calls Christians to the world in ways that are both incidental and intentional.	STRATEGIZING God calls Christians to personalize the gospel for the diverse peoples in and near their homeland.		
Cultures	PEOPLE GROUPS God's mission to the world includes all people groups.	POPULATION SEGMENTS Penetrating a diverse continent or country with the gospel requires a loving understanding of its people and history.		
Church Planting	MOVEMENTS When the gospel is successfully planted, new churches grow and multiply.	LEADERS The unchanging gospel speaks to diverse cultures and generations through new leaders and new methods in new churches.		
Cooperation	GIVING Taking the gospel to the world is costly.	KNOWING AND PRAYING Informed churches pray God's power into God's mission.		
Challenges	RULERS Many kingdoms oppose God's kingdom, but God has sovereign authority over all.	SOCIETY Negative cultural influences require both scriptural proclamation and spiritual confrontation.		

homeland. Philip was one of these mobilized witnesses who "went on their way proclaiming the message of good news" (Acts 8:4). The Holy Spirit mightily empowered this "wherever you go" deacon for His mission in the nearby but complex land of Samaria.

The Samaritan people were a diverse mixture of many backgrounds; yet the Bible says that "the crowds paid attention with one mind to what Philip said" (Acts 8:6). Why the unified response? The Holy Spirit was already at work in the hearts of the Samaritan people. He helped Philip communicate effectively and demonstrated through signs and miracles that Philip had a unique message for them from God.

Those signs and miracles met many of the Samaritans' physical and emotional needs, but the Holy Spirit's interest in the lost people of Samaria went much deeper. He knew that years of alienation and second-class citizenship in the eyes of devout Jews had taken their toll, even on the Samaritans who sought to worship the true God. Jesus' conversation with the Samaritan woman in John 4 had clearly demonstrated the historical religious and racial rift between Jews and Samaritans. Even those who had received the gospel message during Jesus' visit must have wondered whether Philip's good news would improve their status. The Samaritans needed acceptance, legitimacy, and a relationship with God that did not depend on race, national origin, or family heritage.

The Holy Spirit understood the deep longings of the Samaritan people. So did the early church leaders who were sensitive to His loving leadership. The Bible says that "when the apostles who were at Jerusalem heard that Samaria had welcomed God's message, they sent Peter and John to them" (Acts 8:14). What a wonderful, symbolic, personal mission action this was! What a loving way to welcome the Samaritan people into the family of God! Philip had served as the scattered witness, the traveling deacon who brought the initial good news. Now the Jerusalem church sent two of the leading apostles—two devout Jews—to lay hands on the new converts and to witness the Holy Spirit flooding into their lives.

In the Samaria mission field, missionaries and other on-mission Christians are often called to cross more than the obvious barriers of geography or language. Even nearby people can be very far from the gospel if churches do not bridge racial, ethnic, religious, or socioeconomic barriers. When the Holy Spirit called Philip, then Peter and John, to cross similar barriers, He gave them exactly what they needed to penetrate the predominant culture of Samaria: the ability to deliver the gospel with love and humility.

> "Those who were scattered went on their way proclaiming the message of good news. Philip went down to a city in Samaria and preached the Messiah to them. The crowds paid attention with one mind to what Philip said, as they heard and saw the signs he was performing. For unclean spirits, crying out with a loud voice, came out of many who were possessed, and many who were paralyzed and lame were healed. So there was great joy in that city." **Acts 8:4-8**

9. Ask a volunteer to read Acts 8:4-8. Ask: Who were the people scattered? What scattered them? Why were the apostles not scattered? What did the people do as they were scattered? Who was Philip (see Acts 6:1-6)? Where did he go? What did he preach to the people? What was the people's response to Philip's preaching? Why do you think the people were unified in their response? What were some of the signs Philip performed? What was the city's response to Philip's preaching? The Holy Spirit is not mentioned specifically in the passage; what evidence do we have that He was at work among the Samaritans?

State how the following factors can be barriers to reaching people with the gospel.

Language: _____

Geography: _____

Race, ethnicity: _____

Religion: _____

Culture: _____

Subculture: _____

Socioeconomics: _____

Much like North America today, Samaria was a melting pot of mixed religious practices and secular options. The historically bitter, battered Samaritans probably expected condescension and superiority from the Jewish messengers, but they found in Philip, Peter, and John the Holy Spirit's truth, power, and love. In that hardened, prejudiced culture, calloused Samaritan hearts were softened because the Holy Spirit and Jesus' witnesses met them at the point of their deepest needs.

The Cultures Principle from Samaria

Penetrating a diverse continent or country with the gospel requires a loving understanding of its people and history. While the Book of Acts gives us several insightful glimpses into the Samaria mission field of the first-century churches, we can also learn from Jesus' visit to Samaria during His earthly ministry. His conversation with the Samaritan woman at the well, recorded with wonderful detail in John 4, helps us better understand how the early churches and their predominantly Jewish members might have felt about being Jesus' witnesses in Samaria.

Read John 4:1-42. Why do you think Jesus needed to go through Samaria (see v. 4)?

_____

Why was the woman surprised that Jesus talked with her (see v. 9)?

_____

10. Lead a discussion of the activity at the top of page 60.
11. Ask the group to list the barriers the Jewish believers faced as they reached out to Samaria with the gospel. List these on a large sheet of paper or on a marker board.
12. Add to the Acts 1:8 visual a placard with the cultures principle, *Penetrating a diverse continent or country with the gospel requires a loving understanding of its people and history.* Call on the three persons you have enlisted to read John 4:1-42 as a role play, using three copies of study sheet 3, "Living Water," that you gave them in

What barriers did Jesus cross in reaching out to the Samaritan woman?

_____

Why do you think Jesus used the figure of living water (see vv. 10,13)?

_____

Why do you think Jesus mentioned the woman's immoral lifestyle (see vv. 17-18)?

_____

Why did the woman attempt to change the subject (see vv. 16-20)?

_____

How did Jesus answer the woman's attempt to engage in religious debate (see vv. 19-24)?

_____

How did Jesus model a deep love for the woman that looked beyond her race, background, and lifestyle?

_____

_____

How did Jesus demonstrate an understanding of the woman's needs?

_____

Why were the disciples surprised to find Jesus talking with the woman (see v. 27)?

_____

What was the food Jesus referred to in verses 31-34? _____

Why did the woman leave her water jar and go back to her village (see v. 28)?

_____

61

advance. One person plays the part of the narrator; the second person, Jesus; and the third, the woman. Presenting the passage this way will make the account come alive in members' minds.

13. Beginning on page 60, lead the group to discuss the answers to the questions in the activities based on John 4. End the discussion by emphasizing Jesus' perception of the woman's deep needs and His understanding of her culture.

What impact did the woman's testimony have on her village (see vv. 30,39-42)?

_____

How do you think Jesus' love and concern for the Samaritan woman influenced His disciples (see vv. 40-41)?

_____

Because of the generally accepted segregation between Jews and Samaritans, neither the Samaritan woman (see John 4:9) nor Jesus' Jewish disciples (see John 4:27) could believe that Jesus even initiated a conversation with her (see John 4:5-9). Most Jews hated Samaritans because many of them had intermarried with foreign conquerors over the years, often adopting their religions and cultures. Most Samaritans hated Jews because of their superior attitude and because of bitter disagreements over where to worship God (see John 4:19-20). In addition, it was socially inappropriate for Jesus to speak to a woman, especially one of her reputation.

Although no one expected Jesus to reach out to this Samaritan woman, He didn't allow social, racial, or religious barriers to keep Him from doing so. Jesus did not condone Samaria's history of religious compromise (see John 4:22) or the woman's history of moral compromise (see John 4:16-18). Yet through a very personal conversation, Jesus modeled an intentional, pursuing love for the woman, a love that looked beyond her race and background.

Jesus demonstrated an understanding of the woman's history, needs, and identity, both as an individual and as a Samaritan. He understood, for example, that centuries of idolatry, oppression by other kingdoms, and rejection by Jews had left many Samaritans with a deep spiritual thirst. Some Samaritans sought to quench that thirst through religious effort. They strictly observed their own version of the Mosaic law and worshiped on Mount Gerizim, a rival to Jerusalem. The Samaritans believed not only that Abraham and Jacob had worshiped on Mount Gerizim but also that Abraham had offered Isaac on an altar there. Other Samaritans sought to quench their spiritual thirst with any number of carnal alternatives offered by their idolatrous or secular culture. The Samaritan woman's five husbands and current relationship give us a picture of those futile pursuits (see John 4:18).

Jesus also understood Samaria's history and culture enough to cut through the smokescreen of religious debate behind which the woman tried to hide her immoral behavior (see John 4:17-19). His questions demonstrate that He understood the emptiness of the woman and her countrymen. Still, He accepted her as a Samaritan, as a woman, and as a sinner, offering her life-changing forgiveness. By offering her living water (see John 4:10-14), Jesus demonstrated how deeply He understood

14. Introduce the two members you have enlisted to role-play an interview of the Samaritan woman after her encounter with Jesus. Both members should have been assigned to prepare by reading pages 62–63. One member, the interviewer, should ask five questions he has prepared in advance. The other member, playing the role of the woman, should respond to the questions. After the interview, give the group an opportunity to make comments or to ask questions.

3 » THE LOST CONTINENT

her thirst. And when the villagers arrived, He obviously met them at the same point of need (see John 4:39-42).

Jesus' encounter with the Samaritan woman gives us a picture of a people who were seeking to quench their spiritual thirst with either religious legalism or moral license. The result was a prevailing culture that was an odd blend of religious pride (for having built their own places to worship the God of Abraham, Jacob, and Joseph) and religious guilt (for having adopted either false religions or pagan morality). When the Samaritans of Sychar came face-to-face with Jesus, they discovered that in His presence they could lay down both their pride and their guilt (see John 4:40-42). Personally meeting the Messiah of grace, they learned that God seeks worshipers in spirit and in truth, regardless of their location, race, or personal history.

Have you ever felt like the woman at the well, seeking things that cannot satisfy? ❑ Yes ❑ No What are some ways Americans try to quench their spiritual thirst?

_____

Jesus' example reveals several qualities that should characterize our efforts to reach our modern-day Samaria:

- Jesus' approach to reaching the Samaritans was *intentional*. John wrote that Jesus "had to travel through Samaria" (John 4:4), meaning not that Jesus was forced to go there but that He felt compelled to go. His example reminds us that there are population segments in or near our homeland with whom we rarely come in contact unless we make a point of doing so. Our normal pathways will not lead us there.
- Jesus was *informed*. He knew what life was like in Samaria, and He was ready to contextualize His message within the history and prevalent culture of the land.
- Ignoring prejudices that kept others away, Jesus was *interested* in the people He met there, acknowledging that their culture was unique and different from His.
- As Jesus interacted with the Samaritans, He was *insightful* into their deep spiritual needs. Therefore, He was able to translate the good news into a context they could understand and accept.
- Because Jesus was *impassioned* to see the people of Samaria come back to God, He didn't remain isolated from them. He entered the culture for the sake of its inhabitants, giving many Samaritans the true identity for which they searched.

As we saw in chapter 2, the early churches' mission to the ends of the earth reveals the *breadth* of obstacles that separate the world's vast people groups from the gospel and the lengths to which churches need to go to overcome those obstacles. The early churches' mission to Samaria reveals the *depth* of historical and cultural layers that often insulate or callous a people from truly hearing the gospel. Those who go on

15. Lead a discussion of the question in the activity on page 63: What are some ways Americans try to quench their spiritual thirst? Summarize the five bulleted points on page 63 and challenge members to be prepared, as Jesus was, to engage our Samaria.

mission to Samaria today must be ready to penetrate the hard shell of prevailing religious or secular culture and to apply the gospel to lost people's deep spiritual thirst. When Jesus drilled down to the core of one Samaritan woman's spiritual need, many in her village came to believe. Led by Philip and others, the early churches continued drilling down into Samaria, and living water quickly flowed in to satisfy spiritual thirst.

The Church-Planting Principle from Samaria

The unchanging gospel speaks to diverse cultures and generations through new leaders and new methods in new churches. If we follow the account of the early churches' experience from Acts 8:5 to Acts 9:31, the picture being drawn in Samaria would resemble the one being drawn by the Holy Spirit in other parts of the world. When Christ was communicated, converts gathered. When the good news about the Messiah was proclaimed, those who believed were baptized, congregated into new churches, and were nurtured as disciples.

"Philip went down to a city in Samaria and preached the Messiah to them." **Acts 8:5**

"The church throughout all Judea, Galilee, and Samaria had peace, being built up and walking in the fear of the Lord and in the encouragement of the Holy Spirit, and it increased in numbers." **Acts 9:31**

However, as the Holy Spirit's mission into Samaria progressed and the number of converts and churches increased, additional dynamics came into play, some of which are clearly stated in the New Testament and some of which are implied. For example, we see the Holy Spirit release the deacon Philip into a dynamic evangelistic ministry. Consequently, the Samaritans didn't have to go to Jerusalem to hear the gospel, and they also didn't have to hear it from an apostle. Clearly, the Holy Spirit intended the good news to be on every believer's lips, and some—like Philip—would see powerful results in places where apostles and even church leaders were not yet in place.

In this same period of expansion, not every person claiming to speak for Jesus really knew Him (see Acts 19:11-20), and the Jerusalem church and the apostles stepped into a supportive, validating role among the new converts in Samaria. The fact that the Holy Spirit did not manifest Himself until Peter and John arrived (see Acts 8:14-17) confirmed the acceptance of the previously outcast Samaritans into the predominantly Jewish church and validated the early apostles' authority to oversee the doctrinal purity of the early churches' teaching and practice.

It quickly became clear, however, that the number of converts and congregations in Samaria would exceed the number of the apostles or evangelists available to lead them. Philip and later Peter and John led people to initial faith in Christ but must also have trained and equipped Samaritan Christians to lead the new churches that were taking root in "many villages of the Samaritans" (Acts 8:25). As important as it was for the Jewish Christian missionaries to understand the Samaritan culture in

16. Add to the Acts 1:8 visual a placard with the church-planting principle, *The unchanging gospel speaks to diverse cultures and generations through new leaders and new methods in new churches.* Summarize the section "The Church-Planting Principle from Samaria."

which they proclaimed the gospel, it was also important for them to develop church leaders within that culture to lead its many new churches.

After his strategic encounter with an Ethiopian eunuch, "Philip appeared in Azotus, and passing through, he was evangelizing all the towns until he came to Caesarea" (Acts 8:40). Later in Acts, when Paul and Luke were traveling back through Caesarea on the way to Jerusalem, we discover that Philip had apparently settled there at Caesarea and that he had "four virgin daughters who prophesied" (Acts 21:9). We can almost imagine Philip, the evangelist to the Samaritans, in a regional ministry with his daughters serving alongside him. No doubt he was still drilling down to the source of the Samaritans' spiritual needs and still equipping a new generation to evangelize and start new churches in Samaria.

The Bible doesn't provide specific details about the early Samaritan churches or the development of their pastors and leaders. But as we imagine Philip and his family investing their lives there and as we think about the proximity of the Jerusalem church and the maturing of Spirit-filled Samaritan Christians, we can conclude that a great deal of cooperation, regional planning, and equipping must have taken place in the early Samaria mission field. In Samaria the early witnesses were challenged by cities as well as villages, older generations as well as younger, pagan religions as well as Jewish legalism. As the first-century churches and missionaries focused on Samaria's complex culture, they no doubt delivered the unchanging gospel through new methods and new leaders, resulting in dynamic new churches.

The Cooperation Principle from Samaria
Informed churches pray God's power into God's mission.

The following Scriptures describe reports the early Christians received on God's work and their reactions to these reports. Read the Scriptures and complete the chart.

Scripture	Report	Recipient	Response
Acts 8:14	_____	_____	_____
	_____	_____	_____
Acts 11:1-18	_____	_____	_____
	_____	_____	_____
Acts 15:3	_____	_____	_____
	_____	_____	_____
Acts 15:4-29	_____	_____	_____
	_____	_____	_____
Acts 15:30-31	_____	_____	_____
	_____	_____	_____

65

17. Add to the Acts 1:8 visual a placard with the cooperation principle, *Informed churches pray God's power into God's mission.* Ask five members to read the Scriptures listed in the activity on page 65. Call for responses to the activity.

The Jerusalem church must have been amazed to hear that the Samaritans had welcomed God's message (see Acts 8:14). But by the time we reach Acts 15, we find that the Holy Spirit had been active in other amazing ways. He had sent Peter to Cornelius to reveal that salvation is for the Gentiles as well as for the Samaritans and the Jews. And He had chosen Saul the persecutor as an apostle, then as a missionary. When Saul and Barnabas passed back through Samaria "describing the conversion of the Gentiles" (Acts 15:3), the Samaritans must have thought, *Wait until our brothers in Jerusalem hear this!*

Perhaps the Samaritan Christians received the news about the Gentiles' conversion with joy because Samaria itself had so surprisingly benefited from God's unbounded grace when Philip had first brought the gospel. The Jewish Christians, on the other hand, found the same report harder to believe (see Acts 11:1-18; 15:1-35). That is why reporting what God was doing on the world's mission fields was so critical to a local church in the New Testament. These reports not only helped authenticate the genuine and sometimes surprising movement of the Holy Spirit but also encouraged churches' unity and cooperation. As churches invested their leaders, their prayers, and their resources beyond their walls, news about the progress of the mission guided their plans for future missions efforts. Missions education encourages missions cooperation.

By the time Peter and John returned to the Jerusalem church from that first trip to Samaria, for example (see Acts 8:25), they could more fully understand the comprehensive scope of God's mission. Perhaps for the first time they could see that the Samaria of Jesus' Acts 1:8 challenge was not just a geographical location where some Jews would hear the gospel. Non-Jews could also receive salvation and the gift of the Holy Spirit! This expanding view of God's mission was further enlarged by Peter's vision and visit with Cornelius. On these occasions God revealed that He intended salvation to extend not just to the Jews and Samaritans but even to the Gentiles (see Acts 10).

Luke twice recounted the missions-education account of Peter and Cornelius in Acts 10–11, almost as if to say, "You won't believe this the first time, so let me tell you again!" The second account, of course, is in the context of Peter's defending Gentile salvation to the Jewish Christians "who stressed circumcision" (Acts 11:2). Peter's eyewitness testimony was that Gentile salvation was a work of the Holy Spirit and a sovereign part of God's comprehensive mission plan. Peter asked, " 'If God gave them the same gift that He also gave to us when we believed on the Lord Jesus Christ, how could I possibly hinder God?' When they heard this they became silent. Then they glorified God, saying, 'So God has granted repentance resulting in life to even the Gentiles!' " (Acts 11:17-18).

Many of the apostle Paul's letters provided news and missions education for the churches that received and shared them. Paul would often chronicle victories,

18. Point out the three ways that reports of the Holy Spirit's mission activity help churches today. These are identified by bullets at the top of page 67.

disappointments, blessings, needs, and stories of faithful and unfaithful workers. Churches that received Paul's letters then knew how to support and participate in the worldwide mission challenge.

Reports of the Holy Spirit's mission activity are also essential to churches today. When churches learn about the Holy Spirit's work on the mission field, they can—

- wisely invest their prayer, leadership, financial support, and other resources;
- support missionaries and missions efforts;
- enlarge their vision of how creatively and surprisingly the Holy Spirit still works in redeeming "Samaritans" and Gentiles today.

The Challenges Principle from Samaria

Negative cultural influences require both scriptural proclamation and spiritual confrontation. A man named Simon, described in Acts 8:9-13, personifies another principle we can learn from the Samaria mission field of the New Testament. Pagan, secular, and demonic influences within a culture can enslave and addict people. Churches must confront the culture's sinful pressures with scriptural truth.

Simon had become engulfed in the evils offered by the sinful culture around him. He worshiped power, popularity, and the profit and pleasures that came with them. By drawing on counterfeit powers that endangered his soul, Simon had convinced himself and others that he had God's power. As a testimony to God's far-reaching grace, Simon accepted Philip's message and committed his life to Jesus. But that was before Peter and John traveled to Samaria and therefore before the Samaritans received the Holy Spirit. The powerful influences of the surrounding culture and Simon's past life still lingered, and his deepest addiction was obviously to power. When Simon saw displays of the Holy Spirit's spiritual power, he relapsed into a selfish desire to broker that kind of power. Read Acts 8:18-24.

Hundreds of years before Simon lived, an unwillingness to abandon an idolatrous, pagan culture had brought God's judgment on the northern kingdom of Israel. Ultimately, the inhabitants had forfeited their identity as the people of God to their Assyrian conquerors because they preferred compromising to their culture over trusting and obeying God.

Therefore, Simon's struggle was not new, and Peter recognized it. His severe rebuke obviously frightened Simon away from his sinful desire. But the event illuminates the serious

> "When Simon saw that the Holy Spirit was given through the laying on of the apostles' hands, he offered them money, saying, 'Give me this power too, so that anyone I lay hands on may receive the Holy Spirit.' But Peter told him, 'May your silver be destroyed with you, because you thought the gift of God could be obtained with money! You have no part or share in this matter, because your heart is not right before God. Therefore repent of this wickedness of yours, and pray to the Lord that the intent of your heart may be forgiven you. For I see you are poisoned by bitterness and bound by iniquity.' 'Please pray to the Lord for me,' Simon replied, 'so that nothing you have said may happen to me.'" **Acts 8:18-24**

67

---

19. Add to the Acts 1:8 visual a placard with the challenges principle, *Negative cultural influences require both scriptural proclamation and spiritual confrontation.* Read Acts 8:9-24 and ask: Did Simon really possess magical powers? Why did the people follow him? Do you think Simon was really converted (see v. 13)? How did Simon misunderstand the work of the Holy Spirit (see vv. 18-19)? Why do you think Peter's rebuke of Simon was so severe (see vv. 20-23)? What does verse 24 indicate about Simon?

strongholds a worldly culture can have on people and the serious responsibility Christians have to confront those strongholds. Paul confronted moral compromise many times, not only in person but also in his letters to churches. Members of the Corinthian church, in particular, allowed cultural depravities to seep back into their behaviors, such as sexual sin (see 1 Cor. 6:9-20) and idolatry (see 1 Cor. 10:1-33). Paul lovingly but directly addressed these issues in his letters to those believers.

Today many new, familiar cultural influences characterize our Samaria mission field. The decline of the family, disregard for the sanctity of life, sexual immorality, substance abuse, racism, and many other evils are endemic to our culture. Philip's faithful proclamation of the gospel and Peter's faithful confrontation of sinful cultural influences were necessary to evangelize first-century Samaria. Those same commitments are necessary for an effective witness in our modern-day Samaria.

Your Church's Samaria

For today's churches, much as it was for the early churches, Samaria is a nearby place that we rarely visit. Samaritans are people who live relatively near us but are not like us. We can legitimately think of our Samaria geographically, racially, ethnically, culturally, or religiously. From all those perspectives, today's closest parallel to Samaria is our own nation and North American continent.

Though North America in many ways has a profound Christian heritage, we cannot ignore the reality that the influence of biblical Christianity on the culture and character of our continent has dramatically weakened, especially in the past generation. In our post-Christian culture it is estimated that more than 235 million North Americans—about 7 of 10 people—do not have a personal relationship with Jesus Christ.[1] Some of those would claim a nominal religious background or label. An increasing number would not even bother to do that.

The population of our continent is growing at a faster rate than our mission force and our churches. As it grows, it is becoming increasingly diverse, secular, and permissive. Chapter 2 taught us that the *breadth* of lostness around the world is staggering. So too is the *depth* of lostness in our diverse homeland, where so many assume they know Christianity but do not know Christ. Consider the following unique challenges to reaching the lost peoples of North America today.

- Many of the lost in North America—more than half—live in the 50 largest metropolitan areas where evangelical churches are often fewest and smallest and where language, cultural, and economic barriers are often largest.[2]
- North America is becoming increasingly ethnic and multicultural. In certain regions of our continent, we may soon be hard pressed to differentiate our Samaria from the ends of the earth.[3] Consider the following statistics.

20. Ask a member to read 1 Corinthians 5:9-11. Ask the group to identify the negative cultural influences that had ensnared some members of the church at Corinth. Record these on a marker board. Point out that in person and in his letters, Paul confronted moral compromise with both scriptural proclamation and spiritual confrontation. Summarize 1 Corinthians 5:1-7; 6:9-20 (sexual sin); 10:1-33 (idolatry). Ask members to name modern-day challenges in our Samaria mission field. List these beside the first-century list on the marker board.

—According to the 2000 census, 1 of 10 residents (11.1 percent) of the United States today was born in another country.[4] About half of them are of Hispanic origin. These more than 31 million foreign-born residents represent a 57 percent increase over the 1990 census.[5]

—The non-Anglo population is growing almost 13 times faster than the Anglo population. Between the 1990 and 2000 censuses the Hispanic population increased by 58 percent.[6] The Census Bureau is projecting that by 2050 the Anglo population will represent only half of the total United States population.[7]

—Numbering around 39 million, Hispanics are the largest minority ethnic group in the United States.[8] As nations, only Mexico, Brazil, Columbia, and Spain are home to more Hispanics than the United States. In fact, the Hispanic population of the United States exceeds the entire population of Canada.[9]

—There are more Jews in America today than in Israel.[10]

—Only five nations in Africa have populations larger than the African-American population of the United States.[11]

—Forty-seven million people in the United States age five and older speak a language other than English at home (18 percent of all people age five and older). Twenty-one million of these do not speak English very well.[12]

—Many of the world's 11,120 ethnolinguistic people groups now live in North America.

• Fewer than three hundred Canadian Southern Baptist churches seek to take the gospel to more than 30 million people. More Christians are in China than in Canada.[13]

• In addition to the national and ethnic diversity of our Samaria, surveys of religious beliefs reveal an increasingly secular culture. The American Religious Identification Survey of 2001, surveying more than 50,000 American households, found that over a 10-year period, the number of U.S. adults who do not claim any religious identification increased from 8 percent to 14 percent, numbering almost 30 million. The number of Americans who describe themselves as Christians declined from 86 percent in 1990 to 77 percent in 2001.[14]

The layers of cultural factors that insulate today's Samaria mission field from the gospel are numerous. Many of these layers of lostness sometimes seem impenetrable. However, churches today have never had more resources to reach their Samaria mission field, and the North American culture is just as ripe for revival today as Samaria was in Philip's day.

Identify the characteristics of today's Samaria.
❑ Godly   ❑ Post-Christian   ❑ Secular   ❑ Homogeneous   ❑ Multicultural

21. Say, Now that we have identified mission principles the early believers followed to reach their Samaria, let's apply these principles to modern-day churches' efforts to reach our Samaria. Call on the member enlisted in advance to summarize the unique challenges to reaching the lost peoples of North America today (pp. 68–69).

Name a community near your home that represents a Samaria—a place you rarely visit or pass through.

_____

Spend a few minutes praying for this community. Be open to the possibility of God's using you to make contact and share the gospel with the people of this community.

What can today's churches do to penetrate the deep lostness of North America? The same biblical principles and the same Holy Spirit that guided the 1st-century churches also guide 21st-century churches to reach their Samaria.

The Calling Principle in Today's Samaria

God calls Christians to personalize the gospel for the diverse peoples in and near their homeland. A church that is on mission in Samaria today sends and supports not only missionaries like Saul and Barnabas but also gifted lay people like Philip and his daughters, who are willing to engage the culture without being absorbed into it. Marketplace ministries and bivocational pathways into fields such as education, law, medicine, and media can provide strategic inroads for everyday witnesses that professional clergy and established churches may not encounter. As evangelistic Christians penetrate the culture, missionaries and existing churches can come alongside them and help, as Peter, John, and the Jerusalem church came alongside Philip to support and celebrate his pioneer ministry.

For example, today thousands of North American missionaries go to their Samaria mission field through the avenue of Mission Service Corps (MSC). Like career missionaries, MSC missionaries receive commissioning, training, and ministry support. But while career missionaries are typically assigned to existing places of service, self-funded MSC missionaries often use an innovative new entry point into the culture to create a place of service.

MSC missionaries have pioneered ministries in jails, weekend motorcycle clubs, urban ministry centers, the NASCAR racing industry, and the professional bass-fishing circuit. They have helped start new churches in unlikely locations ranging from apartment buildings to arts communities to the Arctic Circle. Some travel from place to place, as Philip did in Acts 8. Others invest their lives in one location, as Philip appears to have done in Acts 21.

On page 60 you identified barriers to reaching Samaria with the gospel. On the following page, describe strategies your church can use to overcome those barriers to the gospel. The first one is completed for you as an example.

22. As you discuss modern-day applications of each principle in "Your Church's Samaria," refer to the five placards that you have already placed on the Acts 1:8 visual. Draw attention to the placard with the calling principle, *God calls Christians to personalize the gospel for the diverse peoples in and near their homeland.* Using the material on page 70, describe ways churches can reach their Samaria.
23. Review the barriers to reaching people in the activity at the top of page 60. Then ask for responses to the activity at the top of page 71. Make sure the responses are specific for your church rather than general.

Language: _A church could offer English classes to members of a nearby Laotian community and share Christ's love with them._

Geography: _____

Race, ethnicity: _____

Religion: _____

Culture: _____

Subculture: _____

Socioeconomics: _____

The Cultures Principle in Today's Samaria

Penetrating a diverse continent or country with the gospel requires a loving understanding of its people and history. Just as Jesus modeled this principle during His encounter with the Samaritan woman and her village, today's churches, missionaries, and on-mission Christians can let their compassion for lost people lead them to deeper understandings of the cultures and subcultures of their own Samaria. For example, the various regions of the United States, its territories, and Canada have very different histories that have produced very different cultural norms. A missionary who is a lifelong resident of Oklahoma is more effective starting a church in New York City if he first works hard to understand New York's people and culture. Furthermore, different generations often see life very differently; youth groups on a mission trip to help senior adults would do well to understand some of those differences. Of course, the growing number of ethnic groups in North America brings unique cultural perspectives to our society. A five-generation English-American family may have things to learn about a first-generation Korean-American family in order to win the right to share the gospel with them. An in-depth understanding of the many people groups in our Samaria mission field gives today's witnesses a loving way to communicate the gospel message.

Name some of the cultures represented in your Samaria mission field.

_____

How would one of these cultures see life differently than a believer does?

_____

How can churches gain a greater understanding of the diverse cultures and subcultures in North America?

_____

71

24. Call attention to the placard with the cultures principle, _Penetrating a diverse continent or country with the gospel requires a loving understanding of its people and history_. Call for responses to the activities at the bottom of page 71.
25. Divide members into three small groups and give each group a supply of newspapers and a variety of magazines. Ask groups to discover from these resources everything they can about the diverse cultures and subcultures of our country. Ask each group to report.

A CHURCH ON MISSION

For the people of Red Hills Southern Baptist Church in Cedar City, Utah, Samaria is about 98 percent Mormon. "If you want to get a taste of foreign missions in an English-speaking environment, come to Utah," says Scott Maxwell, the pastor of Red Hills. As it reaches out with the truth of Christ, Red Hills invites Southern Baptists from around the country to minister to this Samaria mission field. "We're seeing more people come to the Lord from the [Mormon] church," says Maxwell. "We're planting seeds, and over the next 15 years, we'll be reaping the harvest."

Old Mormon Rock Church in Cedar City, Utah, reminds members of Red Hills Southern Baptist Church of the challenges they face in their Samaria mission field.

A church youth group from Oklahoma recently came to do evangelism and went home transformed. At least three of the teens committed themselves to full-time Christian service. "They went home saying, 'If we can do it in Cedar City, Utah, we can do it in our hometown,' " Maxwell reports. "They started hitting the streets and sharing the gospel in their town, and they had never done that before."

Red Hills, which has about 115 members, is also trying to stretch its own limits. The church recently sent its first overseas missions volunteer to Russia and plans a youth mission trip to Mexico.[15]

The Church-Planting Principle in Today's Samaria

The unchanging gospel speaks to diverse cultures and generations through new leaders and new methods in new churches. As cultural pioneers and creative missionaries establish relationships and evangelize in North America, today's churches also need to be ready with strategies for establishing relevant new churches and preparing capable new leaders. Many of these new strategies will be very different from those of their partner churches, because they will be designed to make disciples in a different cultural context.

72

26. Call attention to the placard with the church-planting principle, *The unchanging gospel speaks to diverse cultures and generations through new leaders and new methods in new churches.* Ask members to brainstorm ways the unchanging gospel could meet the needs of some of the diverse cultures and subcultures the group discovered in step 25.

Give an example of the way the unchanging gospel would adapt to a culture or generation in your North American mission field.

Today's churches have valuable partners in seminaries and in the North American Mission Board, who work together with state and local associations of churches to better understand North American culture, to develop coordinated church-planting methods and strategies, and to prepare tomorrow's church planters. Some of tomorrow's pastors and church leaders will serve churches and communities similar to the ones in which they grew up and were trained. But in the years ahead many churches that reach the millions of lost people in North America will be innovative models led by pioneer leaders who are trained and willing to intentionally cross barriers.

The Cooperation Principle in Today's Samaria

Informed churches pray God's power into God's mission. Today's Samaria mission field is too large and complex for a single church to undertake alone. As is true in reaching the ends of the earth, reaching the Samaria mission field is a responsibility that many cooperating churches share. Southern Baptist churches support a unified giving plan called the Cooperative Program, as well as a special Annie Armstrong Easter Offering® for North American missions. These resources enable the North American Mission Board to place more than five thousand missionaries in strategic locations throughout North America. These missionaries provide the infrastructure for churches to be personally involved in North American missions. These resources also help fund evangelistic and church-planting strategies, enabling Southern Baptists to establish new congregations throughout North America.

Churches can increase their comprehensive support of North American missions not only by financially supporting missions but also by providing missions education for their members. Missions education equips church members for prayer, for giving, and for personal evangelism just as Paul's letters and the early missionaries' reports equipped first-century churches.

How well informed is your church about North American missions?
❏ Not well informed   ❏ Somewhat informed   ❏ Very well informed

How often does your church pray for North American misions?
❏ Never   ❏ Seldom   ❏ Faithfully

Rate the effectiveness of North American missions education in your church.
❏ Ineffective   ❏ Somewhat effective   ❏ Very effective

73

27. Call attention to the placard with the cooperation principle, *Informed churches pray God's power into God's mission*. Summarize this section on page 73. Lead the group to brainstorm ways your church can stay better informed about North American missions. Emphasize the importance of regularly praying for North American missions.

The Challenges Principle in Today's Samaria

Negative cultural influences require both scriptural proclamation and spiritual confrontation. To make an impact on today's Samaria mission field, churches must also forcefully confront the powerful cultural influences that contribute to North America's moral decline and its rejection of a biblical worldview. Pornography, abortion, homosexual marriage, and other symptoms of cultural decay are rampant in North America. Government leaders, journalists, and educators seem increasingly unable or unwilling to delineate right from wrong, and the unified voice of our churches is too often silent or too soft to be effective. Just as Peter confronted Simon with his sin and called him to repent, today's churches and church leaders must hold church members to a biblical standard of morality. Churches must also fulfill their prophetic role in society by proclaiming biblical morality to the surrounding culture.

What are some evil strongholds or evidences of moral decay prevalent in our society?

_____

How can churches confront cultural influences that contribute to moral decline?

_____

How Deep Will We Go?

When the Samaritan woman met Jesus, she at first hid behind superficial religious and political issues, but she soon revealed her desperate spiritual thirst—a thirst her sometimes religious, sometimes idolatrous Samaritan culture couldn't satisfy. Nor were the other Samaritans in that town satisfied with a superficial, secondhand, or second-rate relationship with Jesus. They wanted something deeper. After time with Jesus, their thirst had been exposed and quenched as well (see John 4:39-42).

The question the Samaria mission field asks of churches today is not just "How far are you willing to go?" but also "How deep are you willing to go? Are you willing to understand people in all their complexity and with all their baggage, knowing that they're not exactly like you?" We must understand that a Samaritan would never have walked into a Jerusalem church to hear the gospel. Yet when the Holy Spirit led Philip and others out of the Jerusalem church and into the Samaritan culture, they found a surprisingly receptive audience. In the same way, today's churches are often most effective in reaching their Samarias when they forfeit home-court advantage and creatively take the gospel into a new culture, whether that culture is ethnic, socioeconomic, religious, geographic, or all of these.

28. Call attention to the placard with the challenges principle, _Negative cultural influences require both scriptural proclamation and spiritual confrontation._ As members name strongholds and evil influences in our culture, list these on a marker board. Ask members to share specific examples of what your church is doing to confront cultural influences that contribute to moral decline. Ask, How would you answer someone who claims that churches should stick to preaching the gospel and not get involved in culture?

Because North America's lostness is deepening under layers of cultural decline, digging down to the heart of lost people's needs is getting harder and harder. Millions of people in the United States, its territories, and Canada desperately need Christ. They need the gospel presented in ways they can understand. And they need churches to which they can relate.

Think about the circles in which you and your church normally travel. Are you intentionally engaging your Samaria, or are you walking around it and, in your heart, even scorning it a little? Does your church see your Samaria as Jesus sees it?

In chapter 4 our missions perspective will zoom in and focus on the Judean mission field. In many ways Judea will look more familiar than Samaria or the ends of the earth. But surprisingly, the Judean mission field doesn't necessarily look any friendlier.

Fill in the blanks to complete the mission principles for carrying the gospel to Samaria. Try to do this from memory. If you have difficulty, refer to the chart on page 58.
Calling principle: God calls Christians to _____ the gospel for the diverse peoples in and near their homeland.
Cultures principle: Penetrating a diverse continent or country with the gospel requires a loving understanding of its _____ and _____.
Church-planting principle: The unchanging gospel speaks to diverse cultures and generations through new _____ and new _____ in new _____.
Cooperation principle: Informed churches _____ God's power into God's mission.
Challenges principle: Negative cultural influences require both scriptural _____ and spiritual _____.

Complete this sentence: Believers have a responsibility to carry the gospel to Samaria because—

_____

_____

Think about the lostness of the United States and Canada. Spend a few minutes praying for these countries. Commit to pray each day that the peoples of these countries will be reached with the gospel of Jesus Christ and that churches will become more involved in reaching out to their Samarias.

Recite Acts 1:8 and Matthew 28:19-20 from memory. Write Mark 16:15 on a card. Keep the card with you and memorize the verse this week. Read it, along with Acts 1:8 and Matthew 28:19-20, at least once each day during this study.

75

29. Say: I would like for you to meet someone who deeply cared about reaching her Samaria. Annie Armstrong, who lived from 1850 to 1938, motivated our entire denomination to give stronger support to North American missions. Southern Baptists' Easter offering for North American missions is named for her. The enlisted member should stand and present the dramatic monologue on page 149.
31. Ask volunteers to read the teaching posters on the walls and to comment on the meanings of selected statements.
32. Ask members to work in pairs to recite the previous memory verses, Acts 1:8 and Matthew 28:19-20.

[1]Research Team Statistics. North American Mission Board of the Southern Baptist Convention.

[2]U.S. Census Bureau, "Population in Metropolitan and Micropolitan Statistical Areas, (Table) 3a. Ranked by 2000 Population for the United States and Puerto Rico: 1990 and 2000" [online], 30 December 2003 [cited 30 April 2004]. Available from the Internet: *www.census.gov/population/www/cen2000/phc-t296.html*.

[3]U.S. Census Bureau, "Projected Population of the United States, (Table) 1a. by Race and Hispanic Origin: 2000 to 2050" [online], 18 March 2004 [cited 30 April 2004]. Available from the Internet: *www.census.gov/ipc/www/usinterimproj*.

[4]U.S. Bureau of the Census, "Profile of Selected Social Characteristics: 2000, (Table) DP-2. Geographic area: United States," Census 2000.

[5]Mike Bergman, "Foreign-Born a Majority in Six U.S. Cities; Growth Fastest in South, Census Bureau Reports," U.S. Census Bureau [online], 17 December 2003 [cited 30 April 2004]. Available from the Internet: *www.census.gov/Press-Release/www/releases/archives/census_2000/001623.html*.

[6]U.S. Bureau of the Census, "Profile of General Demographic Characteristics: 1990, (Table) DP-1. Geographic Area: United States" and "Profile of General Demographic Characteristics: 2000, (Table) DP-1. Geographic Area: United States," Census 1990 and Census 2000.

[7]U.S. Census Bureau, "Projected Population of the United States, (Table) 1a. by Race and Hispanic Origin: 2000 to 2050" [online], 18 March 2004 [cited 30 April 2004]. Available from the Internet: *www.census.gov/ipc/www/usinterimproj*.

[8]U.S. Census Bureau, "Annual Resident Population Estimates, (Table) 2. of the United States by Sex, Race, and Hispanic or Latin Origin: April 1, 2000, to July 1, 2002" [online], 18 June 2003 [cited 30 April 2004]. Available from the Internet: *eirc.census.gov/popest/data/national/tables/asro/NA-EST2002-ASRO-02.php*.

[9]"Demographic Statistics," *The Daily* [online], 1 January 2004 [cited 30 April 2004]. Available from the Internet: *www.statcan.ca/Daily/English/040322/d040322e.htm*. U.S. Bureau of the Census, "Profile of General Demographic Characteristics: 2000, (Table) DP-1. Geographic Area: United States," Census 2000.

[10]Lawrence Grossman and David Singer, eds., *American Jewish Year Book: 2001*, vol. 101 (New York: The American Jewish Committee, 2001), 540–42.

[11]Population Reference Bureau, "2003 World Population Data Sheet of the Population Reference Bureau," Chart. U.S. Census Bureau, "Annual Resident Population Estimates, (Table) 2. of the United States by Sex, Race, and Hispanic or Latin Origin: April 1, 2000 to July 1, 2002" [online], 18 June 2003 [cited 30 April 2004]. Available from the Internet: *eirc.census.gov/popest/data/national/tables/asro/NA-EST2002-ASRO-02.php*.

[12]U.S. Bureau of the Census, "Profile of Selected Social Characteristics: 2000, (Table) DP-2. Geographic area: United States," Census 2000.

[13]"Demographic Statistics," *The Daily* [online], 1 January 2004 [cited 30 April 2004]. Available from the Internet: *www.statcan.ca/Daily/English/040322/d040322e.htm*. Research Team Statistics, North American Mission Board of the Southern Baptist Convention.

[14]Ariela Keysar, Barry A. Kosmin, and Egon Mayer, "Self Described Religious Identification (Exhibit) 1. of U.S. Adult Population: 1990–2001," American Religious Identification Survey 2001. New York: The Graduate Center of the City University of New York.

[15]Appreciation is expressed to Erich Bridges, International Mission Board, for providing this account.

Answers to matching activity on page 56: 1. e, 2. c, 3. b, 4. a, 5. f, 6. d, 7. b, 8. i, 9. h

32. Show cel 10 of Mark 16:15. Lead the group to read the verse in unison. Challenge members to memorize the verse before the next session.

33. Ask volunteers to complete this sentence: "Believers have a responsibility to carry the gospel to Samaria because ..." (activity, p. 75).

34. Close by praying that each group member and your church will realize the deep spiritual thirst of people in your Samaria mission field and will respond with compassionate, Spirit-led action.

Chapter 4

A State of Concern:
Your Church's Judea

YOUR MISSION

After completing this chapter, you will be able to—

• summarize mission principles the early churches followed to reach Judea with the gospel;

• apply these principles to modern-day churches' efforts to reach their Judeas;

• characterize your state as a modern-day Judea;

• summarize believers' responsibility to carry the gospel to Judea;

• commit to pray for the people of your state.

In the small town where I grew up, sandlot baseball occupied almost every summer day. A boy who lived down the street from the field was widely known to be spoiled and obnoxious. I'll call him Jimmy. Jimmy never played baseball with us but would frequently ride his bike past the ball field while we were playing. Often he would coast to a stop beside the fence near home plate to watch and taunt us.

At first my friends and I exchanged verbal barbs with Jimmy, but eventually we learned to ignore him. That's when he started throwing rocks. One day the verbal barbs became particularly sharp, and Jimmy's rocks came out early. Jimmy let one fly just as the batter was smashing a ground ball to the infield. As our shortstop leaned over to field the ground ball, the rock struck him squarely on the forehead. As the blood and tears started to flow, everyone on the field turned with an angry scowl to face Jimmy, who looked startled and scared. Then someone yelled, "Get him!" and the chase was on.

Because he had a head start and was already on his bike, Jimmy reached his house a few seconds before our pack of vigilantes could catch up with him. Dropping his

Group Session 4

1. Display a large map of your state. Ask: Is there a biblical mandate for believers to reach their states with the gospel? Is there a strong Christian presence in our state? What missions work in our state are you aware of? Call attention to the title of chapter 4. Read "Your Mission" for chapter 4 on page 77. Ask a member to lead in prayer.

2. Ask members to recite to a partner the three Great Commission verses they have learned. Show cel 11 of Luke 24:47 and read the verse in unison. Ask members to memorize this verse before the next session.

bike in his front yard, Jimmy ran up the front steps and across the porch screaming for his mother. When Jimmy's mom appeared at the front screen door, I prepared to present our case. I had a tearful, bloodied friend by my side. I had a pack of eyewitnesses who would testify not only to the attack but also to weeks of slander, annoyance, and reckless endangerment we had endured from Jimmy. *When his mom hears what I have to say,* I thought, *she's really going to let him have it.*

Boy, was I wrong. Jimmy's mom immediately ordered us out of their yard. I blurted out a few words about rocks and blood and injustice, but she wasn't listening. I was filled with indignity that she wouldn't hear our case against Jimmy, and as I remounted my bike, I argued that we were in her yard only because her bratty son had launched a rock that could have killed one of us. Her response was to reach behind the door and pull out a baseball bat of her own. I began to see where Jimmy got both his tactics and his charm.

When I got home, I told my own parents what had happened. After being scolded about my role in the escapade, I asked my mother why Jimmy's mom wasn't open to the truth. With a faint smile, my mom answered, "Haven't you ever heard the saying 'Blood is thicker than water'?"

My experience with Jimmy certainly brought home the meaning of that saying. Today many people are willing to blindly take care of their own interests and defend their own relationships or values, even if doing so means creating new definitions of what is true or right. People are sometimes more committed to protecting the status quo and their own rationalized beliefs than accepting truth that would necessitate change. And sadly, many people manufacture their own definitions of religious truth, regardless of what God has revealed through Christ and in the Bible. These are the realities that confront us when we enter the Judea mission field.

False Security

The early churches' Judea mission field was dominated by leaders who valued preserving the religious state of affairs in the name of self-interest. For instance, the Romans who ruled the region served their own interests by encouraging the Jewish people to quietly practice their religion and forget about fighting for independence. Subservient Jewish authorities like Herod and Caiaphas served their own interests by keeping order among the Jewish people. And religious leaders like the Pharisees and Sadducees served their own interests by creating a system of religious rituals that gave them power and influence. To these groups the "blood" of Jewish tradition and political power was thicker than the life-giving "water" that Jesus offered.

For 21st-century churches the Judea mission field represents the immediate state, province, or region in which the church is located. Like the early churches' Judea, your state (the term we will use for the sake of simplicity) no doubt has many irreli-

3. Ask members to recall what *ends of the earth, Samaria,* and *Judea* represent for 21st-century churches (the world, North America, and our state, respectively). Call attention to the Acts 1:8 visual you have developed in sessions 2–3 and say: We have been studying principles for reaching the four mission fields in Jesus' Acts 1:8 challenge. This session focuses on our Judea—our state.

4. Show cel 12 with the terms *Self-Serving Religion, False Security, Cultural Christianity.* Define these terms according to the material on pages 78–79.

gious people in it. But it also has a religious status quo that might include non-Christian religions whose leaders do not want their people to be evangelized. Also included in the Judea mission field are cultural Christians—people who claim the label of Christianity but do not a have a personal relationship with Jesus Christ.

Whether through the legalistic Judaism of the first century or the cultural Christianity or false religions of today, sinful humankind has always tended to distort sincere faith into self-serving religion. A particularly challenging barrier to the true gospel, self-serving religion gives masses of people the false assurance that they are right with God. Especially in America today, churches often find that their Judea mission field, while so near, is as difficult to penetrate as Jimmy's house was to my friends and me. Guarding the door may be a religious "parent" who is more interested in protecting the status quo than in receiving the truth about Jesus. Even the people we are trying to reach may hide behind belief systems that wrongly condone their values or lifestyle.

Many of the people who live in our state seem like us: they may call themselves religious or even Christian. But without having personally placed their faith in Jesus, they are on a path of false security that leads to eternal separation from God.

How would you describe a self-serving religion? _____

_____

How does a self-serving religion give false assurance that people are right with God?

_____

_____

How would you describe a cultural Christian? _____

_____

In this chapter as we zoom in closer to the Judea mission field, we will see that the barriers of Judea are not always the high walls of distance, language, culture, or race but often the thick walls of presumed—yet false—religious security. Many people in first-century Judea left their seemingly secure religious systems and discovered the freedom of a personal relationship with Jesus Christ. From the example of the New Testament churches, we will discover ways to offer hope to those who need a relationship of grace rather than a religion of self-effort.

5. Ask three previously enlisted members to summarize Acts 5; 8:9-24; 19:11-17 and to point out examples of cultural Christianity and self-serving religion.
6. Point to the heading *Self-Serving Religion* on cel 12 and ask: How would you describe a self-serving religion? How does a self-serving religion give false assurance that people are right with God? What is an example of a self-serving religion today? Can Christianity become a self-serving religion? If so, how? How can faith, prayer life, worship services, and Christian service become self-serving?

The Early Churches' Judea

Many characteristics of Samaria and the ends of the earth were also true of first-century Judea. Judea was a crossroads region through which many travelers came for military, commercial, or religious reasons, and the early churches in Judea encountered many barriers—language and cultural differences—that existed outside their home state. But the Judea mission field, both in ancient and modern times, presents its own unique challenges.

The following Scriptures give background information about the Judean mission field. Read each passage and match it with the correct statement.

___ 1. Genesis 49:9-10   a. Jesus was born in Judea.

___ 2. Joshua 15:20   b. Men of Judah captured Jerusalem.

___ 3. Judges 1:1-20   c. David was from the tribe of Judah.

___ 4. Ruth 4:12,16-22   d. Many people from Judea came to hear Jesus teach.

___ 5. 2 Samuel 2:4   e. The Messiah would come from the tribe of Judah.

___ 6. Jeremiah 52:27   f. David was anointed king over the house of Judah.

___ 7. Matthew 2:1   g. The tribe of Judah inherited this land.

___ 8. Matthew 3:1   h. Jesus was from the line of David and Judah.

___ 9. Mark 3:7-10   i. The people of Judah were carried into captivity.

___ 10. Luke 3:23-38   j. John the Baptist preached in the desert of Judea.

Of all the places in His Acts 1:8 challenge where Jesus said His disciples would be witnesses, Judea must have seemed the most inviting. Judea represented the remnant of the southern kingdom of Judah. Judah had survived the Assyrian assault to which the northern kingdom, Israel, had succumbed in 721 B.C., but later the Babylonians conquered even Judah, destroying Jerusalem in 586 B.C. and leaving Solomon's magnificent temple in ruins. Most of the population was deported to Babylon, but the Jewish race and culture were allowed to remain largely intact.

> "You will receive power when the Holy Spirit has come upon you, and you will be My witnesses in Jerusalem, in all Judea and Samaria, and to the ends of the earth.'" **Acts 1:8**

Years later when Cyrus established his Medo-Persian empire, Ezra and Nehemiah were allowed to return with thousands of Jews, most of whom were from the tribe of Judah, to what would come to be known as the Persian province of Judea. There they were allowed to rebuild the wall of Jerusalem and to reestablish Jewish culture and worship. In fact, from the time of Ezra and Nehemiah forward, God's people were commonly referred to as Jews (see Ezra 4:12).

The Bible's first reference to Judea is when Matthew wrote that "Jesus was born in Bethlehem of Judea" (Matt. 2:1). John the Baptist also began his ministry in "the wilderness of Judea" (Matt. 3:1). Although precise geographic boundaries for Judea were not established, the territory was generally understood to extend from the

7. Point to the heading *False Security* on cel 12 and ask: What are some indications that someone places trust in a false form of security? Is it possible for a Christian to have false security? What is a Christian's basis for security?
8. Point to the heading *Cultural Christianity* on cel 12 and ask: How would you describe a cultural Christian? What is evidence in our society of cultural Christianity? Why do you think cultural Christianity is prevalent? How can believers guard against practicing cultural Christianity?

Mediterranean Sea on the west to the Dead Sea on the east, with its northern boundary at Joppa and its southern boundary a few miles south of Gaza and the southern portion of the Dead Sea. Thus, Judea had a fairly small, square geography of about 55 miles from north to south and about the same from east to west.

When the early churches looked around their home region of Judea, they saw many familiar people and practices. Certainly, generations of conquest and resettlement had produced diversity in the people and their customs. But more than any place, Judea was the home country of the loyal people of God who had protected their race, religious practices, and cultural traditions.

Jews who lived in Judea and found their identity with the tribe of Judah had a rich heritage of which they were proud. The blessing Jacob gave to Judah as he was dying (see Gen. 49:9-10) was considered a prophecy of the Messiah's coming. The faithful spy Caleb was from the tribe of Judah (see Num. 13:6; 34:19), and after Joshua's death this tribe appears to have been the first to occupy the territory it had been given, including Jerusalem (see Judg. 1:1-20). King David came through the tribe of Judah, and beginning with Rehoboam, the Davidic dynasty ruled over the southern kingdom for centuries after the northern kingdom was conquered and assimilated by the Assyrians. And of course, Jesus performed many miracles and taught throngs of people in Judea (see Mark 3:7-10; Luke 5:17).

> "Judah is a young lion—
> my son, you return from
>   the kill—
> he crouches; he lies down like
> a lion
> and like a lioness—who wants
>   to rouse him?
> The scepter will not depart
>   from Judah,
> or the staff from between
>   his feet,
> until He whose right it is comes
> and the obedience of the
>   peoples belongs to Him."
> **Genesis 49:9-10**

How surprised the early churches must have been to find the greatest resistance to the good news about Jesus the Messiah among the devout Jewish people around them! Certainly, many Judean Jews became Christ-followers as the believers proclaimed the gospel to them. But the New Testament shows that in town after town the Jewish leaders were the most resistant to the gospel message, even to the point of persecuting the apostles and the early Christians. And nowhere were those Jewish leaders more numerous and influential than in Judea.

Much of our study of the early churches' response to the Acts 1:8 challenge can focus on the Book of Acts, which chronicles the acts of the Holy Spirit, from Jerusalem to Rome, in detail. Interestingly, the Book of Acts provides fewer specific details about the early churches' mission to Judea than about its efforts to reach Jerusalem and Samaria. However, the New Testament Gospels and Epistles offer numerous insights not only into the Judea mission field but also into the opportunities and barriers that the Jewish religion presented.

Like Samaria, Judea is significant not just as a specific nearby geographical location in biblical times. It also represents a significant mission field for churches

81

9. Ask members to identify how self-serving religion, false security, and cultural Christianity are barriers to reaching people for Christ.
10. Overview the background of Judea by asking volunteers to read the Scriptures in the activity on page 80 and to select the statement that matches each Scripture. Answers: 1. e, 2. g, 3. b, 4. c, 5. f, 6. i, 7. a. 8. k, 9. d, 10. h.
11. Say, Now let's examine some principles the first-century churches used to reach their Judea. Refer to the Acts 1:8 visual you have used in the two previous sessions. Under *Judea* add a placard with the calling principle,

today. While the mission to Samaria is often a mission across culture, the mission to Judea is often a mission within the same culture. Judea was the home state where the Jewish people shared the same laws, traditions, and interests, practicing religious beliefs that influenced all who lived around them.

Look at the chart on page 83 and notice the mission principles we will study about the Judea mission field. Remember that the key mission concepts of calling, cultures, church planting, cooperation, and challenges apply to each of these principles.

What timeless principles can we learn from New Testament churches that were Jesus' witnesses in Judea?

The Calling Principle from Judea

God calls Christians to penetrate surrounding regions and their predominant religions with the true gospel. In addition to calling early churches to travel to the ends of the earth and to climb high over many barriers in Samaria, the Holy Spirit also clearly called early churches to penetrate the thick fortress of nominal religion and empty traditions that kept the people of Judea from hearing the liberating gospel. This task was difficult and dangerous, for Jewish leaders like Saul were so outraged at the Jesus movement that they "persecuted God's church to an extreme degree and tried to destroy it" (Gal. 1:13). The "Judean churches in Christ" (Gal. 1:22) were formed by courageous, mostly Jewish converts who accepted and shared the gospel at their own peril. In fact, many had been scattered from Jerusalem during the persecution that followed Stephen's death (see Acts 8:1-3).

In Galatians 1:11-17,22-24 Paul described to the Galatian church his conversion and call to become an apostle. He also referred to "the Judean churches in Christ" who "glorified God" (Gal. 1:22) because of his conversion. On-mission Christians like Ananias (see Acts 9:10-19) and Barnabas (see Acts 9:26-31), following the Holy Spirit's leadership, were called to come alongside Paul during the early days after his conversion.

Although trusting the sincerity of Paul's early testimony was difficult, these Judean disciples courageously trusted the Holy Spirit's leadership and call to their Judea mission field, embracing the man who personified their religious and political opposition.

Early churches faced a unique challenge in responding to their call to Judea. Some of those early Jewish believers, having always been subject to the *externally* enforced boundaries of the Jewish law, had difficulty accepting a new authority: the *internal* guidance of the Holy Spirit.

Read Acts 15:1-5. What were believers in Judea trying to add to the plan of salvation?

_____

God calls Christians to penetrate surrounding regions and their predominant religions with the true gospel. Use the chart on page 83 as a guide for attaching the placards to the wall during this session.

12. Say, The task of reaching Judea was difficult and dangerous and required trusting the Holy Spirit. Mount sentence strips with the following statements in a column on the wall: *Saul was converted. The churches in Judea praised God because of the change in Paul. The Judean disciples saw Paul preaching boldly under persecution. A great persecution broke out against the Judean believers. Ananias ministered to Paul. Saul was a leader in perse-*

PRINCIPLES FROM THE MISSION'S FIELDS

Mission Concepts	Ends of the Earth	Samaria	Judea
Calling	STARTING God calls Christians to the world in ways that are both incidental and intentional.	STRATEGIZING God calls Christians to personalize the gospel for the diverse peoples in and near their homeland.	STRENGTHENING God calls Christians to penetrate surrounding regions and their predominant religions with the true gospel.
Cultures	PEOPLE GROUPS God's mission to the world includes all people groups.	POPULATION SEGMENTS Penetrating a diverse continent or country with the gospel requires a loving understanding of its people and history.	RELIGIOUS LOST Those depending on works-based religion rather than a grace-based relationship don't understand the gospel.
Church Planting	MOVEMENTS When the gospel is successfully planted, new churches grow and multiply.	LEADERS The unchanging gospel speaks to diverse cultures and generations through new leaders and new methods in new churches.	SUPPORT Regional support and cooperation strengthen new churches for multiplication.
Cooperation	GIVING Taking the gospel to the world is costly.	KNOWING AND PRAYING Informed churches pray God's power into God's mission.	GOING Mission-minded churches mobilize to meet human needs in the name of Christ.
Challenges	RULERS Many kingdoms oppose God's kingdom, but God has sovereign authority over all.	SOCIETY Negative cultural influences require both scriptural proclamation and spiritual confrontation.	SELF-RIGHTEOUSNESS Opposition from religious systems and leaders should be expected and met with spiritual resolve.

83

cuting the early believers. Believers in Jerusalem were initially afraid of Paul. Barnabas helped the Jerusalem church accept Paul. Distribute small slips of paper with the following Scripture references: (1) Acts 8:1; (2) Acts 8:3; 9:1-2; Galatians 1:13; (3) Acts 9:1-6; (4) Acts 9:10-19; (5) Acts 9:26; (6) Acts 9:26-27; (7) Acts 9:28-29; (8) Galatians 1:22-24. Ask members to read their assigned verses in numerical order. After each Scripture or group of Scriptures is read, ask the group to match it with the correct sentence strip on the wall.

At the Jerusalem Council recorded in Acts 15, the apostle Peter, supported by missionaries Barnabas and Paul, spoke against returning to the law as a requirement for righteousness, asking, " 'Why, then, are you now testing God by putting on the disciples' necks a yoke that neither our forefathers nor we have been able to bear?' " (Acts 15:10). This event demonstrates that the early churches accepted the call to boldly proclaim and clarify the true gospel rather than return to a religious system that had become legalistic and burdensome.

The early churches' missionaries to the ends of the earth show us the importance of *starting* new churches among converts who respond with faith to the gospel message. The early churches' missionaries and evangelists in Samaria remind us that the call to reach diverse peoples is often a call to *strategize*—to go out of our way and think differently. An up-close view of the Judea mission field shows us the call to *strengthen* a region's churches so that they not only withstand the world's pressures and persecution but also rescue people from the false assurances of empty religion and secular society.

The Cultures Principle from Judea

Those depending on works-based religion rather than a grace-based relationship don't understand the gospel. As early churches went into their Judea mission field, they found many people who were relying on their own identity or performance for personal security and right standing with God. Often, those who were royal, rich, or Roman felt privileged and self-sufficient. Many led secular lives, giving only nominal attention to religious matters.

But average Jews, whose religion and culture were predominant in Judea, also had many reasons to resist the gospel:

- Pharisees like Saul, priding themselves on their knowledge and observance of every detail of Jewish law, were spiritually blinded by religious pride and self-righteousness.
- The Sadducees, a wealthy, conservative political group from the Jewish aristocracy, were no doubt concerned that the growing Christian movement would unravel temple worship and their privileged status in the Greco-Roman culture.
- Jewish Zealots, committed to armed resistance of the Romans, must have been puzzled and dissatisfied by the church's subordinate, nonviolent posture.
- The Essenes were Jews who simply retreated to the Judean wilderness to study the Scriptures in secluded communities and prepare for God's coming kingdom.[1]

13. Ask a volunteer to read Acts 15:1-5. Call for responses to the activity on page 82. Briefly summarize Acts 15:6-31 to identify the way the problem was resolved. Point out that problems like these arise when Christians begin to penetrate surrounding regions with the true gospel.
14. Call attention to the concepts of starting, strategizing, and strengthening on page 84.
15. Add to the Acts 1:8 visual a placard with the cultures principle, *Those depending on works-based religion rather than a grace-based relationship don't understand the gospel.* Display four poster strips with the terms *Pharisees,*

Match the Jewish parties with their characteristics.

a. Pharisees   b. Sadducees   c. Zealots   d. Essenes

___ 1. Simon, one of the disciples, belonged to this group (see Luke 6:15).
___ 2. Jesus said our righteousness must be greater than that of this group
(see Matt. 5:20).
___ 3. Sought to convert Gentiles (see Matt. 23:15)
___ 4. Did not believe in life after death (see Acts 23:8)
___ 5. Committed to armed resistance to the Romans
___ 6. Paul belonged to this group before he was a Christian (see Acts 23:6; Phil. 3:5).
___ 7. Questioned Jesus about His disciples' breaking the tradition of the elders
(see Matt. 15:1)
___ 8. Strictly observed God's law
___ 9. Jesus called them hypocrites (see Matt. 23:13).
___ 10. Denied the existence of angels and demons (see Acts 23:8)
___ 11. Studied Scriptures in secluded communities

All of these groups shared a common Jewish heritage and culture, but all were committed to a works-based religion that depended on Jewish identity as God's chosen people and obedience to His law. The various forms of piety they pursued gave them a sense of status and control they would have had to abandon to accept the claims of the gospel and enter a relationship with the risen Christ. In many cases they were unwilling to let go of the security of their hollow religion and their status as Jews to believe in the promise of eternal life through Christ.

In Acts 15:1-2 we see that even the early church struggled to accept the truth that a right relationship with God is a gift provided by Jesus' sacrificial death. Some people attempted to accept Christianity as a Jewish sect in which they could believe in Jesus but must also continue earning righteousness by obeying the Jewish law. One responsibility of first-century churches in the culture of their Judea mission field was to strongly proclaim that the new covenant Jesus made possible is a covenant of grace, not position or performance.

A great challenge that was common to the culture of the Judea mission field was the barrier of presumed familiarity that people have with the gospel. People who were lost in a works-based religion in the first century were likely to declare, "I'm Roman" or "I'm Jewish," just as those lost in the Judea mission

"Some men came down from Judea and began to teach the brothers: 'Unless you are circumcised according to the custom prescribed by Moses, you cannot be saved!' But after Paul and Barnabas had engaged them in serious argument and debate, they arranged for Paul and Barnabas and some others of them to go up to the apostles and elders in Jerusalem concerning this controversy." **Acts 15:1-2**

85

Sadducees, Zealots, Essenes. Say, These groups are examples of people who practiced works-based religion in the first century. Ask four volunteers to read aloud the descriptions of these groups on page 84.

16. Write this statement on a marker board: *The new covenant Jesus made possible is a covenant of grace, not position or performance.* Explain the concept of a new covenant of grace, contrasting it with position and performance.

17. Assign four small groups Luke 3:8; John 8:30-59; Acts 15:5-11; Galatians 3:11-12. Ask each group to discover how the persons in these passages dealt with misunderstandings about the gospel.

field of churches today might declare, "I'm a Baptist" or "I'm a Catholic." Sometimes those statements mean that who I am, who my parents are, what I'm doing, or where I live makes me good enough for God's approval. Although cultural Christians believe in God and may try to live moral lives, they have not entered a relationship with God through the blood of His Son, Jesus Christ.

Match the Scriptures with their teachings.

___ 1. John 1:12; Romans 10:13   a. Good works cannot save.
___ 2. Luke 3:8; John 8:30-40   b. Money cannot save.
___ 3. Acts 4:12   c. There is only one way to be saved.
___ 4. Acts 15:5-11   d. Rules and laws cannot save.
___ 5. Romans 10:1-2   e. Family tree cannot save.
___ 6. Galatians 3:11   f. Zeal cannot save.
___ 7. Ephesians 2:8-9   g. A person is saved by trusting Jesus Christ.
___ 8. 1 Peter 1:18

> "All who rely on the works of the law are under a curse, because it is written: 'Cursed is everyone who does not continue doing everything written in the book of the law.' Now it is clear that no one is justified before God by the law, because the righteous will live by faith." **Galatians 3:11-12**

John the Baptist faced a similar challenge in his dealings with the proud Jews of Judea (see Luke 3:8), and so did Jesus (see John 8:30-59). We have seen the way Peter addressed this issue as he defended the conversion of the Gentiles (see Acts 15:5-11), and Paul's letter to the Galatians is almost entirely devoted to the meaning of true religion (see Gal. 3:11-12).

Churches and individual Christians who are on mission in Judea must relentlessly clarify that a redemptive relationship with Jesus, not a religion of works, brings a right relationship with God. The prevalent notion that a person can achieve enough goodness to earn God's acceptance is still a huge challenge in penetrating the culture of today's Judea mission field.

The Church-Planting Principle from Judea

Regional support and cooperation strengthen new churches for multiplication. We have seen that the culture of the Judea mission field of the first century presented unique barriers to the gospel. But Judea's common culture and religion also created bridges to the gospel. After Saul's conversion brought a time of peace to Judea and the surrounding areas, the Bible says the churches there quickly grew stronger and more numerous (see Acts 9:31).

With few barriers of language, culture, or religious history and tradition, the early disciples could easily get straight to the point with a Judean Jew: the Messiah had come, and a new covenant was now in effect. Jesus' life, death, and resurrection fulfilled the Old Testament prophecies and the requirements of the law, and

18. Call for the answers to the activity on page 86 (1. g, 2. e, 3. c, 4. d, 5. f, 6. d, 7. a, 8. b). Point out examples of cultural Christianity.
19. Add to the Acts 1:8 visual a placard with the church-planting principle, *Regional support and cooperation strengthen new churches for multiplication.* Point out that even though barriers to reaching Judea existed, a common culture and religion also created bridges to the gospel.

people no longer needed to depend on keeping the law to attain right standing before God. They simply needed to repent of their sin, place their faith in Jesus, and receive the Holy Spirit. They could then be baptized and join a congregation of maturing disciples in worshiping, serving, and proclaiming the gospel. For many devoted Jews (see Acts 2:37-47) and even many priests (see Acts 6:7), the gospel made perfect sense, and they came to faith in Christ by the thousands (see Acts 4:4).

Read Peter's sermon on the Day of Pentecost in Acts 2:14-41. What were some bridges Peter used to communicate with his audience?

_____

When Peter stood to deliver his first sermon on the Day of Pentecost, his proclamation was to " 'Jewish men and all you residents of Jerusalem' " (Acts 2:14). He quoted from the prophet Joel and from the psalms of David, knowing that his audience would be familiar with these references (see Acts 2:14-36; Joel 2:28-32; Ps. 16:8-11; 110:1). Even those from remote parts of the world were likely in Jerusalem because of their Jewish faith, and Peter eagerly and effectively delivered the gospel message across the bridge of common background and understanding.

No doubt the many travelers who passed through the crossroads of Judea perceived the impact that followers of "the Way" (Acts 9:2) had on the region. Often those who didn't reject the message became either converts or spiritual seekers, as in the case of the Ethiopian eunuch to whom the Holy Spirit called Philip.

Read Acts 8:26-40. What bridge of common understanding did Philip use in witnessing to the Ethiopian official?

_____

Heading home to Ethiopia from Jerusalem on a Judean roadway, the Ethiopian queen's treasurer was investigating Isaiah's prophecy about Jesus. The Jewish culture of Judea had apparently piqued his interest in Scripture, and "Philip proceeded to tell him the good news about Jesus, beginning from that Scripture" (Acts 8:35).

The Judean audience may be thousands, like the multitude Peter addressed, or an individual, like the Ethiopian Philip met. But in each case the on-mission Christian found a bridge of common understanding and walked across it with the gospel message. The result was a network of growing, multiplying churches that were bold enough to proclaim the gospel of grace throughout their region and strong enough to endure the resulting persecution and hardship.

20. Divide members into five groups and make these assignments: Jesus (Matt. 6:25-34), Peter (Acts 2:14-41), Philip (Acts 8:26-40), Paul (Acts 17:15-34), Paul (Acts 21:33-40; 22:1-2). Ask the groups to summarize the passages and to tell how the speakers built on bridges of common understanding.

The Cooperation Principle from Judea

Mission-minded churches mobilize to meet human needs in the name of Christ. For first-century churches the Judea mission field was like the fertile soil of a flood plain. Often, the seeds of the gospel easily took root in rows of Jewish culture that had been well prepared for their Messiah. At other times floods of persecution or hardship washed in, frustrating the young churches' efforts.

The Judea mission field of the first-century church demonstrated that local churches can receive as well as provide benevolent mission action.

Read Acts 11:27-30. What physical calamity was coming? _____

What did the disciples at Antioch decide to do? _____

_____

How do you think the Jewish Christians in Judea felt when they received the gift from the Gentile believers? Check all that apply.
❏ Overwhelmed ❏ Resentful ❏ Angry ❏ Humble ❏ Grateful ❏ Suspicious

When the Holy Spirit revealed that a severe famine was coming, the more affluent church in Antioch demonstrated its compassion, generosity, and unity with the Judean churches by sending a relief offering (see Acts 11:27-30). The selection of Barnabas and Saul for this mission of mercy foreshadowed the event recorded in Acts 13, when the Holy Spirit called out these same two men for what would become a lifetime of missionary service. This would not be the only time in church history that the Holy Spirit used a short-term mission trip to cultivate a lifelong missions commitment.

Read Romans 15:25-27. What was the attitude of the Gentile Christians in Europe toward the poor Christians in Judea?

_____

What actions had the churches in Europe taken toward the Christians in Jerusalem?

_____

How had the Gentile Christians in Europe been blessed by the Christians in Jerusalem?

_____

21. Add to the Acts 1:8 visual a placard with the cooperation principle, *Mission-minded churches mobilize to meet human needs in the name of Christ*. Have members read the Scriptures in the activities on page 88. Call for responses to the related activities. Emphasize that the early churches' cooperation and unity were expressed in ministry.

The famine gave the churches outside Judea an opportunity to mobilize their resources and members for ministry and to demonstrate compassion and unity among Christianity's increasingly diverse churches. Perhaps even more importantly, it gave the sometimes proud Jewish Christians an opportunity to trust God during adversity and to humbly receive help from mostly Gentile Christians.

At the same time, many Gentile churches realized that they had spiritually benefited from the Jewish Messiah and that He had come to them through the tribe of Judah and the churches of Judea. So when the Judean churches had material needs, the churches they had nurtured at the ends of the earth were pleased to do all they could to help. Romans 15:25-27 describes their reciprocal love and cooperation.

The growing network of churches spreading throughout Judea, Samaria, and the ends of the earth was increasingly diverse and widespread yet remarkably unified. The churches readily exchanged resources, leaders, and letters. Their sensitivity to one another's needs revealed the new love the Holy Spirit had placed in their hearts. That love equipped them to add benevolent ministry to their evangelistic mission.

The Challenges Principle from Judea

Opposition from religious systems and leaders should be expected and met with spiritual resolve. As the early churches moved out from Jerusalem, they had opportunities to confront the challenges of the Judea mission field beyond the borders of Judea itself. The scene described in Acts 13:44-52, for example, is from Paul and Barnabas's experience in Antioch of Pisidia.

Read Acts 13:44-52. What motivated the Jews' opposition? _____

What was Paul and Barnabas's response? _____

How did the Jews react to Paul and Barnabas's statement? _____

_____

How did Paul and Barnabas respond when they were expelled from the district?

_____

From this account we see that the opportunities and challenges of the Judea mission field emerged not only in Judea but also in the Jewish communities outside Judea. Wherever Paul went, he sought out a town's Jewish population, whether it gathered formally at a local synagogue, as in Antioch of Pisidia (see Acts 13:14), or informally for prayer, as in the Roman colony of Philippi (see Acts 16:13-15).

89

22. Add to the Acts 1:8 visual a placard with the challenges principle, *Opposition from religious systems and leaders should be expected and met with spiritual resolve.* Ask a member to read Acts 13:44-52. Discuss the activities on page 89.

The early missionaries had a love and compassion for the Jewish people, considering them a priority audience for the gospel message. They also understood that most Jews knew Old Testament Scriptures and had a commitment to moral conduct based on God's law. This theological foundation gave Jews a context in which to receive the good news about Jesus the Messiah, and many did so joyfully.

First-century churches also quickly learned that religious systems and leaders are often the true gospel's most mean-spirited enemies.

Match the Scriptures with the incidents of opposition they describe.

____ 1. Acts 13:44-52   a. Paul and Silas were put in prison.
____ 2. Acts 14:1-7   b. More than 40 men conspired to kill Paul.
____ 3. Acts 14:19-20   c. Jealous Jews persecuted Paul and Barnabas.
____ 4. Acts 16:16-24   d. Jews and Gentiles plotted together against Paul
____ 5. Acts 19:23-31   and Barnabas.
____ 6. Acts 21:26-36   e. Roman soldiers had to rescue Paul from an angry mob.
____ 7. Acts 23:12-15   f. Craftsmen who made false gods and shrines incited a riot
         against Paul.
     g. Paul was stoned and left for dead.

In Antioch of Pisidia (see Acts 13:44-52) and in many other towns and cities thereafter (see Acts 14:1-7; 17:5-9; 18:5-6; 21:26-36; 23:12-15), jealousy and a rejection of the gospel message led the Jews to oppose, insult, and stir up persecution against the early churches and their missionaries. The gospel threatened the power and status of the religious establishment and its leaders, whose authority was often much more political than spiritual.

The first-century churches and their missionaries repeatedly navigated volatile political situations, relying on the overriding power of the Holy Spirit and the courage He provided. The apostle Paul, writing to the church at Thessalonica, compared their sufferings (see Acts 17:5-9) to those of "God's churches in Christ Jesus that are in Judea" (1 Thess. 2:14). He went on to describe the destructive role that self-serving religious leaders played by "hindering us from speaking to the Gentiles so that they may be saved" (1 Thess. 2:16). Paul's next sentence then delivered a chilling indictment of those who hide behind religious fences and throw rocks at the gospel: "As a result, they are always adding to the number of their sins, and wrath has overtaken them completely" (1 Thess. 2:16).

"You, brothers, became imitators of God's churches in Christ Jesus that are in Judea, since you have also suffered the same things from people of your own country, just as they did from the Jews." 1 Thessalonians 2:14

The early churches understood that to be effective in the Judea mission field was to be savvy about the religious and governmental forces that influence a region and that have political interest in the spiritual decisions of the people. Twenty-first-

23. Ask members to read the Scriptures listed in the activity on page 90. Call for the answers to the activity as the Scripture passages are read (1. c, 2. d, 3. g, 4. a, 5. f, 6. e, 7. b).

century churches would be wise to learn this lesson as well. John 10 and Acts 13 teach us that we must love all people and go to those ready to receive our message.

Your Church's Judea

For today's churches, as for the early churches, Judea can be seen as the surrounding state, region, or province in which people tend to share or adapt to a predominant language, culture, and regional identity. If Samaritans are seen as those who live relatively near us but are not like us, Judeans may be seen as those who live relatively near us and in many ways are like us.

The biblical principles we have learned from the first-century churches are equally applicable to today's efforts to reach our Judea mission field.

The Calling Principle in Today's Judea

God calls Christians to penetrate surrounding regions and their predominant religions with the true gospel. Today many people identify themselves as Hoosiers or Gators or Yankees or Razorbacks, deriving a sense of identity not merely from where they live but also from a membership or interest. More than Illinoisans, people may identify themselves as Cubs fans. More than Coloradoans, they may consider themselves outdoorsmen. Those kinds of common identities can pull people together who have little else in common. No doubt you and your church members have certain alma maters, hobbies, or passions that link you to many like-minded people in your Judea mission field.

Name common identities of people in your state—sports, schools, professions, and so on.

_____ _____ _____

How can these identities become bridges for sharing the gospel?

_____

Just as first-century Christians could traverse their Judea in a few days, you can probably drive across your Judea in a short time. The people of your Judea are not geographically or culturally distant from you. In fact, many of them may be easy to relate to and talk to—until your conversation turns to spiritual things. Then you may find familiarity to be an obstacle because people assume that you are like them, having no more knowledge of spiritual truth than they do. The early churches found that many Judean people thought they knew everything they needed to know about a carpenter's son from Nazareth who had died a criminal's death on

24. Calling attention to the five principles under *Judea* on the Acts 1:8 visual, say, Let's apply these principles to our Judea today. As you discuss modern-day applications of each principle in "Your Church's Judea," refer to the five placards that you have already placed on the Acts 1:8 visual. Call attention to the placard with the calling principle, *God calls Christians to penetrate surrounding regions and their predominant religions with the true gospel.* Ask members to name common identities in your state—sports, schools, industries, and so on— as you write them on a marker board. Discuss how these identities can become bridges for sharing Christ.

a cross. Likewise, unbelievers in our own Judea today may view Christianity as another legalistic religion rather than a life-giving relationship with God. The surface similarities between Christians and those who live in their Judea make the spiritual differences more critical if today's disciples are to be effective witnesses.

How can presumed familiarity with the gospel in your Judea mission field be a barrier to placing faith in Christ?

_____

How can churches reach out and free people from the false assurance of empty religion and secular society?

_____

The Cultures Principle in Today's Judea

Those depending on works-based religion rather than a grace-based relationship don't understand the gospel. Today many states or regions of our country have predominant religious traditions that are not based on a personal relationship with Jesus Christ. When we talk with others about Jesus, a response like "I'm a Catholic" or "I'm a Methodist" may not mean that someone has a relationship with Him. In fact, in some regions "I'm a Mormon" or "I'm a Muslim" is an increasingly common claim from families and coworkers who may otherwise have lifestyles and interests very much like those of Christians.

If we try to depict the religious beliefs of today's Judea mission field, we could not paint every state or region with the same broad stroke. For example, the religious heritage of Tennessee is very different from that of the Canadian province of British Columbia. Arizona's religious climate is very different from that found in the northeastern United States. Those differences are one reason churches in various states or regions often band together and specialize in reaching the predominant culture around them. To focus on the Judea mission field is to ask, "What religious beliefs and practices do most people in our state have in common, and how might understanding those dynamics help us reach them with the true gospel of grace?"

Name some religious beliefs and practices of the people in your church's Judea, including cults and non-Christian religions.

_____

_____

25. Call for responses to the activities at the top of page 92.
26. Referring to the placard with the cultures principle, *Those depending on works-based religion rather than a grace-based relationship don't understand the gospel,* summarize the material on page 92. Call for responses to the activity at the bottom of that page.

Consider the religious character of North America's Judea mission fields:

- In the United States the number of Southern Baptist churches pales in comparison to the growing population. Even in states with a greater Southern Baptist presence like Mississippi (one church for every 1,378 in population) or Kentucky (1:1,632), much of the Judea mission field is still unreached. In states like Rhode Island (1:95,302) or Minnesota (1:72,345), the ratio of Southern Baptist churches to population is even higher.[2]
- In Canada, which has far fewer Protestant churches than the United States, one Canadian Southern Baptist church exists for every 151,338 people.[3] Some Canadian provinces have few or no churches.
- Not only do many people in the Judea mission field not know Christ, but many also haven't heard the gospel presented in a relevant way because they don't attend church, listen to Christian media, or know a faithful witness. Many people in our Judea mission field possess only a cultural Christianity: they rationalize that nominal church membership or the faith of a parent or grandparent gives them right standing with God.
- Because religious freedom prevails in North America, people feel that they have many options from which to choose. Many default to cultural Christianity. Others adopt a works-based religion, whether in the form of a cult like Mormonism or Jehovah's Witnesses or of a world religion like Islam. Still others consider their morality or acts of charity sufficient for salvation, proudly asserting that they don't need a church to practice their religion. Just as in the first century, these lost people in our Judea mission field are leaning on works-based religion rather than a grace-based relationship with Jesus.

What do some religious groups today add to God's plan of salvation?

_____

Although the people of our Judea may look a lot like us, many have not yet received God's grace. We have the responsibility and privilege of showing our Judea mission field that true religion consists of a relationship with God through Jesus Christ.

Check characteristics of your Judea.
❑ People in many ways are like you.
❑ Most people have a relationship with Jesus.
❑ Many rely on works-based religion.
❑ Churches keep pace with population growth.
❑ Cultural Christianity characterizes this mission field.
❑ Religious freedom leads people to consider Jesus just one of many options.

27. Call on a member enlisted in advance to present the examples of the religious character of North America's Judea mission field on page 93. Emphasize that many people in your state do not have a grace-based relationship with Jesus Christ.

The Church-Planting Principle in Today's Judea

Regional support and cooperation strengthen new churches for multiplication. When we think about missionaries, we naturally picture pioneers like Paul or evangelists like Philip. But the Book of Acts reminds us that strengtheners and encouragers like Barnabas and Ananias are also vital to the spread of the gospel. Today's Judean missionaries may be administrators, strategists, or equippers who help churches multiply, grow stronger, and reach their Judea mission field. The Judea mission field certainly needs pioneers and evangelists, but as a region becomes populated with cooperating churches, the need to coordinate strategies, equip leaders, exhort one another with sound doctrine, and mobilize existing churches for the missions task also becomes important.

Churches that share a Judea mission field benefit greatly and are more effective when they cooperate together to reach the people of their common state or region. This is often accomplished through state conventions of churches, in which autonomous congregations combine their resources and coordinate their strategies to evangelize and start new churches in the Judea mission field they share. Established state conventions may have several thousand churches focusing on their Judea mission field, while emerging states may have only a few dozen. But without cooperation and coordination, individual churches have great difficulty reaching beyond their immediate community.

Each state has a predominant culture that is influenced by its own religious, political, and historical makeup. Yet Judea may have as much diversity and ethnicity as the Samaria mission field. For this reason churches must focus on evangelism and church-planting strategies that are contextualized—that is, methods that make sense within that setting.

Describe the culture of your state—its religious, political, socioeconomic, and historical makeup.

_____

_____

As churches cooperate in state conventions today, numerous regional ministries can be undertaken. These might include urban ministries in the state's largest cities, student ministries on the state's college and university campuses, or prison ministries within the state's correctional system. The state's population can be studied to plan effective evangelism and church-planting strategies. Struggling or suffering churches within the state can be strengthened and supported through training, leadership development, or volunteer ministries and gifts from other

28. Call attention to the placard with the church-planting principle, _Regional support and cooperation strengthen new churches for multiplication._ Summarize the material on page 94. Lead the group to discuss the activity on that page. Ask members to share examples of regional ministries they know about. Call for responses to the activity on page 95.

churches. These strategies should help the Christians and churches of that state grow stronger and the number of effective new churches multiply, so that the unreached people of the region can hear the gospel in a way they can understand.

What are some ways your state convention helps churches reach their Judea?

A CHURCH ON MISSION

For University Baptist Church, Judea is Alaska—diverse, lost, and searching. "Sometimes we talk about end-of-the-roaders here," says Gary Cox, pastor of the Fairbanks congregation. "This is their last chance at life."

The church has about 240 regular attenders. But every Sunday service—morning and evening—attracts people Cox has never seen. "They come into the church searching," Cox explains. Fairbanks has among the highest suicide, alcoholism, sexual abuse, and domestic violence rates in the nation. University Baptist ministers to all of the victims."

As its name indicates, University Baptist also actively ministers to students—especially students from around the world. The church, reaching out to University of Alaska's campus, has a Friday-night worship service for mainland Chinese students—

"Our purpose is simply the Great Commision," says Pastor Gary Cox of University Baptist Church. The church ministers to people from all over the world in Fairbanks, Alaska.

most of whom are not Christians—and a Filipino congregation. Sixteen new Chinese believers have been baptized. For 15 years church volunteers have operated a language school for new English speakers. Its current class of 80 students represents 28 nationalities.

"Six days a week people in the church do some kind of ministry," reports Cox. "Our purpose is simply the Great Commission. You don't have to be clever and flashy in Alaska. You just hammer away at the basics, and God blesses it."[4]

95

The Cooperation Principle in Today's Judea

Mission-minded churches mobilize to meet human needs in the name of Christ. During times of natural disaster or economic difficulty, human needs in a particular region can be severe. Often those needs are more than a single church can meet, but mission groups and trained volunteers from multiple churches can band together to bring relief and assistance. Timely, compassionate ministry can earn credibility to share the gospel with people whose pain has opened their hearts. And churches that are prepared to minister and share with those who are hurting can transform times of pain and need into opportunities for eternal life change.

How does your church work with other churches to meet needs in your state?

The Challenges Principle in Today's Judea

Opposition from religious systems and leaders should be expected and met with spiritual resolve. The more churches determine to impact their Judea mission field with the gospel, the more they can expect opposition. Self-serving government or religious leaders may be reluctant to lose control over people and resources. People who accept Christ may affect the livelihoods of local or regional authorities, and those authorities may not be kind to churches that attempt to change the status quo.

Name one way a change to a Christlike lifestyle could affect a state's economy or government.

New converts may decide to stop gambling, to speak up about the sanctity of life, or to influence the local school system or chamber of commerce. They may participate more actively in the government for reasons that are moral and spiritual, not just political. New churches may even find opposition from existing churches that express jealousy or fear rather than a desire to cooperate to advance God's kingdom.

A church that seeks to influence lives with the gospel will inevitably begin to influence education, media, law, government, and other arenas with new moral, ethical, and spiritual standards. As worldly, self-serving religious systems resist, churches must stand with spiritual resolve and defend the true gospel of Jesus Christ.

What forms of opposition might churches face today as they evangelize their Judea?

29. Refer to the placard with the cooperation principle, *Mission-minded churches mobilize to meet human needs in the name of Christ.* Summarize the corresponding topic on page 96. Call for responses to the activity.

30. Call attention to the placard with the challenges principle, *Opposition from religious systems and leaders should be expected and met with spiritual resolve.* Lead a discussion of "The Challenges Principle in Today's Judea," including the activities in that section. Ask members to identify any forms of opposition that are specific to your state. Write these on a marker board and challenge members to pray for spiritual victory in these areas.

How can churches strengthen believers to withstand opposition and persecution?

How Much Will We Sacrifice?

Read Romans 15:30-32 in the box. Underline three prayer requests Paul made.

> "I implore you, brothers, through the Lord Jesus Christ and through the love of the Spirit, to agonize together with me in your prayers to God on my behalf: that I may be rescued from the unbelievers in Judea, that my service for Jerusalem may be acceptable to the saints, and that, by God's will, I may come to you with joy and be refreshed together with you." **Romans 15:30-32**

Paul's words express to one Roman church his mixed feelings about his trip back to Judea. On one hand, he knew from experience that the Jews of Judea who valued religion over the gospel were his most dangerous enemies. Paul asked his friends in Rome to pray for him to be "rescued from the unbelievers in Judea" (Rom. 15:31). He also asked them to pray that his service to the saints in Jerusalem would be acceptable. He was willing to sacrifice and even suffer to help the Jewish Christians in Judea and to continue inviting the hostile, unbelieving Jews there to accept the truth about the risen Lord Jesus.

Paul's letter reminds us that the Judea mission field can be just as challenging as Samaria or the ends of the earth. At the end of chapter 2 we posed the ends-of-the-earth question "How far will we go?" Are we willing to take the gospel to the uttermost parts of the world, where many have little or no access to the gospel? At the end of chapter 3 the Samaria question was "How deep will we go?" Are we willing to drill past cultural differences and other barriers that separate us from people who are not like us in order to intentionally go to our Samaria?

The question for our involvement in our Judea mission field is "How much will we sacrifice?" Although our Judea may at first seem familiar and even religious, we must recognize that Judea is often prevented from hearing the true gospel by people "holding to the form of religion but denying its power" (2 Tim. 3:5). To press past the facade; to challenge the superficial religion that is based on tradition, works, and self-interest; to call instead for a spiritual relationship and life change based on God's transforming grace—these are the countercultural claims of the gospel.

In chapter 5 our missions perspective will focus further as we look at the Jerusalem mission field. This is the first mission field we find when we walk out the door of our church; yet we often ignore our Jerusalem because in many ways it forces us the greatest distance beyond our comfort zone.

Review the chart on page 83. Now without referring to the chart, summarize each Judea mission principle in your own words on the following page.

97

31. Review the session by asking volunteers to read the teaching posters on the walls and to comment on their meanings.
32. Say: A well-known missionary can bring a fresh perspective to the subject of state missions. David Brainerd, who lived from 1718 to 1747, has perhaps had a greater influence on Christian missions than any other person since New Testament times. Sickly all of his life, Brainerd died of tuberculosis in the home of famed preacher Jonathan Edwards. Upon the young man's death, Edwards published his diary, which has influenced Christians

Calling principle: _____

_____

Cultures principle: _____

_____

Church-planting principle: _____

_____

Cooperation principle: _____

Challenges principle: _____

Practice saying Acts 1:8; Matthew 28:19-20; and Mark 16:15 from memory. Write Luke 24:47 on a card. Keep the card with you and memorize the verse this week. Read it, along with the other three Scriptures, at least once each day during this study.

Complete this sentence: Believers have a responsibility to carry the gospel to Judea because—

_____

_____

Pray for your state and commit to God that you will pray for it each day.

------

[1]Merrill C. Tenney, *New Testament Survey*, Rev. Walter M. Dunnett (Grand Rapids: William B. Eerdmans Publishing Company, 1985), 105–12.
[2]North American Mission Board, "Population, Southern Baptist Congregations, Population per Congregation, Resident Members, and Population per Resident Member by State and Canadain [sic] Province, 2000." Photocopy.
[3]"About Us," Canadian Convention of the Southern Baptists [online] [cited 30 April 2004]. Available on the Internet: *www.ccsb.ca/about/stats.htm*. "Demographic Statistics," *The Daily* [online], 1 January 2004 [cited 30 April 2004]. Available from the Internet: *www.statcan.ca/Daily/English/040322/d040322e.htm*.
[4]Appreciation is expressed to Erich Bridges, International Mission Board, for providing this account.

Answers to matching activity on page 80: 1. e, 2. g, 3. b, 4. c, 5. f, 6. i, 7. a. 8. k, 9. d, 10. h
Answers to matching activity on page 85: 1. c, 2. a, 3. a, 4. b, 5. c, 6. a, 7. a, 8. a, 9. a, 10. b, 11. d
Answers to matching activity on page 86: 1. g, 2. e, 3. c, 4. d, 5. f, 6. d, 7. a, 8. b
Answers to matching activity on page 90: 1. c, 2. d, 3. g, 4. a, 5. f, 6. e, 7. b

around the world. The member you enlisted in advance should come forward and present the dramatic monologue on page 150.

33. Ask members to summarize why believers have a responsibility to carry the gospel to Judea (activity, p. 98).

34. Close by praying that members will accept responsibility for their state and will seek to overcome the barriers that are keeping its residents from a true relationship with Jesus Christ.

Chapter 5

The World Next Door:
Your Church's Jerusalem

YOUR MISSION

After completing this chapter, you will be able to—

- identify mission principles the early churches followed to reach Jerusalem with the gospel;
- apply these principles to modern-day churches' efforts to reach their Jerusalems;
- characterize your community as a modern-day Jerusalem;
- summarize believers' responsibility to carry the gospel to Jerusalem;
- commit to pray for your community.

Not long ago I was sitting on an airplane, waiting to take off for Dallas. Our departure had been delayed on the runway, giving me an opportunity to talk with the man in the seat beside me. We soon discovered that we had been married the same number of years, had the same number of children, and were about the same age. We were both frequent flyers, enjoyed the same sports, and had watched the same TV program the previous evening.

I was anxious to find out whether Bill was a Baptist like me. When I asked him whether he and his family were active in a church, though, his smile faded a little. "No, not for several years," he responded—not since he attended church with his parents before getting married. He figured he had gotten all the church he needed as a child; he and his wife considered their family their highest priority.

I nodded as if I understood, but I also told Bill I was surprised that, considering everything else we had in common, he wasn't involved in church. Sensing my genuine interest and concern for him and his family, Bill cautiously but openly listened as I named the benefits I gain from my church. Unfortunately, he replied

Group Session 5

1. Show cels 2, 9, 10, and 11 and have the group read the verses in unison. Point out that all of these verses teach that our responsibility is to tell people everywhere about Jesus.
2. Show cel 2 of Acts 1:8. Underline the four mission fields as you say: We are responsible for the ends of the earth. We are responsible for Samaria. Where is our Samaria? As the response is made, write *North America* on the cel and draw a line to *Samaria*. Say: We are responsible for Judea. Where is our Judea? As the response is made,

that none of those benefits sounded as good to him as his weekend activities of sleeping late, catching up on home projects, enjoying outdoor recreation, and relaxing with his wife and kids.

"My family and I like doing a lot of those things too," I responded. "But church is really important to us because we've found that it helps answer our deepest needs in life. Do you ever feel that you and your family also have spiritual needs?"

Though more uncomfortable than at the start of our conversation, Bill asked, "What do you mean?"

"For example," I said, "do you ever think about what happens after you die? Have your kids every worried about that?"

Bill shrugged at my question, then offered an answer that broke my heart: "I try to be a good person, and I think I'm better than most people. I think that if there is a God who is fair, He will be able to distinguish the good people from the bad."

For most of the flight, I tried to gently but persuasively present what the Bible says about salvation, pointing out that Bill's view of fairness didn't match what God has revealed in the Bible. Bill listened somewhat patiently, but he remained convinced that he and his family would be fine without making religious commitments. As we parted, I gave Bill my business card, suggested a couple of churches in his area, and asked for him to e-mail or call me if he had any questions. But Bill didn't offer me his business card, and I never heard from him again.

Bill's refusal hit me hard because I saw in him what my life would have been if I had not accepted Christ. Bill's Christian upbringing, education, family, career, and stage of life were very much like mine. He could have been me; I could have been him.

As I traveled back through the airports, highways, and streets of my own Jerusalem mission field a few days later, I thought about Bill. I prayed for him and hoped that someone else in the Jerusalem mission field of Dallas was watering the seed I had planted and would even lead Bill to personal faith in Christ.

Falling Through the Cracks

" 'You will receive power when the Holy Spirit has come upon you, and you will be My witnesses in Jerusalem, in all Judea and Samaria, and to the ends of the earth.' " **Acts 1:8**

The final mission field we will examine from Jesus' Acts 1:8 challenge is Jerusalem. The Jerusalem mission field is the surrounding community where we live, work, shop, play, and go to school. Although Jerusalem is our closest mission field, reaching it for Christ requires as much intentionality as the mission fields of Judea, Samaria, and the ends of the earth. The cities and counties where we live are the most accessible mission field to our church members. Therefore, Jerusalem calls for believers to be continually involved in reaching out with the good news. Our daily and weekly routines regularly bring us into contact with people who don't

100

write *Our State* on the cel and draw a line to *Judea*. Say: We are responsible for Jerusalem. Where is our Jerusalem? As the response is made, write *Our Community* on the cel and draw a line to *Jerusalem*. Say, This session focuses on our responsibility to the world next door, our church's Jerusalem.

3. Read "Your Mission" for chapter 5 on page 99. Ask a member to lead in prayer.
4. Distribute copies of study sheet 4, "Agree or Disagree?" Read the first statement and ask members who agree with it to raise their hands. Then ask those who disagree to raise their hands. If the group is divided, hold a debate.

know Jesus. Whether anonymous faces, casual acquaintances, or established relationships, people in our Jerusalem need to hear the spiritual truth we possess.

The Jerusalem mission field is often fraught with presumption: I presume that you know what I know, and you presume that I know what you know. For example, I presume that you, like me, know what it means to be a Christian and have an opportunity to participate in a church. And falling into the cracks between such presumptions may be many lost people like Bill. Instead of taking for granted that residents of our Jerusalem are believers, we must listen for both expressed and unexpressed spiritual needs.

What are some presumptions churches today make about people in their Jerusalem?

_____

Our Jerusalem mission field is filled with many people who, for a variety of reasons, might never attend our church. Still we must reach out to them, not to populate our fellowship halls but to populate the kingdom of God. Part of our Jerusalem mission is to cooperate with other churches to reach people. In many cases, in fact, our Jerusalem mission may even involve starting a new church that can reach people whom existing churches cannot.

The proximity of our Jerusalem mission field presents many opportuniites for as-you-go evangelism.

Give an example of as-you-go evangelism from each Scripture passage.

Acts 3:1-10: _____

Acts 9:32-35: _____

Acts 16:13-15: _____

Most of us travel through our Jerusalem every day, even on the way to church. That's what Peter and John were doing as they walked to daily prayer at the temple (see Acts 3:1). But on the way they noticed a man who was not part of their church—though very much a part of their Jerusalem mission field. The man, lame from birth, wanted money; instead, Peter healed him in the name of Jesus (see Acts 3:2-10).

Name two opportunities you had for as-you-go evangelism during the past week.

1. _____   2. _____

101

Allow 20 seconds for a spokesperson representing the agree side to defend that position. Then allow 20 seconds for someone representing the disagree side. Follow this pattern for the other statements. Answers are on page 145.
5. Summarize the paragraph at the top of page 101. Ask, What are some presumptions we tend to make about our community? Write responses on a marker board.
6. Ask, What is as-you-go evangelism? Divide members into five groups and give each group a three-by-five-inch card with the following Scripture references: (1) Mark 10:17-22; Luke 17:11-19. (2) John 3:1-16. (3) Acts 3:1-10;

First-century witnesses like Peter and John did not keep the good news about Jesus a secret (see Acts 4:8-16). They did not merely huddle in Jerusalem's upper rooms to enjoy fellowship with one another and their risen Lord. Instead, the early witnesses went into the streets and public places of their Jerusalem, ministering to people in need (see Acts 3:1-10) and boldly proclaiming the risen Christ (see Acts 4:1-12). Threatened by the religious establishment and ordered not to preach or teach in Jesus' name, Peter and John answered, " 'Whether it's right in the sight of God for us to listen to you rather than to God, you decide; for we are unable to stop speaking about what we have seen and heard' " (Acts 4:19-20).

If the Jewish Christians had been content to worship at the temple, obey Jewish law and ritual, meet behind closed doors, and assimilate into Jewish culture, the religious and secular authorities would probably have tolerated the Jesus movement. Likewise, in today's Jerusalem, churches that are content to keep their practices within their walls without "imposing their beliefs" on society or secular culture can expect a fairly comfortable existence. But when churches take the life-changing gospel into the culture, they find the Holy Spirit ready to work through them in miraculous ways that even the gospel's opponents cannot deny.

The Early Churches' Jerusalem

Jerusalem is mentioned more than any other city in the Bible. No place has been more significant and central to God's purposes. Jerusalem, the holy city, became the capital of Israel under David's united kingdom and, during Solomon's rule, became the site of the magnificent, long-awaited temple—the resting place for the ark of the covenant. As the center of Jewish worship and culture, Jerusalem was the destination for devoted Jewish families who visited the city several times a year for religious festivals.

Match the Scriptures with the statements to discover Jerusalem's role in God's plan.

___ 1. 2 Chronicles 6:6   a. Jesus began His church in Jerusalem.
___ 2. Matthew 21:1-11   b. Jesus will return to Jerusalem.
___ 3. Matthew 23:37-39   c. Every nation in the world was represented in Jerusalem.
___ 4. Mark 15:22-25   d. God chose Jerusalem for His name to be there.
___ 5. Luke 19:45-48   e. Jesus made a triumphal entry into Jerusalem.
___ 6. Acts 2:4   f. Jesus taught in Jerusalem.
___ 7. Acts 2:5   g. The Holy Spirit came to the disciples at Jerusalem.
___ 8. Acts 2:40-47   h. New Jerusalem is a name for heaven.
___ 9. Revelation 21:1-4   i. Jesus was crucified in Jerusalem.

8:4-8. (4) Acts 8:26-35; 8:40; 9:32-35. (5) Acts 11:19-21; 16:13-15; 16:16-18. Ask the groups to read their passages and to tell how they illustrate as-you-go evangelism. Call for responses to the activity at the bottom of page 101.
7. Summarize the two paragraphs at the top of page 102. Ask someone to read Acts 4:12. Ask: What does this verse say about the exclusiveness of the way of salvation? What does this verse imply about the non-Christian religions of the world? About the responsibility of those who know the way to tell those who do not? About the responsibility of Christian denominations to witness to other groups?

Only five miles from Jesus' birthplace of Bethlehem, Jerusalem was where Jesus taught, ministered, suffered, died, and was buried. Jesus first sent the Holy Spirit to believers in Jerusalem (see Acts 2:1-11), and He established His church there (see Acts 2). Jesus will return to Jerusalem in the future (see Matt. 23:37-39), and one day we will live together with Him in the New Jerusalem (see Rev. 21).

Jerusalem was also where the disciples were to wait for the promised Holy Spirit. Whatever was going to happen next in God's redemptive mission was going to begin there. When the Day of Pentecost arrived, Jerusalem became ground zero for the explosive power of Spirit-filled New Testament churches.

Whether in the 1st century or the 21st century, a church that is committed to its Jerusalem mission field must ask:

- Who in our community does not know Jesus?
- What will be required to communicate the gospel to the lost people in our Jerusalem and to involve them in a local fellowship of believers where they can grow, serve, and reach out to others?

In many cases the answers to these questions involve sending or supporting a local missionary, providing sacrificial ministries in the community, or starting new churches to reach the lost with the gospel. As with the other mission fields, churches must work cooperatively to evangelize Jerusalem.

In this chapter we will zoom in for a closer look at the Jerusalem mission field and will discover that many characteristics of Judea, Samaria, and the ends of the earth are also true of Jerusalem. Therefore, the same principles we examined in chapters 2–4 often apply to the Jerusalem mission field. At the same time, our Jerusalem presents its own unique challenges to today's on-mission churches.

The chart on page 104 includes the mission principles we will examine and apply to our Jerusalem mission field. Again we see that the key mission concepts of calling, cultures, church planting, cooperation, and challenges form a backdrop for understanding these principles.

What timeless principles can we learn from the New Testament churches that were Jesus' first witnesses to the Jerusalem mission field?

The Calling Principle from Jerusalem
God calls Christians to establish a lasting Christlike influence in their local communities. Some churches have signs at their exits that read, "You are now entering your mission field."

Suppose your 10-year-old child saw that sign as you were leaving church and asked what it meant. Write your response.

_____

8. Ask members to read the Scripture references in the activity at the bottom of page 102. Call for the answer as each Scripture passage is read (1. d, 2. e, 3. b, 4. i, 5. f, 6. g, 7. c, 8. a, 9. h).
9. Display a large sheet of paper on which you have recorded the two bulleted questions on page 103: *Who in our community does not know Jesus? What will be required to communicate the gospel to the lost people in our Jerusalem and to involve them in a local fellowship of believers where they can grow, serve, and reach out to others?* State that these questions will be answered as we examine principles for reaching our Jerusalem.

PRINCIPLES FROM THE MISSION'S FIELDS

Mission Concepts	Ends of the Earth	Samaria	Judea	Jerusalem
Calling	**STARTING** God calls Christians to the world in ways that are both incidental and intentional.	**STRATEGIZING** God calls Christians to personalize the gospel for the diverse peoples in and near their homeland.	**STRENGTHENING** God calls Christians to penetrate surrounding regions and their predominant religions with the true gospel.	**STAYING** God calls Christians to establish a lasting Christlike influence in their local communities.
Cultures	**PEOPLE GROUPS** God's mission to the world includes all people groups.	**POPULATION SEGMENTS** Penetrating a diverse continent or country with the gospel requires a loving understanding of its people and history.	**RELIGIOUS LOST** Those depending on works-based religion rather than a grace-based relationship don't understand the gospel.	**NEIGHBORS** Reaching a community trains a church to reach the world.
Church Planting	**MOVEMENTS** When the gospel is successfully planted, new churches grow and multiply.	**LEADERS** The unchanging gospel speaks to diverse cultures and generations through new leaders and new methods in new churches.	**SUPPORT** Regional support and cooperation strengthen new churches for multiplication.	**SACRIFICE** Disciples sacrifice for the sake of new believers and new churches.
Cooperation	**GIVING** Taking the gospel to the world is costly.	**KNOWING AND PRAYING** Informed churches pray God's power into God's mission.	**GOING** Mission-minded churches mobilize to meet human needs in the name of Christ.	**LIVING** Participating in God's mission is a local, life commitment.
Challenges	**RULERS** Many kingdoms oppose God's kingdom, but God has sovereign authority over all.	**SOCIETY** Negative cultural influences require both scriptural proclamation and spiritual confrontation.	**SELF-RIGHTEOUSNESS** Opposition from religious systems and leaders should be expected and met with spiritual resolve.	**COMPLACENCY** Many Christians need help to understand and obey Jesus' Acts 1:8 challenge.

10. Refer to the Acts 1:8 visual you have used in the three previous sessions. Under *Jerusalem* add a placard with the calling principle, *God calls Christians to establish a lasting Christlike influence in their local communities.* Use the chart on page 104 as a guide for attaching the placards to the wall during this session. Ask members to name Christians from your church, already in heaven, who left a lasting Christlike influence on the community. Point out that now it is our responsibility to influence our community. Ask a member to read Matthew 5:13-16. Ask, How do the metaphors of salt and light illustrate this principle?

That message is consistent with the attitude and practice of first-century churches as they fluidly moved from the upper room to the streets of Jerusalem. First-century Christians were not content to stay behind closed doors to worship, pray, fellowship, study, and serve one another. They wanted every person in their community to hear the gospel, come to faith in Christ, and unite with a local congregation of believers.

It probably isn't accurate to think of the Jerusalem church as one huge congregation of five thousand or more people, although we know at least that many came to Christ soon after Pentecost (see Acts 4:4). Many of those new believers no doubt continued to worship at the Jerusalem temple and in the temple complex. But the Jerusalem church might be more accurately described as an association of churches that met "from house to house" (Acts 2:46), probably organized around language or neighborhood location. Historians tell us that, in addition to the main temple, there were an estimated 460 Jewish synagogues in Jerusalem at that time, such as the Freedmen's Synagogue referred to in Acts 6:9. Therefore, it is likely that new Christian churches and house churches formed in similar neighborhoods or communities.

What was happening in Jerusalem in the days following Pentecost was more than local-church evangelism; it was community-wide missions (see Acts 2:46-47). This distinction is important. Evangelism—sharing the good news—should be a primary activity in every mission field. But so should church planting, discipleship, ministry to physical and emotional needs, leadership development, and other mission activities. A church that is active in Jerusalem missions seeks to make disciples of all the lost in its community, and that task is broader than evangelism. Making disciples may also require a church to use new methods. For example, some new believers' needs for spiritual growth may best be met in a church other than the one that initially brought them to Christ. A church in the Jerusalem field must be willing to take responsibility for the health of the entire community, not just for its own growth.

> "Every day they devoted themselves to meeting together in the temple complex, and broke bread from house to house. They ate their food with gladness and simplicity of heart, praising God and having favor with all the people. And every day the Lord added those being saved to them." **Acts 2:46-47**

A significant obstacle churches face in embracing their Jerusalem mission field is the mind-set that they are competing against other churches rather than cooperating with like-minded churches to win the lost. A church can certainly grow by evangelizing and making disciples of those who, when converted, would easily fit into the life of the church. Yet the church also needs to support efforts to start churches that can more effectively reach people who are not currently being reached.

What kinds of churches might be needed to reach lost people in our Jerusalem?
• Churches that worship and teach in languages other than English
• Churches that use various styles of music and Bible-teaching methods
• Churches that offer specialized ministries not offered elsewhere

105

11. Call for responses to the activity at the bottom of page 103.
12. Point out the difference between evangelism and community-wide missions, emphasizing that the latter includes church planting, discipleship, ministry to needs, leadership development, and other mission activities (p. 105).
13. Emphasize the importance of cooperation among churches rather than competition. Help members understand the implications of this idea (p. 105).

"On that day a severe persecution broke out against the church in Jerusalem, and all except the apostles were scattered throughout the land of Judea and Samaria." **Acts 8:1**

As we discovered when we studied the ends of the earth, Samaria, and Judea, God calls missionaries to go, start, strategize, and strengthen. But the Jerusalem mission field reminds us that many missionaries are also called to stay, investing their lives in a particular community. After Stephen's stoning, being a Christ-follower in Jerusalem became increasingly dangerous. Being a Christian church leader was even more dangerous. Yet the apostles—the Jerusalem missionaries—had staying power (see Acts 8:1). Jesus' half-brother, James, in particular, became not only a pastor but also a sort of director of missions in Jerusalem.

Read Acts 15:12-21; 21:17-18; Galatians 2:8-10; and James 1:1.

How did Paul refer to James? _____

How did James refer to himself? _____

What counsel did James give the early church about the salvation of the Gentiles?

_____

How did James encourage Paul and Barnabas in their ministry to the Gentiles?

_____

Why do you think Paul reported to James and the elders what God had done among the Gentiles through his ministry?

_____

As James strengthened and encouraged the persecuted but faithful churches of Jerusalem, the influence of their scattered witnesses began changing the world through the power of the Holy Spirit.

The Cultures Principle from Jerusalem

Reaching a community trains a church to reach the world. Often we focus on Stephen's martyrdom and the subsequent scattering of witnesses (see Acts 7:54–8:2) while overlooking the huge impact that Stephen's life and ministry had on the culture of his Jerusalem mission field. But Acts 6:8-10 indicates that Stephen had a particular impact on what came to be known as Hellenistic Jews. Because these

14. Explain that the calling principle may require missionaries to stay and minister in the community. Use the activities on page 106 to illustrate how James was such a missionary.
15. Add to the Acts 1:8 visual a placard with the cultures principle, *Reaching a community trains a church to reach the world.* Summarize "The Cultures Principle from Jerusalem."

Greek-speaking Jews had come to Jerusalem from all over the Roman Empire, they had long been exposed to Greek culture. Therefore, they were well educated; were more open to new, nontraditional ideas than the Hebraic Jews; and mixed easily with Gentiles who shared their Greek culture.

The Hellenistic synagogues in Jerusalem were not only an important mission field but were also an important training ground for the early churches. In those settings the believers learned to reason with and reach out to people from all over the world who had Greek culture in common. As Stephen worked wonders and signs in Jerusalem's Hellenistic synagogues, he also learned to answer the Jewish arguments against the gospel with "wisdom and the Spirit" (Acts 6:10). In fact, he was so effective that his frustrated opponents incited a riot against him that led to his death. Many scholars believe that the converted Hellenistic Jews were the primary believers who were scattered from Jerusalem following Stephen's martyrdom and that the Hebraic Jews, including most of the apostles, were allowed to stay.

> "Stephen, full of grace and power, was performing great wonders and signs among the people. Then some from what is called the Freedmen's Synagogue, composed of both Cyrenians and Alexandrians, and some from Cilicia and Asia, came forward and disputed with Stephen. But they were unable to stand up against the wisdom and the Spirit by whom he spoke." **Acts 6:8-10**

The Jerusalem mission field served as a training ground in several ways:

- It providentially prepared the Hellenistic Jews for the scattering that would follow Stephen's death.
- It taught the early witnesses to meet the opposition of Jewish authorities.
- It taught the churches to assimilate believers from many different language groups and cultures.
- It taught church leaders, guided and empowered by the Holy Spirit, to solve problems, clarify church doctrine and practice, and meet one another's needs.

The early witnesses discovered that Jerusalem was the home to many people who might not normally come into contact with Christians. Whether in the Hellenistic synagogues, the streets full of beggars, or the courts of the Sanhedrin, the early churches learned that Jerusalem was full of a variety of subcultures. This mission field, then, was a valuable training ground for reaching other areas to which the Holy Spirit would later lead the witnesses.

The Church-Planting Principle from Jerusalem

Disciples sacrifice for the sake of new believers and new churches. The Jerusalem mission field of the first century gives us an inspiring picture of ways the disciples of that community were willing to accommodate the spiritual and physical needs of those around them.

107

16. Add to the Acts 1:8 visual a placard with the church-planting principle, *Disciples sacrifice for the sake of new believers and new churches.* Call for responses to the activity at the top of page 108. Ask: Do our church members sacrifice to develop new believers and new churches? If not, why not? If so, in what ways?

Read Acts 2:41-45; 4:32-37; 6:1-7. List some ways the disciples sacrificed for the sake of new believers and new churches.

_____

When thousands of new converts came into the church (see Acts 2:41; 4:4), special financial needs arose. Travelers stayed longer in Jerusalem than they had intended, and workers lost their jobs because of their new faith. The early disciples willingly contributed everything they had for the Jerusalem mission of reaching new people with the gospel and assimilating them into a local congregation. Consequently, "every day the Lord added to them those who were being saved" (Acts 2:47).

Through these acts of sacrificial service, the disciples in first-century Jerusalem supported the coordinated evangelism and church-planting strategies of a growing number of local churches in their community. In doing so, they overcame the distractions of persecution (see Acts 3–5), hypocrisy (see Acts 5:1-11), and administration (see Acts 6:1-4). Working together under the Holy Spirit's leadership, they were able to saturate their community with the gospel and to start new churches.

How could the following distractions impede the work of a church?

Persecution: _____

Hypocrisy: _____

Administration: _____

The backdrop for this Jerusalem church-planting movement was the reconstruction of the Jewish temple, begun by Herod the Great in 20 B.C. The Jews commented to Jesus in John 2:20 that the temple had been under construction for 46 years. In fact, the complete remodeling and enlargement project was not completed until A.D. 64. So while Jesus was building His church in the hearts and lives of people, the Jewish authorities were visibly investing in a magnificent structure that would facilitate the fruitless sacrifice of animals for sins.

In that volatile setting Stephen, a Hellenistic Jewish Christian, attracted a great deal of attention through wonders, signs, and wisdom in the Hellenist synagogues (see Acts 6:8-10). When dragged before the Sanhedrin (see Acts 6:11-14), Stephen recited Jewish history and quoted Jewish Scriptures through the time of Solomon's building the original Jewish temple (see Acts 7:47). But when Stephen declared, " 'The Most High does not dwell in sanctuaries made with hands' " (Acts 7:48), quoting the prophet Isaiah to validate his point (see Acts 7:49-50), his statement

17. Call on three previously enlisted members to use Acts 3–5; 5:1-11; 6:1-4 to explain how persecution, hypocrisy, and administration could have served as distractions to the early churches. Show how the churches overcame these distractions through sacrificial service. Point out the way God used Stephen's life and martyrdom to spread the gospel.

was more than the temple-building Jewish authorities would tolerate. Stephen, who had learned in his Jerusalem mission field to sacrifice everything for the advancement of the gospel, made the ultimate sacrifice: his life. Just as God used the sacrificial gifts of other Jerusalem disciples to start and strengthen new churches throughout Jerusalem, He used Stephen's martyrdom to accelerate that process throughout Judea and Samaria (see Acts 8:1).

The Cooperation Principle from Jerusalem
Participating in God's mission is a local, life commitment.
The first few chapters of Acts record mission actions the early witnesses performed in their Jerusalem mission field. They prayed, gave, went, proclaimed, and sacrificed. But Acts 4:32-35 shows that participating in God's mission is not just an occasional activity. It is a life commitment that is daily and local, actively unfolding wherever believers live.

Read Acts 4:32-35. Identify evidence that the early believers had made a life commitment to participate in God's mission.

"The multitude of those who believed were of one heart and soul, and no one said that any of his possessions was his own, but instead they held everything in common. And with great power the apostles were giving testimony to the resurrection of the Lord Jesus, and great grace was on all of them. For there was not a needy person among them, because all those who owned lands or houses sold them, brought the proceeds of the things that were sold, and laid them at the apostles' feet. This was then distributed to each person as anyone had need." **Acts 4:32-35**

In the Jerusalem mission field of the first century, disciples shared and sacrificed for one another and for the sake of the mission. They neither insulated themselves from unbelievers nor reserved their witness for certain locations and times of the year. Rather, they had daily opportunities to minister in Jesus' name; to share the good news; and to guide new believers to a local congregation in which they could grow, serve, worship, and become witnesses. These opportunities were available in the community where the witnesses lived. When believers walked from their place of worship to their homes, they literally went through their Jerusalem mission field.

For instance, John and Peter demonstrated their life commitment in their daily routine of walking to the temple complex for prayer (see Acts 3:1–4:31). Sensitive to the need of a lame man by the gate, they made eye contact with him, healed him in Jesus' name, and then used the opportunity to proclaim the gospel to the awestruck onlookers and even to the angry Jewish authorities. Barnabas also demonstrated the depth of his life commitment to the mission by liquidating a major asset and laying it at the apostles' feet (see Acts 4:36-37). And the first seven deacons demonstrated their life commitment through a willingness to do whatever the church needed (see Acts 6:1-7). Of course, Stephen demonstrated the same commitment by investing his

109

18. Add to the Acts 1:8 visual a placard with the cooperation principle, *Participating in God's mission is a local, life commitment.* Call for responses to the activity on page 109. Use the examples at the bottom of that page to show how early Christians demonstrated a life commitment to the community.

life in daily ministry to the Hellenistic Jews and ultimately by laying down His life for the sake of the gospel.

The 1st-century witnesses did not compartmentalize their lives, separating their church, Christian activities, and believing friends from the lost world around them. Jesus had promised to return. And in their lifetime, in their Jerusalem, they had a responsibility to tell lost people about the resurrected Christ and His offer of forgiveness and eternal life. For the 1st-century witnesses the Jerusalem field called daily for their attention and their compassion. The people of their marketplace, schools, neighborhoods, and workplaces needed to know that the Messiah had come and that He provided the one way to a right relationship with God.

What are some ways Christians today sometimes compartmentalize their lives, separating their Christian activities from the lost world around them?

_____

The Challenges Principle from Jerusalem
Many Christians need help to understand and obey Jesus' Acts 1:8 challenge.
The term *cocooning* describes our growing tendency to stay in the comfort of our homes, enjoying our families, possessions, and comfort rather than socializing in public settings. Sadly, that same tendency can exist in local churches.

How is cocooning a threat to the spread of the gospel? _____

_____

Believers enjoy the fellowship, worship, and spiritual growth that take place in their local congregations. But over time, relationships with believers gradually replace relationships with unbelievers. We unintentionally begin to compartmentalize church life, keeping it separate from the rest of our lives.

Stephen's martyrdom probably occurred a year or two after Jesus' Acts 1:8 challenge. Maybe this was just the right amount of time for the young church at Jerusalem to cocoon before emerging to spread the gospel in Judea, Samaria, and the ends of the earth. Or perhaps the Jerusalem witnesses should have more immediately obeyed Jesus' Acts 1:8 challenge. Perhaps the persecution following Stephen's death was necessary to move the witnesses beyond Jerusalem.

In any case one important lesson we learn from the first-century Jerusalem mission field is that growing comfortable within the walls of the church is always a threat to the spread of the gospel. The Jerusalem mission field beckons believers to leave their comfort zones and reach out with the good news of Jesus Christ.

110

19. Explain that the first-century believers did not compartmentalize their lives but infused their everyday activities with a vibrant witness of Christ. Brainstorm ways Christians sometimes compartmentalize their lives (see first activity, p. 110). List these on a marker board. Ask members to examine their lives and determine which of these ways might be true of them.

20. Add to the Acts 1:8 visual a placard with the challenges principle, *Many Christians need help to understand and obey Jesus' Acts 1:8 challenge.* Ask a volunteer to define *cocooning* (p. 110). Ask: What are some indications of

As they go into their Jerusalem, believers can gain valuable experience and on-the-job training to go to all the world. Church leaders can encourage church members to reach beyond the walls of their church by providing the biblical teaching and experiential training they need to respond to Jesus' Acts 1:8 challenge.

In each mission field of Jesus' Acts 1:8 challenge, we see unique spiritual, governmental, cultural, and religious barriers. The close-to-home Jerusalem mission field reminds us that a church's comfort or complacency can also be a barrier that inhibits its obedience to the mission. We may also settle for poor substitutes, such as offering social ministry without evangelism or traveling to see the world instead of to share the gospel, rather than fully obeying the Great Commission. Church leaders must challenge members to authentic missions involvement under the Holy Spirit's authority.

The law of inertia states that an object tends to remain at rest or continue moving in a straight line until a directional force acts on it. One of the church's greatest barriers to effective missions involvement is spiritual inertia. A church tends to remain at rest within its walls until biblical conviction and the Holy Spirit's prompting motivate it to action. But once the church is moving on mission in the power of the Holy Spirit, nothing can stand in its way.

Your Church's Jerusalem

Beyond the walls of the church but within the reach of ministry and missions involvement, a church's surrounding community is its 21st-century Jerusalem mission field. In their Jerusalem, worshipers and disciples can daily express themselves as witnesses, and local churches can work together through regional associations to reach the community with the gospel.

A church that is intent on reaching its Jerusalem focuses on people who may never enter the church building. It is active in the schools, apartment complexes, shopping malls, and neighborhoods. Such a church knows that missions is local as well as remote and that barriers such as language, culture, economic status, and age can be as imposing as barriers like oceans or mountains.

Jerusalem is the first place you go when you step out the door of your church. It includes the people you drive by on your way home from worship. And it includes the people who live between your church and the next church but attend neither. In urban areas like ancient Jerusalem, today's Jerusalem might be defined as a city or a metropolitan area. In rural areas it might be better defined as several counties.

A helpful way to define a church's Jerusalem is simply to ask, "Where are the closest like-minded churches, and how can our church cooperate with them to reach our extended community with the gospel?" Usually, Southern Baptist churches form regional associations of churches whose Jerusalem work is coordinated by a director of missions or an associational missionary. Just as state conventions of churches

111

cocooning? How is cocooning a threat to the spread of the gospel? Are there signs of cocooning in our church? How can a church avoid cocooning?

21. Write this sentence on a marker board: *One of the church's greatest barriers to effective missions involvement is spiritual inertia*. Ask a volunteer to define *spiritual inertia* (p. 111).
22. Call on the member enlisted to characterize today's Jerusalem mission field, using the material on pages 111–14.

cooperate to reach the people of a particular state, region, or province, associations of churches focus on an even more specific geographic region and group of people.

In North America there are around 1,200 regional associations of Southern Baptist churches. Quite diverse, these associations range in size from fewer than 5 churches with about 100 resident members (members who live close enough to a congregation to attend) to more than 500 congregations with more than 200,000 resident members. (The median size is 28 churches with around 5,500 resident members.)[1] Making generalizations about the Jerusalem mission field or even a Baptist association is difficult. Nevertheless, we can make the following observations about today's Jerusalem.

- Not all Jerusalem mission fields or associations of churches geographically equate with a county, but many do, and data available by county give us one picture of lostness in today's Jerusalem mission field. In a typical (median) U.S. county, 43 percent of the population is unclaimed by any religious group, Christian or otherwise.[2] Of course, a much larger percentage, around 70 percent, is estimated not to have a personal relationship with Jesus Christ.[3] Yet 89 percent of U.S. adults say they believe in God or a universal spirit, and only 6 percent say they do not believe.[4] So although many people are indifferent or have only nominal religious beliefs, they are not necessarily closed to spiritual conversation or hostile to a Christian witness.

- Many of today's Jerusalem mission fields or associations might be considered metropolitan areas. Of the 362 metropolitan areas in the United States—

—4 of 5 people in the United States live there;

—49 of these areas are home to one million or more, and these 49 account for more than half of the total U.S. population;

—the largest populations are in the cities and surrounding areas of New York (18.3 million), Los Angeles (12.3 million), Chicago (9.1 million), and Philadelphia (5.7 million);

—all but four of the top one hundred fastest-growing metropolitan areas are in the south and the west.[5]

- Of the 27 metropolitan areas in Canada—

—6 of 10 people in Canada live there;

—5 of these areas are home to one million or more, and these 5 account for 40 percent of the total Canadian population;

—the largest populations are in the cities and surrounding areas of Toronto (5 million), Montreal (3.6 million), Vancouver (2.1 million), Ottawa-Gatineau (1.1 million), and Calgary (1 million).[6]

- Many large cities in North America contain larger concentrations of people groups that are second only to the country in which that people group originated. For example, the Polish population in the larger Chicago metropolitan area is second only to the Polish population in Warsaw. Southern California has the largest Vietnamese population outside Vietnam.[7]

• Although metropolitan areas are home to a majority of North America's population, the more expansive geographies of its town and country populations present their own challenges. In land area, for example, Canada is the largest nation in the western hemisphere and one of the most sparsely populated. The majority of the U.S. population is concentrated on about 20 percent of the land area, while the 20 percent of the population classified as nonmetropolitan is dispersed throughout the other 80 percent of the land area.[8] Sometimes the Jerusalem mission field is a tall tower of urban concentration. Sometimes it is a vast sprawl of farms, ranches, countryside, or wilderness. Whatever a church's Jerusalem mission field looks like, a large percentage of the inhabitants do not know Jesus as Savior and Lord and do not have a relevant church within reach.

Characterize your church's Jerusalem mission field by describing its—

geography: _____

population: _____

age distribution: _____

languages: _____

subcultures: _____

socioeconomic conditions: _____

_____

• Many people in today's Jerusalem mission field would not consider attending a church because they are preoccupied with survival needs, like the lame man Peter and John healed in Acts 3:1-10. For example, one in five adult Americans cannot read a newspaper.[9] About 12 percent of the U.S. population lives below poverty thresholds, and slightly less than half of these are children and the elderly.[10] Survival needs are either barriers or bridges to hearing the gospel.

How can survival needs become bridges to hearing the gospel? _____

_____

23. Call for responses to the activity in the middle of page 113.

- The diverse, growing population and needs of today's Jerusalem mission field call for many new ministries and new congregations. Yet 39 percent of Southern Baptist associations report no church-type missions among their congregations,[11] and only around 5 percent of Southern Baptist churches are involved in sponsoring a church-type mission.[12] In today's associations it is estimated that almost 30 percent of churches are served by bivocational pastors[13] and that another 10 percent do not have pastors.[14] Clearly, we need more churches and more leaders to serve and reach the lost in our Jerusalem mission field.

It might have been easy for the first-century witnesses to assume that everyone in Jerusalem knew about Jesus. But the early believers did not take a passive and presumptuous attitude toward the lost. Instead, they were bold in ministry and proclamation outside the temple and beyond the walls of their house churches. And as churches spread to Antioch, Ephesus, Corinth, Rome, and beyond, each newly established congregation became a new mission outpost from which the gospel radiated to the local community. Because local churches took seriously their responsibility for the Jerusalem mission field, the gospel spread very quickly in the first century. Churches today can learn from their example. Let's apply the biblical principles used by the first-century churches to our Jerusalem mission field today.

The Calling Principle in Today's Jerusalem

God calls Christians to establish a lasting Christlike influence in their local communities. Churches in a Jerusalem mission field must have leaders—not just career missionaries but also pastors and key lay leaders from local churches—who recognize the lostness around them. These leaders must also challenge their churches to do more than maintain or grow themselves in order to reach everyone who needs Christ. Mission-minded Christians from all walks of life must invest themselves beyond their own church walls to reach their Jerusalem mission field. Working with other churches in a regional association, a church can reach its Jerusalem more effectively than it could alone.

Name persons or groups in your community who do not know Jesus.

_____

Give examples of ways your church influences its Jerusalem through—

evangelism: _____

discipleship: _____

114

24. Calling attention to the five principles under *Jerusalem* on the Acts 1:8 visual, say, Let's apply these principles to our Jerusalem today. As you discuss modern-day applications of each principle in "Your Church's Jerusalem," refer to the five placards that you have already placed on the Acts 1:8 visual. Call attention to the placard with the calling principle, *God calls Christians to etablish a lasting Christlike influence in their local communities.* Discuss the activities on page 114 and at the top of page 115.

ministry to physical and emotional needs: _____

_____

leadership development: _____

church planting: _____

The Cultures Principle in Today's Jerusalem

Reaching a community trains a church to reach the world. To be cooperative and intentional in reaching the Jerusalem mission field, churches must train leaders and other witnesses for all of the churches' mission fields.

Rate your church's effectiveness in training members in doctrine.

_____

Neglects training   Offers some training   Aggressively trains

Rate your church's effectiveness in training members in leadership skills.

_____

Neglects training   Offers some training   Aggressively trains

In addition to teaching biblical doctrine and leadership skills, churches should train their members to look with missionary eyes for pockets of lost people whom no church is reaching. Churches must learn to think evangelistically as they plan events, ministry actions, and Bible-study opportunities. Believers can receive on-the-job training in multihousing neighborhoods, school campuses, crisis-pregnancy centers, upscale corporate environments, and other community ministries. Often they discover people groups in their own Jerusalem whom God will use to equip them for later missions efforts in other parts of the world. Experiences in the Jerusalem mission field frequently prepare believers for service to Judea, Samaria, and the ends of the earth.

List ways your church's Jerusalem mission field serves as a training ground to help church members reach the world.

_____

_____

115

25. Refer to the placard with the cultures principle, *Reaching a community trains a church to reach the world.* Call for responses to the activity at the bottom of page 115. If members have difficulty answering, give examples from the material on that page.

A CHURCH ON MISSION

Immanuel Baptist Church in Wichita, Kansas, has a rich history of taking the gospel to the ends of the earth. But this thriving inner-city church also discovered a closer mission field right outside its doors. When God opened the doors for the church to partner with nearby schools, members began taking the gospel to their Jerusalem.

Providing school supplies to local schools has allowed Immanuel Baptist Church to share the gospel with its neighbors in Wichita, Kansas.

Church members began by providing back-to-school supplies for every child in the two elementary schools. The church's youth ministry then began leading a weekly Bible club at the middle school. The church ministers to the teaching staffs by providing lunches, prayer notes, and special recognitions. Members also volunteer as mentors and tutors for dozens of students each week.

Immanuel's school ministries opened a variety of other opportunities. The congregation now sponsors free meals and concerts in a park adjoining its property. The church works with the police department and neighborhood association to clean up the community, sponsor a carnival, and provide home improvements for the elderly. With an Air Force base nearby, Immanuel teams with military church members to minister to people in the armed services.

These ministries have earned Immanuel the privilege of leading evangelistic teams into homes to share the gospel. And they have become tangible reminders that the global mission field begins just outside the church's walls.[15]

The Church-Planting Principle in Today's Jerusalem

Disciples sacrifice for the sake of new believers and new churches. Today's churches that are active in their Jerusalem mission field find many opportunities for sacrificial ministry. Although many new converts will find church homes in existing congregations, in some cases new congregations may need to be formed.

116

26. Call attention to the placard with the church-planting principle, *Disciples sacrifice for the sake of new believers and new churches.* Discuss the sacrifices necessary to disciple new believers and establish new congregations.

Name sacrifices that would be needed to establish a new congregation.

_____

Sometimes churches must share their facilities with new congregations. In fact, many churches have two or more congregations worshiping in different languages under the same roof. Other churches, cooperating with other churches in their regional association, establish new congregations in different locations to effectively reach and assimilate the people being reached. When an existing church sacrifices time, people, money, and other resources to establish a new congregation, God blesses its kingdom-minded generosity.

The Cooperation Principle in Today's Jerusalem
Participating in God's mission is a local, life commitment. One of the most challenging, wonderful discoveries churches make about the Jerusalem mission field is that it's always around them.

What are some arenas in your Jerusalem in which believers can share the gospel?

_____

Christians can spread the gospel on local-school campuses, in hard-to-penetrate apartment complexes, and in local prisons. The mission may focus on a language or ethnic group or on groups with special needs, such as illiteracy, poverty, or isolation. Many churches equip their members to be chaplains in local corporations, hospitals, or military bases. Other churches commission missionaries from their congregations to enter new communities or to reach groups with special needs. Often these Jerusalem missionaries create pathways for more witnesses to become involved in their Jerusalem mission field.

How does your church cooperate with other churches to reach its Jerusalem?

_____

The Challenges Principle in Today's Jerusalem
Many Christians need help to understand and obey Jesus' Acts 1:8 challenge.
Helping all church members understand and obey their call to be witnesses is a critical task. The failure of churches and Christians to go into the Jerusalem mission field can undermine the mission fields of Judea, Samaria, and the ends of the earth. Recall Jesus' sadness when Jerusalem persistently rejected His message of truth

117

27. Refer to the placard with the cooperation principle, *Participating in God's mission is a local, life commitment.* Ask members to name ways your church cooperates with other churches to reach the community. List these on a marker board and challenge members to find places of service through which they can share Christ in their community.

(see Matt. 23:37; 24:2; Luke 13:33; 19:42). Jesus knew that Jerusalem's need was urgent and that the role of His church in that mission field was critical. Jerusalem was not just the holy, historical city where so much had already happened. Jerusalem was the place where He would first send the Holy Spirit to empower His disciples to go from the upper room into the world. Jerusalem was the current location of the local church and the launching pad for God's mission to all the world. No more critical need exists today than for believers to awaken to the same calling and power that will spill them from the comfort of their churches into the streets of their Jerusalem and, ultimately, their world.

Cocooning, comfort, and complacency are three barriers on-mission churches must overcome to reach beyond their walls. What can a church do to overcome them?

How Long Will We Wait?

In first-century Jerusalem, some Jewish Christians felt that circumcision and keeping the Mosaic law were necessary elements of the Christian faith. As described in Acts 15, Paul and Barnabas returned from their first missions journey to help settle the controversy. Notice the wonderful snapshot in verse 4, which shows that the local Jerusalem church, the called-out missionary apostles, and the local-church pastors or elders gathered and celebrated the amazing things God had done through them. Almost 20 years had passed since Jesus had issued His Acts 1:8 challenge, and the report from Paul and Barnabas was perhaps a reminder that faithful witnesses were spreading the gospel throughout Judea, Samaria, and the ends of the earth. And, as promised in Luke 24:46-48, it had all begun in Jerusalem.

"When they arrived in Jerusalem, they were welcomed by the church, the apostles, and the elders, and they reported all that God had done with them."
Acts 15:4

The Jerusalem field is also where my mission began. When I was a young pastor's son, our associational missionary occasionally spoke to our congregation about the ways several churches in our area were working together to reach out to the community. That's when I realized that our mission was larger than just our church.

Years later when my dad became a director of missions and when I became an associational youth director, I saw several churches working and sacrificing together to reach people. I saw encouraging fellowship between pastors and other church leaders. I saw a kingdom perspective and a commitment to congregations who spoke different languages, had special needs, or were too new to support themselves.

When I attended annual associational meetings, I felt much closer to God's mission because I heard church leaders, pastors, and missionaries talk about the

28. Call attention to the placard with the challenges principle, *Many Christians need help to understand and obey Jesus' Acts 1:8 challenge*. Ask members to evaluate whether cocooning, comfort, and complacency are obstacles preventing your church from reaching your Jerusalem. Discuss what your church can do to overcome these obstacles and to reach beyond the church walls.

lostness of our community, what strategies we could implement together to reach lost people with the gospel, and where we could start new churches. The more I learned about the needs of our Jerusalem mission field, the less complete my own church involvement seemed. Although I wasn't specifically trained or experienced, I felt called to help start an outpost church designed to reach people in our community whom existing churches were not reaching. Within a year after launching the new church, we saw it become about twice the size of its sponsoring church!

Helping start a new church was the most challenging and rewarding spiritual experience of my life to that point. I discovered what escapes many devoted Christians: although a church's worship, fellowship, discipleship, and ministry have intrinsic value for the life of the church, they also prepare the church to go on mission. For years I had been a pastor's son, a missionary's son, a deacon, a Sunday School teacher, a youth director, a choir director—an active church participant. But I had rarely seen people come to Christ. I didn't even know many people who weren't Christians until I went into my Jerusalem mission field.

When we hear Jesus' Acts 1:8 challenge, we cannot look at the ends of the earth without asking, "How far will we go?" The many cultural barriers that separate us from people in our Samaria mission field force us to ask, "How deep will we go?" In our nearby Judea mission field, with its religious traditions and relativism, we must ask, "How much will we sacrifice to convey that a personal relationship with Jesus is the only pathway to God?" But the question posed by the Jerusalem mission field is perhaps the most critical. Because it surrounds us every day, the Jerusalem mission field forces us to ask ourselves and our churches, "How long will we wait?"

More and more churches are responding: "We will not wait another day. We are ready for the Holy Spirit to turn our church inside out, spilling us out into the streets of our Jerusalem." For those churches and for those that are already active in Jerusalem, Judea, Samaria, and the ends of the earth, we bring our spaceship to a landing for our final chapter of study. Now that we have a biblical view of God's worldwide, history-long mission and a clearer understanding of each mission field in the Acts 1:8 challenge, we will consider how a 21st-century church can pursue a comprehensive missions strategy that honors the One who issued the great challenge.

Review the chart on page 104. Now without referring to the chart, fill in the blanks to complete the mission principles for carrying the gospel to Jerusalem.
Calling principle: God calls Christians to establish a lasting Christlike _____ in their local communities.
Cultures principle: Reaching a community trains a church to reach the _____.
Church-planting principle: Disciples sacrifice for the sake of new _____ and new _____.
Cooperation principle: Participating in God's mission is a local, life _____.

119

29. Refer to the teaching posters on the wall. Ask members to read posters that capture the heart of this session's study.
30. Ask members to summarize why believers have a responsibility to carry the gospel to Jerusalem (activity, p. 120).
31. Show cel 13 of John 20:21 and have the group read the verse in unison. Ask members to memorize the verse before the next session.

Challenges principle: Many Christians need help to _____ and _____
Jesus' Acts 1:8 challenge.

Practice saying Acts 1:8; Matthew 28:19-20; Mark 16:15; and Luke 24:47 from memory.
Write John 20:21 on a card. Keep the card with you and memorize the verse this week.
Read it, along with the other four Scriptures, at least once each day during this study.

Complete this sentence: Believers have a responsibility to carry the gospel to
Jerusalem because—

_____

_____

Pray for your community and commit to God that you will pray for it each day.

____

[1]Research Team Statistics, North American Mission Board of the Southern Baptist Convention.

[2]Dale E. Jones et al., "Religious Congregations & Membership in the United States 2000: An Enumeration by Region, State and County Based on Data Reported for 149 Religious Bodies" (Nashville, Glenmary Research Center, 2000). Research Team Statistics, North American Mission Board of the Southern Baptist Convention.

[3]Research Team Statistics, North American Mission Board of the Southern Baptist Convention.

[4]The Gallup Organization, "Religion" [online], 30 May 2003 [cited 3 May 2004]. Available from the Internet: *www.gallup.com/content/print.aspx?ci=1690*.

[5]U.S. Census Bureau, "Population in Metropolitan and Micropolitan Statistical Areas, (Table) 3a. Ranked by 2000 Population for the United States and Puerto Rico: 1990 and 2000" [online], 30 December 2003 [cited 3 May 2004]. Available from the Internet: *www.census.gov/population/www/cen2000/phc-t296.html*.

[6]Canadian Statistics, "Population of census metropolitan areas, 2001 Census boundaries" [online] 23 April 2004 [cited 3 May 2004]. Available from the Internet: *www.statcom.ca/english/Pgdb/demo05a.htm*. Canadian Statistics, "Population, provinces, and territories" [online], 23 April 2004. Available from the Internet: *www.statcan.ca/english/Pgdb/demo02.htm*.

[7]U.S. Bureau of the Census, "Profile of General Demographic Characteristics: 2000, (Table) DP-1. Geographic area: Los Angeles—Riverside—Orange County, CA CMSA," Census 2000. U.S. Bureau of the Census, "Profile of Selected Social Characteristics: 2000, (Table) DP-2. Geographic area: Chicago, IL PMSA," Census 2000.

[8]U.S. Bureau of the Census, "Statistical Abstract of the United States: 2000, (Table) 31. Metropolitan and Nonmetropolitan Area Population: 1970 to 1998," Census 2000.

[9]National Institure for Literacy, "National Adult Literacy Survey 1992" [online], [cited 4 May 2004]. Available from the Internet: *www.nifl.gov/nifl/facts/NALS.html*. Research Team Statistics, North American Mission Board of the Southern Baptist Convention.

[10]Jospeh Dalaker and Bernadette D. Proctor, "Poverty in the United States: 2002" U.S. Census Bureau (September), 1, 6.

[11]Research Team Statistics, North American Mission Board of the Southern Baptist Convention.

[12]Ibid.

[13]Ibid.

[14]Ibid.

[15]Appreciation is expressed to Gayle Tenbrook, Immanuel Baptist Church, Wichita, Kansas, for providing this account.

Answers to matching activity on page 102: 1. d, 2. e, 3. b, 4. i, 5. f, 6. g, 7. c, 8. a, 9. h

32. If you invited your associational director of missions to speak to the group, introduce him.
33. Thank the director of missions for sharing with the group. Close by praying that members will take more responsibility for their community and will reach out with the love of Christ.

Chapter 6

Embrace the Challenge:
Your Church on Mission

YOUR MISSION

After completing this chapter, you will be able to—
• write your personal mission statement;
• identify your church's partners in the Acts 1:8 challenge;
• pray for your Acts 1:8 mission partners;
• evaluate your personal and church involvement in the Acts 1:8 challenge;
• identify actions you or your church can take to reach the Acts 1:8 mission fields;
• commit to become more personally involved in the Acts 1:8 challenge.

A few years ago the world was shocked when Christopher Reeve, who had played the part of Superman in several movies, became paralyzed from the neck down after being thrown from a horse. Reeve has fought to overcome his physical challenges, but each time I see his atrophied body wheeled to a microphone so that he can speak a few strained words, I sadly remember the virile images from his Superman movies.

Occasionally I wonder whether Jesus looks at some churches with that same sadness. Although superhuman power is available to them through the Holy Spirit, some churches appear to be mere shells of the mighty forces Jesus intended them to be. As we think about Jesus' Acts 1:8 challenge for churches today, the mission's *Founder* continues to call. The mission's *fields* are clear. What else is needed? The mission's *followers* must respond.

Throughout this study we have met many followers of Jesus who accepted His Acts 1:8 challenge and became His witnesses at the ends of the earth, in Samaria, in Judea, and in Jerusalem. As Peter, John, Philip, Barnabas, and Stephen came onto the scene in the Book of Acts, each demonstrated a passionate, sacrificial commit-

121

Group Session 6

1. Read this statement about the mission's Founder: God's history-long, worldwide mission is to redeem and reclaim the sin-enslaved peoples of the earth. Through the family of Abraham, the nation of Israel, Jesus, and the church, God has revealed Himself and restored relationships with those who come to Him in faith. One day the mission will end, but the fruit of the mission—eternal worshipers who reflect God's glory—will live forever. Say, We are a part of that worldwide mission. Ask five volunteers to recite the memory verses in this order:

ment to the Lord Jesus and to His redemptive mission. Perhaps no one expressed that commitment in more personal, absolute terms than the apostle Paul: "I reckon my own life to be worth nothing to me; I only want to complete my mission and finish the work that the Lord Jesus gave me to do, which is to declare the Good News about the grace of God" (Acts 20:24, GNT). Paul considered his life of no value apart from the mission Jesus gave him. Nothing would stop him from pursuing its completion. Commenting on this verse, Oswald Chambers wrote:

> *Joy comes from seeing the complete fulfillment of the specific purpose for which I was created and born again, not from successfully doing something of my own choosing. The joy our Lord experienced came from doing what the Father had sent Him to do. And He says to us, "As the Father has sent Me, I also send you" (John 20:21). Have you received a ministry from the Lord? If so, you must be faithful to it—to consider your life valuable only for the purpose of fulfilling that ministry. Knowing that you have done what Jesus sent you to do, think how satisfying it will be to hear Him say to you, "Well done, good and faithful servant" (Matthew 25:21).[1]*

Many people write statements of their missions in life. As you read the following Scriptures, think about your own mission.

Read Acts 20:24 in several translations. Write in your own words Paul's mission.

_____

Read Joshua 24:15 from several translations. Write Joshua's mission statement for himself and his family.

_____

Read John 4:34; 5:30; 9:4; 17:4. Write in your own words Jesus' mission in the world.

_____

_____

Say aloud the five Great Commission Scriptures you have memorized in this study.

On a separate sheet of paper, write a mission statement for your life. Before writing, ask God to help you express what He wants your mission to be.

Matthew 28:19-20; Mark 16:15; Luke 24:47; John 20:21; Acts 1:8. Show cel 2 with Acts 1:8 and circle the four mission fields where we are to be witnesses.

2. Say, This session focuses on embracing the Acts 1:8 challenge and putting it into action. Call attention to "Your Mission" for chapter 6 on page 121. Ask a member to lead in prayer.

3. Ask a member to hold up poster 1, which you prepared in advance (see "Posters for Session 6," p. 146). Ask members to explain the statement.

With today's missionary force, today's technology and travel resources, the affluence and education of today's North American churches, and today's mission boards and other Great Commission partners, you and your church have every reason to be personally involved in reaching all four of your Acts 1:8 mission fields. Every Christian should be a witness where he or she lives— an obedient participant in Jesus' Acts 1:8 challenge. And every local church should be a worldwide missions center that equips its witnesses to fulfill God's call.

> " 'You will receive power when the Holy Spirit has come upon you, and you will be My witnesses in Jerusalem, in all Judea and Samaria, and to the ends of the earth.' " **Acts 1:8**

No matter how many important activities take place within the church walls, a church's primary, most urgent mission is beyond those walls—at the ends of the earth, in Samaria, in Judea, and in Jerusalem, among the lost peoples whom Jesus sees so clearly and loves so much. Churches that are nearsighted may have meaningful worship services and gifted pastors. They might take good care of our kids and provide us with encouraging Christian friends. We can receive many benefits from being part of a nearsighted church. But a church that allows Jesus to correct its vision also sees the enormous needs that exist outside its walls. A church that embraces Jesus' Acts 1:8 vision motivates and trains us to give our lives away in His mission to the world. Are you and your church following the mission's Founder into the mission's fields?

Your Church's Reflection in the Acts 1:8 Challenge

God's Word provides a perfect mirror in which we can view our reflection (see Jas. 1:22-25). As we hold up the mirror of God's Word, we should ask ourselves: *Does our church look like the bold, on-mission churches of the New Testament? Are we following the Holy Spirit's leadership as the early churches did?* Jesus' last words on earth in Acts 1:8 should be the words that are freshest in our ears and nearest to our hearts.

Examine the chart on page 124, which summarizes what we studied in chapters 1–5. Do you see your church's reflection in this biblical mirror?   ❏ Yes   ❏ No
Does your church have a biblical understanding of and commitment to God's history-long, worldwide mission?   ❏ Yes   ❏ No
Has your church identified and taken responsibility for its ends of the earth, Samaria, Judea, and Jerusalem?   ❏ Yes   ❏ No
In the four Acts 1:8 mission fields is your church pursuing a comprehensive strategy that involves more and more church members?   ❏ Yes   ❏ No

4. Write on a marker board, *"You were made for a mission."*—*Rick Warren*[a] State, It is important for every believer to have a mission statement that reflects his or her involvement in God's mission. Call for responses to the activities on page 122. Ask volunteers to share their personal mission statements.
5. State, It is also important for churches to be involved in God's mission. Call for responses to the activities on pages 123–24.

JESUS' ACTS 1:8 CHALLENGE

The Mission's Founder	God's history-long, worldwide mission is to redeem and reclaim the sin-enslaved peoples of the earth. Through the family of Abraham, the nation of Israel, Jesus, and the church, God has revealed Himself and restored relationships with those who come to Him in faith. One day the mission will end, but the fruit of the mission—eternal worshipers who reflect God's glory—will live forever.

The Mission's Fields	MISSION CONCEPTS	ENDS OF THE EARTH	SAMARIA	JUDEA	JERUSALEM
	Calling	Starting	Strategizing	Strengthening	Staying
	Cultures	People Groups	Population Segments	Religious Lost	Neighbors
	Church Planting	Movements	Leaders	Support	Sacrifice
	Cooperation	Giving	Knowing and Praying	Going	Living
	Challenges	Rulers	Society	Self-Righteousness	Complacency

Rate your church's current involvement in each of the four mission fields you have studied. 1 = not involved; 3 = somewhat involved; 5 = very much involved.

Taking the gospel to the ends of the earth   1 2 3 4 5
Taking the gospel to lost people in our continent   1 2 3 4 5
Taking the gospel to lost people in our state   1 2 3 4 5
Taking the gospel to lost people in our community   1 2 3 4 5

The first step toward reflecting the biblical model of an on-mission New Testament church is to recognize that you and your church belong at the forefront of God's mission to the world. Your church is one of the Holy Spirit-led bodies through which God has chosen to take the gospel to the world in these last days before Jesus' return. And you are one of the witnesses whom Jesus has sent into that world.

In this study we have looked at Jesus' Acts 1:8 challenge first from the perspective of the early churches and their surrounding geography and cultures. But we have also looked at each mission field from the perspective of a local North American church today, emphasizing that every local church has a community; a state, province, or region; a country or continent; and an ends of the earth. Are we to interpret Jesus' words about these four places literally? Symbolically? Geographically? Ethnically? Culturally? Yes! No matter how you categorize the peoples of the world, every local church has responsibility for them. God wants your local church to have a radiating influence throughout your unique Acts 1:8 mission fields.

Wherever those mission fields may be for your church, the key mission concepts we identified in this study provide a framework for planning your involvement there:

- *Calling.* Through missionaries, other on-mission Christians, your church's direct involvement, and your personal obedience, God is calling you and your church to leave your comfort zone and help take the gospel to the world.

- *Cultures.* God calls you to the people groups of the world, to the population segments within a country or continent, to religious people who do not personally know Jesus, and to the neighborhoods you pass every day.

- *Church planting.* The consistent New Testament pattern is for converts to be baptized into a local body of believers in which they can worship, encourage and support one another, and grow in Christlikeness. Like new believers, new churches must continually multiply if the gospel is to reach all the peoples of the world. New leaders and new methods are constantly required to reach new people.

- *Cooperation.* While every church has responsibility for taking the gospel to the world, no church can accomplish this task alone. The body of Christ most effectively continues His mission when it cooperatively gives, prays, and sacrifices for the sake of God's worldwide mission.

- *Challenges.* Many obstacles and opponents stand between a church and the delivery of the gospel. Many are external powers and influences, but some are our own traditions, fears, or complacency. The Holy Spirit gives us all we need to overcome any challenge, but we must depend on His power and guidance.

These key mission concepts apply to the Acts 1:8 mission fields of the early churches, but they also provide a biblical mirror for viewing our mission involvement today.

Describe one specific action your church is taking to reach each mission field.

Your ends of the earth: _____

_____

Your continent: _____

_____

Your state: _____

_____

Your community: _____

6. Show cel 8 and review the mission concepts, indicated by bullets, on page 125. Ask for responses to the activity on page 125. Draw attention to areas in which your church is not already involved.

Your Church's Resources for the Acts 1:8 Challenge

Accepting Jesus' Acts 1:8 challenge today is a daunting task for an individual church. Even the largest churches' financial and human resources are dwarfed by the size and complexity of the worldwide mission. But by cooperating together, Southern Baptist churches are uniquely positioned and organized to respond to Jesus' Acts 1:8 challenge. In every Acts 1:8 mission field, your local church has at least one primary partner that is ready to assist you in the Great Commission task. As you read about your partners for reaching your Acts 1:8 mission fields, see page 142 for information on contacting them.

Your Partner for Reaching Your Ends of the Earth

When the Southern Baptist Convention first convened in 1845, two of its most far-reaching actions were to create foreign and domestic mission boards. The foreign board, now called the International Mission Board (IMB), has appointed more than 15,000 missionaries since its first commissioning service in 1846, and today more than a third of that number actively serve in 15 major regions around the world. As we saw in chapter 2, those missionaries engage more than 1,500 of the 5,000 Last Frontier people groups, adding almost 200 people groups each year.

The IMB is uniquely positioned to help your church learn, pray, give, and go to the ends of the earth. This infrastructure of missionaries and ministries throughout the world gives your church a network in which to operate and inside information on which to build your ends-of-the-earth strategy. When the Holy Spirit places a people group or world region on your church's heart, the IMB can help you connect with missionaries, adopt one or more people groups for focused prayer, and plan mission trips to touch those people's lives. The IMB can also connect you with other churches that may have similar missions strategies or interests and can provide you with resources to inform, awaken, and mobilize your church members.

Stop and pray for the more than five thousand IMB missionaries around the world; their safety; their ministry; their loved ones in this country; the people to whom they minister; and the IMB staff at the headquarters in Richmond, Virginia.

Your Partner for Reaching Your Samaria

The Southern Baptist domestic mission board that was formed in 1845 is now called the North American Mission Board (NAMB). With more than 5,000 missionaries throughout the United States, its territories, and Canada, the NAMB is uniquely positioned to assist your church in reaching your Samaria mission field. As we saw in chapter 3, today an estimated 7 of 10 people in North America don't have a

7. Say: Our churches must work together to obey the Acts 1:8 challenge. We have partners to help us meet the challenge. Assign the five sections on pages 126–28 to five small groups. Ask each group to work together to summarize the work of its assigned missions partner.

8. As the small group reports on the International Mission Board, show cel 14 and read the IMB mission and vision. Read the prayer request for the IMB on page 126 and ask a member to lead in prayer.

personal relationship with Christ, in spite of the fact that more than 43,000 Southern Baptist churches are located in this continent. Many of these lost people are in the northern and western regions, and many are in the cities and metropolitan areas, where Southern Baptist churches are just emerging. With the help of the NAMB and its state and Canadian partners, you and your church can identify your Samaria mission field and can become involved where the Holy Spirit leads you.

The NAMB can help your church connect with missionaries and established ministries throughout the United States, its territories, and Canada, providing an experienced and reliable network in which to operate. The missionaries and new churches in emerging regions of North America desperately need your church's prayer support. Many are close enough for your church to work alongside them on mission trips or in long-term partnerships. You might help a church planter launch a new church or help a brand-new church build or improve its facilities. You could help an urban ministry center reach out to the poor or a resort ministry center reach out to the isolated affluent. The NAMB can also connect you with other churches that may have similar missions strategies or interests in North America and can provide you with resources to inform, awaken, and mobilize your church members.

Stop and pray for the the more than five thousand NAMB missionaries; their ministry; the NAMB staff at the headquarters in Alpharetta, Georgia; and the lost people in the United States, its territories, and Canada.

Your Partner for Reaching Your Judea

In North America each of more than 40 state and regional Baptist conventions brings together hundreds of churches to cooperate in reaching their Judea mission field. For many churches, Judea missions means working with their state conventions to start and strengthen new churches. State conventions also coordinate many volunteer missions opportunities, such as disaster-relief ministries, church-construction ministries, or special ministries to groups ranging from campers to auto-racing enthusiasts.

The missionaries and staff you consult in your state convention may be starters or strategists, but many are strengtheners who provide training, resources, or renewal for new or needy churches. The organization and structure of state conventions vary because each Judea mission field has its own unique history and needs. Therefore, each group of churches forms its own unique state strategies. But in most cases your church can find help in reaching its Judea through a missions or church-planting department, a volunteer-missions or missions-mobilization group, the state Woman's Missionary Union®, or other state-convention staff.

Stop and pray for your state Baptist convention staff, its ministry, and the lost people of your state.

127

9. As the small group reports on the North American Mission Board, show cel 15 and read the NAMB mission statement. Read the prayer request for the NAMB on page 127 and ask a member to lead in prayer.

Your Partner for Reaching Your Jerusalem

As we saw in chapter 5, more than 1,200 local Baptist associations help Southern Baptist Convention churches cooperate to reach their Jerusalem mission fields. Associations provide networks and coordinated, cooperative strategies that concentrate on each church's local community.

Many churches' Jerusalem missions efforts through their local association may focus on starting and strengthening new churches. For example, approximately two-thirds of associations committed to start at least one new congregation through a Convention-wide "Light Up the Nation" emphasis. Your local association can involve you and your church in starting a new church and in supporting new churches and ministries that boldly reach out to new people in your community.

Having studied your Jerusalem mission field, your local association probably knows where pockets of unreached people live and what they need. In addition to planning new churches for them, your association may have evangelistic and ministry strategies for building bridges to the gospel. Your church can join these initiatives or help formulate new strategies. Together the churches in an association have more resources for reaching their Jerusalem than any single church has.

Stop and pray for your Baptist association's director of missions and the ministries your association coordinates.

Your Other Mission Partners

Other Southern Baptist entities assist churches to fulfill Jesus' Acts 1:8 challenge.

- Woman's Missionary Union® (WMU®) works on the international, national, state, and local levels to promote missions awareness and missions involvement through praying, giving, learning about, and doing missions. WMU also produces resources that equip men, women, students, boys, and girls to live God's mission and to support missions and missionaries.
- The Executive Committee of the Southern Baptist Convention helps churches understand and promote the Cooperative Program, which funds cooperative missions efforts.
- LifeWay Christian Resources produces resources that equip churches to grow in Christ, strengthen the body of Christ, witness to the lost, and minister to others.
- Six Southern Baptist Convention seminaries play vital roles in equipping Christians for mission service.
- Several ethnic fellowships, some of which predate the Southern Baptist Convention, work with Southern Baptists to help ethnic leaders connect and work cooperatively with others.

10. After the work of the state Baptist convention and association is presented, ask a member to lead in prayer for the state convention and the local association.
11. Ask the small group to report on "Your Other Mission Partners."

Stop and pray for the WMU organization in your church and for the staff at the head-quarters in Birmingham, Alabama; the Executive Committee of the Southern Baptist Convention, located in Nashville, Tennessee; LifeWay Christian Resources, also in Nashville; and the six Southern Baptist seminaries: Southern, Southwestern, New Orleans, Southeastern, Golden Gate, and Midwestern. Thank God for our denomination and its leaders.

With the assistance of Southern Baptist mission boards, agencies, resources, state conventions, and local associations, churches can combine their efforts to reach all four arenas in Jesus' Acts 1:8 challenge.

Identify one or more denominational partners that can assist you and your church in reaching each mission field.

Your ends of the earth: _____

_____

Your continent: _____

_____

Your state: _____

_____

Your community: _____

_____

Your Church's Response to the Acts 1:8 Challenge

When a church understands and accepts Jesus' Acts 1:8 challenge, what steps does it take to fulfill God's mission at its ends of the earth, in its Samaria, in its Judea, and in its Jerusalem? We will examine eight responses to Jesus' Acts 1:8 challenge that were modeled by New Testament churches. The same approaches are equally relevant and effective for on-mission churches today.

12. Show cel 16. Point out that your church can make eight responses to the Acts 1:8 challenge.

"Be strengthened by the Lord and by His vast strength. Put on the full armor of God so that you can stand against the tactics of the Devil. For our battle is not against flesh and blood, but against the rulers, against the authorities, against the world powers of this darkness, against the spiritual forces of evil in the heavens." **Ephesians 6:10-12**

Prepare

Empower a designated leader of missions and develop mission teams, strategies, and plans to take the gospel to your community, state, continent, and world. Each church needs a vision of its unique ends of the earth, Samaria, Judea, and Jerusalem and a strategy for joining God's activity in each field. That vision comes first and foremost from God's Word and from the Holy Spirit, but it is communicated through spiritual leaders who seek God's direction from those sources. When these missions leaders emerge, they can marshal the church's resources and help the body move in response to the Holy Spirit's direction.

The primary vision and commitment to Jesus' Acts 1:8 challenge should come from the pastor and flow to other staff and leaders. A church must also identify gifted, called, Spirit-led missions leaders who can serve as a team to help the church develop strategies and plans for reaching its unique mission fields. Fulfilling God's mission to the world is the frontline of battle in spiritual warfare. Preparing for that warfare requires spiritually mature leaders who study God's Word and rely on the Holy Spirit's power and leadership (see Eph. 6:10-12).

Read Ephesians 6:10-12. Who or what is our adversary in reaching a lost world?

_____

Read Zechariah 4:6. What is our primary resource for reaching a lost world?

_____

Your Church Can Prepare
From IMB, NAMB, or WMU, obtain resources for forming or equipping a missions leadership team (see p. 142). A free resource for planning your church's Acts 1:8 strategy is available at www.actsone8.com.

Most church members enthusiastically accept Jesus' Acts 1:8 challenge because it is a biblical way to express God's love for the world. Acts 1:8 also encourages churches to customize their strategies for their unique mission fields. But for many church members who have been preoccupied with their own lives and with internal church life, venturing outside the walls can be new and frightening. A church's missions leadership team must discern the Holy Spirit's leadership and vision for the church. It must also implement that vision in creative, practical ways that will capture the imagination and involvement of every church member.

13. Summarize the section "Prepare." Ask two members to hold up posters 2 and 3. Relate the statements to the need for your church to have a vision of its mission. Ask a volunteer to read Zechariah 4:6 and identify our primary resource for reaching a lost world.

Learn

Bring missions awareness and interaction to the entire church body, train members for service, and connect them to missionaries and mission needs.

As the writer of the most detailed Gospel account and the Book of Acts, Luke was a missions educator. He knew that unless Christians learned about Jesus' mission on earth and His vision for the church, they would not fully support the mission.

The following Scriptures illustrate the importance of learning about God's activity in the world. Read each passage and match it with the correct statement.

___ 1. Luke 1:1-4

___ 2. Acts 11:19-24

___ 3. Acts 14:25-28

___ 4. Acts 15:1-3

a. Paul and Barnabas reported to the church at Antioch about their missionary trip.

b. Luke realized the importance of accurately teaching believers about events in Jesus' life.

c. The Jerusalem church sent Barnabas to Antioch to help new converts.

d. The believers in Phoenicia and Samaria were happy when they learned that Gentiles were being saved.

Churches need an ongoing awareness of and education about God's redemptive mission and activity. That message should be delivered year-round to church members of all ages.

Church-based organizations such as Mission Friends® for preschoolers, Children in Action for boys and girls, Royal Ambassadors for boys, Girls in Action® for girls, Challengers and Acteens® for teens, Youth on Mission for students, Adults on Mission, Baptist Men on Mission, and Women on Mission® can provide missions education for church members. Churchwide or associational events such as On-Mission Celebrations and other global missions conferences can expose church members to missions in all four Acts 1:8 fields.

> **Your Church Can Learn**
> Contact IMB, NAMB, or WMU about resources your church can use to educate members about God's mission in the world today (see p. 142).

Churches can stay in touch with God's mission activity through missionary speakers, missions videos, missions publications, and bulletin inserts. With advances in technology and travel, every local church can stay aware of the status and needs of their church's mission in all four Acts 1:8 mission fields.

Most missionaries would testify that their calling to missions first came in a local church, where someone informed them about God's mission and educated them about becoming involved. Many were moved to personal missions involvement when a missionary spoke to their churches. In the New Testament, missionaries frequently reported to churches either in person or in writing, encouraging others to answer the call to missions and eliciting support through prayer and finances. A church's obedience to God's mission is linked to its understanding of that mission.

14. Summarize the section "Learn." Call for responses to the activity on page 131 (1. b, 2. c, 3. a, 4. d). Ask a member to read 2 Peter 3:9. Ask, What does this verse teach us about God's redemptive mission? Identify the ways to learn about missions that are mentioned on page 131.

Pray

Ask God for a kingdom perspective and a worldwide vision as you intercede for Christian workers and unevangelized peoples. As a church learns about God's mission in the world and prepares to join His mission, the most effective action it can take is fervent, focused prayer. Through prayer a church can span the barriers of distance, time, and spiritual opposition. Through prayer God's kingdom can come on earth as it is in heaven. Through prayer Christians can be involved anywhere in God's mission.

The following Scriptures emphasize the importance of prayer. Read each Scripture and match it with the prayer request it describes.

___ 1. Matthew 9:38   a. A prayer that the message would spread rapidly
___ 2. Ephesians 6:18-20   b. A prayer for boldness in speaking
___ 3. 2 Thessalonians 3:1-2   c. A prayer for all believers
                                                          d. A prayer for soul-winners
                                                          e. A prayer for protection from wicked men
                                                          f. An admonition to pray in the Spirit

> **Your Church Can Pray**
> Discover the resources that IMB, NAMB, and WMU offer to help your church pray for missions efforts (see p. 142).

What missions concerns should a church pray about?
- Pray for a kingdom perspective on the world.
- Pray for unevangelized peoples, perhaps adopting a specific people group on which your church can focus. Pray that they will be receptive to the gospel and that new churches will be established to nurture new converts as disciples.
- Pray for the missionaries your church supports through its missions offerings, the Cooperative Program, and perhaps other ways. Also pray for missionaries' families.
- Pray for God to " 'send out workers into His harvest' " (Matt. 9:38) and for Christians to obey His call.
- Pray for boldness in your efforts to share the gospel and for opportunities to do so.
- Pray for all of these things in the contexts of your church's ends of the earth, Samaria, Judea, and Jerusalem.

Missionaries testify that prayer is what they need most to be effective in their mission. And almost any missions leader would identify prayer as the most important resource to help mobilize a local congregation for missions. In addition to individual and group prayers, churchwide prayer ministries provide opportunities for the body of Christ to intercede for the lost peoples of the world.

15. Introduce the section "Pray" and call for the answers to the activity on page 132 (1. d, 2. b, c, f, 3. a, e). Ask volunteers to read the Scripture passages. As you show cel 17, emphasize the bulleted missions concerns on page 132 that churches should pray for.
16. Ask three members to hold up posters 4, 5, and 6. Ask volunteers to read the posters and to suggest their implications for your church.

Give

Increase the financial support of the Cooperative Program and other Southern Baptist cooperative missions. Reading about the sacrificial giving of New Testament churches is both humbling and inspiring.

What does each of the following Scripture passages say about giving?

Acts 2:44-45: _____

Acts 4:32-37: _____

_____

2 Corinthians 8:1-5: _____

_____

Philippians 4:15-19: _____

_____

Time and time again the New Testament churches gave "according to their ability and beyond their ability" (2 Cor. 8:3). Believers like Barnabas sold property and laid the proceeds at the disciples' feet (see Acts 4:36). Acknowledging that all material possessions are temporary, unnamed multitudes gave their combined resources for the sake of God's mission (see Acts 4:32-33).

Today Southern Baptist churches have an effective means of funding missions that is tailor-made to Jesus' Acts 1:8 challenge. Through the Cooperative Program local churches combine their resources to spread the gospel to the ends of the earth, Samaria, Judea, and Jerusalem. Usually sent through Baptist state conventions, these funds are distributed to—

- ends-of-the-earth missions through the International Mission Board;
- Samaria missions through the North American Mission Board;
- Judea ministries and missions within the state;
- Jerusalem ministries and missions conducted by local associations.

In addition to the Cooperative Program, special annual missions offerings such as the Lottie Moon Christmas Offering® for international missions, the Annie Armstrong Easter Offering® for

> **Your Church Can Give**
> Find out how your church can participate in the Cooperative Program and other missions offerings. Contact your Baptist state or Canadian convention office, the Southern Baptist Executive Committee office, IMB, NAMB, or WMU (see p. 142).

133

17. Summarize the section "Give." Ask volunteers to read the Scripture passages and to respond to the activity on page 133. Ask a member to hold up poster 7. Discuss this statement in light of individual giving to missions and in light of your church's involvement in the four Acts 1:8 mission fields. Share with the group how much money your church gives to missions each year through the Cooperative Program, associational missions, the Lottie Moon Christmas Offering® for international missions, the Annie Armstrong Easter Offering® for North American missions, the state missions offering, and other offerings such as gifts for mission trips and designated missions

North American missions, and your state or associational missions offering provide focused channels through which local churches can support targeted missions efforts. Most churches also support their local Baptist associations through direct gifts.

Many churches choose to contribute directly to missionaries, mission projects, and mission trips. Every dollar invested in Jesus' Acts 1:8 challenge is money well spent, but only the Cooperative Program and other cooperative missions offerings provide the infrastructure and denominational assistance that enable churches to work together most effectively. Giving faithfully, generously, and sacrificially through these channels allows churches to have an impact on each Acts 1:8 mission field.

Go

Enable a growing number of members to directly participate in short-term, long-term, and marketplace opportunities to minister and spread the gospel beyond your church walls. Today the Internet, television, radio, and other media provide channels for disseminating the gospel message, and many churches and mission organizations use these tools effectively. However, Jesus' Acts 1:8 challenge states that individual Christians go as witnesses of Jesus Christ. Jesus commanded His witnesses to go (see Matt. 28:19; Acts 22:21), and the Holy Spirit directed the early churches to go (see Acts 8:29; 13:1-3). The New Testament believers' obedience in going to all four Acts 1:8 mission fields defined the church's evangelistic task for the first century and for the future (see Rom. 10:13-15).

The same is true of Jesus' Acts 1:8 witness today. God's witness in us is incarnate. That is, the Holy Spirit literally inhabits us and empowers us to personally bear witness of Jesus among the lost peoples of the world.

The world today is more accessible to more churches than ever. Through brief mission trips or longer volunteer missions efforts, groups and individuals can go to many places that their grandparents could only read about. And they can physically reach people their grandparents could reach only through prayer and missionary support. Churches can equip their members to go into the marketplace as missionaries, whether in corporate settings; in professions such as education, law, or medicine; or in industries such as media or entertainment. To reach the lost peoples of all Acts 1:8 mission fields—especially Jerusalem—churches must recognize that the marketplace is a key mission field.

I once attended a church's missions celebration that made me recognize the necessity of going to the lost people in every mission field. Church members and guest missionaries filled the church's auditorium. As the choir sang a majestic anthem about the supreme lordship of Jesus Christ, flags from all over the world were carried down the aisles. Volunteers who had gone on mission trips during the past year came forward and gathered around the

> **Your Church Can Go**
> Contact IMB, NAMB, or WMU to learn about pathways of direct involvement through mission trips or other volunteer efforts (see p. 142).

giving. Show the total amount of missions giving as a percentage of the total annual church receipts for the year.

18. Summarize the section "Go." Point out the avenues for sharing the gospel and for going to the world that were once unavailable. Ask a member to read Isaiah 6:1-8. Discuss the response the prophet made and the implications of the passage for our involvement in missions today.

19. Ask four members to hold up posters 8, 9, and 10. Discuss each statement. Have a member read Matthew 19:29.

flags of the countries they had visited. As they faced the congregation, a flag bearing the name of Jesus and a royal crown was brought down the middle aisle. When it reached the front of the auditorium, the other flags and the witnesses surrounding them bowed in reverence to this symbolic banner of Jesus their King.

A CHURCH ON MISSION

No Southern Baptist should be left out of missions participation. Through local and international strategies the leaders at First Baptist Church in Woodstock, Georgia, look for ways to plug every member into missions. "Missions is at the core of what this church is about," says Al McMillan, regional missions director at the church. "That is our heart."

In one year the church may participate in 40 to 50 mission trips. In the past the church has sent volunteer missions teams to India, Iraq, Iran, Thailand, Portugal, Russia, and Turkey. The church is equally active on local and national levels. One program reaches out to every home within a 5-mile radius, providing information

First Baptist Church in Woodstock, Georgia, reaches every home in a 5-mile radius and plans to reach even farther.

about the gospel and the church. The program has proved so successful that the church may soon expand its outreach to homes within 10 miles of the church.

The church supports many missions and outreach ministries through financial giving. It also uses a churchwide prayer strategy and Wednesday-night prayer gatherings to provide support for its various missions ministries. The church provides missions education through Grow classes, equipping members to participate in volunteer mission trips.

"Through such efforts church members pray that they can make a difference in their world for Christ," McMillan says. "Our ultimate goal is to find out where God is working and come along beside Him."[2]

20. Say: Let's stop and meet a Southern Baptist who obeyed Jesus' command to go. Lottie Moon went to China as a missionary in 1873, where she served until her death in 1912.[b] When she died, she weighed only 50 pounds; she had stopped eating in order to give food to the Chinese. In 1918 Southern Baptists' Lottie Moon Christmas Offering® for international missions was named in her memory. Introduce the member you enlisted before the session to present the dramatic monologue on page 151.

As I caught a faint glimpse of what worship in heaven must be like, I was moved not only by the symbolism of the ceremony but also by the volunteers' commitment to go and sacrificially invest their lives in God's redemptive mission. Those who had gone were grateful to those who had supported them. Those who had supported them were grateful for those who had gone. And all gratefully worshiped the King for whom the sacrifices had been made and who had taken the most sacrificial mission trip Himself by leaving His throne of glory to die on a cross. When we go to our ends of the earth, Samaria, Judea, or Jerusalem, we model Christlike love and obedience.

Read Isaiah 6:1-8. Write the response the prophet made to God in verse 8.

_____

Spend a few minutes thinking about short- and long-term opportunities to be involved in missions. Make Isaiah's response your prayer to God.

Tell

Involve an increasing number of members in intentional, culturally relevant evangelism. A church that is effective in going to its Acts 1:8 mission fields needs witnesses who are committed to telling God's story and their own stories of the difference God has made in their lives. Like the Apostle Paul, we should always be eager to share the truth of the gospel with everyone we meet (see Rom. 1:16; 1 Cor. 1:18-23). In Paul's letter to Philemon he wrote, "I pray that you may be active in sharing your faith, so that you will have a full understanding of every good thing we have in Christ" (Philem. 1:6, NIV). The implication of Paul's prayer is that we will have "a full understanding of every good thing we have in Christ" only when we are active in sharing our faith. A certain depth of Christian experience is realized only when we discover the joy of leading others to faith in Christ.

> **Your Church Can Tell**
> Check with IMB, NAMB, WMU, and LifeWay Christian Resources to discover tools to help your church train and involve members in personal evangelism and culturally relevant evangelistic strategies (see p. 142).

A church that embraces Jesus' Acts 1:8 challenge equips its members to share their faith and encourages them to do so through training, mentoring, accountability, and opportunities like these:
- Door-to-door witnessing and visitation
- Evangelistic events like block parties or sporting events
- Evangelistic ministries such as a food pantry or clothing ministry
- Evangelistic women's groups or men's groups
- Evangelistic groups or clubs for students on campus

21. Summarize the section "Tell." Call attention to the witnessing opportunities identified with bullets on page 136. Ask members to name other ways they can be involved in telling the good news of Jesus.
22. Ask a member to read Romans 10:12-14 and ask a member to hold up poster 11. Lead members to discuss the verse and the statement. Ask, Does Romans 10:14 say that only preachers can tell others about Christ?

As a church goes on mission, it frequently finds opportunities to meet human needs and relieve human suffering. Responding with compassion to these needs not only demonstrates Christlike character but also builds bridges of credibility and relationship across which the gospel message can flow. Christian compassion also dictates that we faithfully tell the gospel message.

As your church prepares for mission trips or projects in different cultures, you will want to get help from missionaries or other experts to learn how to make culturally relevant presentations of the gospel. Methods like storying can help cross language barriers, and evangelistic tools such as the *Jesus* video or *The Hope* video can help you communicate God's story across language or cultural barriers.[3]

Send

Provide opportunities for members to hear and respond to God's call to vocational missions service. An apostle is someone who has been divinely commissioned to bear witness of the risen Christ and to help establish new churches on sound doctrine. Today we also use the term *missionary* to designate someone who is sent. In 2 Corinthians 11:5-9 Paul reminded the Corinthian church that he didn't have to be an eloquent speaker or a paid staff member to be an effective missionary who served that church. Sent by the church in Antioch (see Acts 13:1-3), Paul was apparently being financially supported by other churches in Macedonia. As a result, he had been able to preach the gospel to the Corinthians free of charge.

Does your church consider missionaries to be superapostles who have extraordinary skills and qualifications but who probably don't come from your church? Or does your church regularly invite members called by God to serve Him on a mission field? A church's obedient response to Jesus' Acts 1:8 challenge is not only to support missionaries whom other churches send but also to send missionaries from its own body. These may be vocational missionaries who are paid through the Cooperative Program or other cooperative missions offerings, or they may be Mission Service Corps or International Service Corps missionaries who are self-funded or retired.

The missionary stereotype leads some churches to believe that their members do not qualify to go on mission. However, most missionaries are not superapostles but ordinary people who have received an extraordinary calling to go to a particular mission field, be a witness of Jesus Christ, and establish new churches on sound doctrine. Many Christians are surprised to discover how much today's mission fields need people just like them. God uses weak vessels in powerful ways, and the pathway to mission service often begins in our own congregation.

> **Your Church Can Send**
> Request resources from IMB, NAMB, or WMU that will teach your church the pathways of mission service and ways to nurture believers into vocational missions (see p. 142).

137

23. Summarize the section "Send." Define the terms *apostle* and *missionary*. Seek to dispel the myth that only superapostles can go on mission.
24. Ask two members to hold up posters 12 and 13. Lead members to explain these statements and to discuss their implications for your church.

Read 2 Corinthians 12:9. What is a biblical response to someone who says he or she is too weak to be involved in missions?

Multiply

Participate in church planting and facilitate church-planting movements.

In the New Testament we read that the number of believers and the number of churches rapidly multiplied (see Acts 14:21-28; 16:5; 2 Tim. 2:2). The same should occur today. As believers move into their Acts 1:8 mission fields, the number of disciples and churches should multiply.

A sad statistic is that only about 5 percent of Southern Baptist churches are actively involved in establishing new congregations.[4] At the same time, about two-thirds of U.S. Southern Baptist churches are plateaued or declining.[5] We may naturally think that churches should cluster inside their walls until they are strong enough to help start a new church or until circumstances are conducive to expansion. But the New Testament pattern does not support such an assumption. First-century churches were often small, poor, and persecuted, with uneducated and unorganized leaders. Most churches probably met in homes as small groups. Transportation was primitive, and technology didn't exist. Believers didn't have the written New Testament Scriptures, much less the wealth of Christian literature and resources available to churches today. Yet the churches multiplied many times over.

> **Your Church Can Multiply**
> Contact IMB, NAMB, your state convention, or your association to get resources on church planting and on facilitating church-planting movements (see p. 142).

To respond obediently and faithfully to Jesus' Acts 1:8 challenge, today's churches must go outside their walls, invest their lives in making disciples, and start new congregations. Our ends of the earth, our Samaria, our Judea, our Jerusalem—all mission fields need new churches. Can Christ be glorified by churches that choose the alternative to multiplication—atrophy and decline?

Consider ways your church can fulfill Jesus' Acts 1:8 challenge by planning your church's mission strategy around these eight biblical responses. The chart on page 139 summarizes the mission concepts and principles we have studied. It also provides blanks for identifying ways your church can apply the eight responses to all four Acts 1:8 mission fields.

Study the chart on page 139. In the blanks at the bottom of the chart, write at least one idea you or your church could take to reach each mission field.

---

25. Summarize the section "Multiply." Contrast the rapid multiplication of the early church with the plateauing and declining status of many Southern Baptist churches today.
26. Ask two members to hold up posters 14 and 15. Discuss the statements and their implications for our personal lives and the life of the church.

RESPONDING TO JESUS' ACTS 1:8 CHALLENGE

The Mission's Founder	God's history-long, worldwide mission is to redeem and reclaim the sin-enslaved peoples of the earth. Through the family of Abraham, the nation of Israel, Jesus, and the church, God has revealed Himself and restored relationships with those who come to Him in faith. One day the mission will end, but the fruit of the mission—eternal worshipers who reflect God's glory—will live forever.

The Mission's Fields

MISSION CONCEPTS	ENDS OF THE EARTH	SAMARIA	JUDEA	JERUSALEM
Calling	Starting	Strategizing	Strengthening	Staying
Cultures	People Groups	Population Segments	Religious Lost	Neighbors
Church Planting	Movements	Leaders	Support	Sacrifice
Cooperation	Giving	Knowing and Praying	Going	Living
Challenges	Rulers	Society	Self-Righteousness	Complacency

The Mission's Followers

Today's churches faithfully respond to Jesus' Acts 1:8 challenge when they prepare, learn, pray, give, go, tell, send, and multiply in their Jerusalem, Judea, Samaria, and ends of the earth. Churches work under the power and leadership of the Holy Spirit and in cooperation with other churches and Great Commission partners so that all peoples have an opportunity to hear the gospel, respond with faith in Christ, and participate in a New Testament fellowship of believers.

Responses to the Acts 1:8 Challenge	ENDS OF THE EARTH International	SAMARIA North America	JUDEA State or Province	JERUSALEM County, Community, or City
	Primary Partner: International Mission Board	Primary Partner: North American Mission Board	Primary Partner: Baptist State Convention	Primary Partner: Baptist Association
Prepare				
Learn				
Pray				
Give				
Go				
Tell				
Send				
Multiply				

27. Call attention to the chart on page 139. Divide members into four small groups and assign each group two of the responses at the bottom of the chart. Ask the groups to identify actions your church can take to go on mission to your ends of the earth, Samaria, Judea, and Jerusalem. Tell groups that ideas are provided in the boxes on pages 130–38, but encourage them to supply their own ideas. Allow time for group work and call for reports.

The International Mission Board and the North American Mission Board, in partnership with cooperating Baptist state conventions and associations, are working together to help local churches respond to Jesus' Acts 1:8 challenge. Contact information for these mission partners is provided on page 142. If your church would like personalized help in responding to the Acts 1:8 challenge, visit *www.actsone8.com* or call (800) 4 ACTS 18 (800-422-8718).

Jesus' Acts 1:8 challenge is for individual believers as well as for churches. Rate your personal involvement in the Acts 1:8 mission through the eight responses you have studied in this chapter. 1 = not involved; 3 = somewhat involved; 5 = very involved.

Prepare	1	2	3	4	5	Go	1	2	3	4	5
Learn	1	2	3	4	5	Tell	1	2	3	4	5
Pray	1	2	3	4	5	Send	1	2	3	4	5
Give	1	2	3	4	5	Multiply	1	2	3	4	5

Your Church's Responsibility to the Acts 1:8 Challenge

The following phrases challenge believers to accept the call to mission service.

Answer His call. God's call to be on mission with Him is not just for missionaries and pastors but for every witness who has had a life-changing encounter with the living Lord Jesus. That call requires that we leave our comfort zones and go to people throughout our Acts 1:8 mission fields, even when they are far away and are different from us. We are called into cultures of people who are separated from God by sin and who are separated from the gospel by barriers that churches are empowered and equipped to cross.

Tell His story. The story of Jesus' redemptive work on the cross and His death-conquering resurrection is the life-changing message that all people need to hear. The story of our changed lives is the story of Jesus' willingness to change every life that comes to Him in faith. We are not responsible for the way people respond to the gospel. However, we are responsible for telling His story.

Change your world. Answering His call and telling His story will inevitably result in changing the world around us, one life at a time. Changing our world is a costly, sacrificial task for local churches, which must cooperate with other churches to make an impact on their Acts 1:8 mission fields. The barriers at the ends of the earth, in Samaria, in Judea, and in Jerusalem are huge, but the Holy Spirit's power can overcome any barrier that stands between the lost peoples of the world and the gospel of Jesus Christ.

28. Review the session by calling attention to the teaching posters on the walls. Ask volunteers to read them and to comment on their meanings.
29. Issue a challenge based on the ideas in "Your Church's Responsibility to the Acts 1:8 Challenge" and "The Mission Accomplished." Urge members to take the Acts 1:8 challenge personally. Distribute copies of study sheet 5, "Acts 1:8 Commitment." Challenge members to commit to being an Acts 1:8 Christian by signing the sheet, carrying it in their Bibles, and implementing the commitments they make.

Are you ready to answer God's call to tell His story and change your world? Pray about becoming more involved in Jesus' Acts 1:8 mission. Then write one action you will take to get started. Ask God to help you follow through on your commitment.

The Mission Accomplished

Thousands of years ago God scattered sinful humankind at the tower of Babel, confounding their language so that people could not cooperate for sinful, self-aggrandizing purposes. Today, because of Jesus' sacrificial death, God is setting apart a people to Himself who will gather others from around the world to worship the Lord God and serve Him forever. Through His Word and the indwelling testimony of His Holy Spirit, God has given us a clear vision of His love for the world. Now He invites us to join Him on mission. And one day God's history-long, worldwide mission through His people will finally be fulfilled. Read the thrilling verses in the box at right.

> "After this I looked, and there was a vast multitude from every nation, tribe, people and language, which no one could number, standing before the throne and before the Lamb. They were robed in white with palm branches in their hands. And they cried out in a loud voice: 'Salvation belongs to our God, who is seated on the throne, and to the Lamb!'" **Revelation 7:9-10**

God deserves nothing less than the praise and adoration of every nation, tribe, people, and language. And this is exactly what He will receive for eternity. In the meantime, in the power of the Holy Spirit, the mission is ours to complete. As Paul wrote to the Corinthian church, "Everything is from God, who reconciled us to Himself through Christ and gave us the ministry of reconciliation: that is, in Christ, God was reconciling the world to Himself, not counting their trespasses against them, and He has committed the message of reconciliation to us" (2 Cor. 5:18-19). God committed the message of reconciliation to us—at the ends of the earth, in Samaria, in Judea, and in Jerusalem. May your church embrace the last earthly words of Jesus—His Acts 1:8 challenge—with new fervor and commitment from now until His glorious return.

---

[1]Oswald Chambers, *My Utmost for His Highest: An Updated Edition in Today's Language* (Grand Rapids: Discovery House Publishers, 1992), March 5.

[2]Appreciation is expressed to Shawn Hendricks, International Mission Board, for providing this account.

[3]The *Jesus* film is available from Jesus Video Project; 275 West Hospitality Lane, Suite 315; San Bernardino CA 92408; (888) JESUS36; *www.jesusvideoproject.com*. Order *The Hope* in DVD or VHS at (866) 407-NAMB or *www.namb.net/catalog*. DVDs can also be purchased at LifeWay Christian Stores.

[4]Research Team Statistics, North American Mission Board of the Southern Baptist Convention.

[5]Research Team Statistics, North American Mission Board of the Southern Baptist Convention.

Answers to matching activity on page 130: 1. b, 2. c, 3. a, 4. d
Answers to matching activity on page 131: 1. d, 2. b, c, f, 3. a, e

141

---

30. Show cel 18 and lead the group to pray the prayer together.

---

[a]Rick Warren, *The Purpose-Driven Life* (Grand Rapids: Zondervan, 2002), 281.
[b]A. Scott Moreau, ed., *Evangelical Dictionary of World Missions* (Grand Rapids: Baker Books, 2000), 658.

Contacting Your Acts 1:8 Mission Partners

The International Mission Board and the North American Mission Board, in partnership with cooperating Baptist state conventions and regional associations, are working together to equip churches to respond to Jesus' Acts 1:8 challenge. For personalized help in responding to the Acts 1:8 challenge, visit *www.actsone8.com* or call (800) 4 ACTS 18 (800-422-8718).

The International Mission Board

3806 Monument Avenue
P. O. Box 6767
Richmond, VA 23230-0767
(800) 999-3113
www.imb.org

The North American Mission Board

4200 North Point Parkway
Alpharetta, GA 30022-4176
(770) 410-6000
Mission projects, (800) 462-8657
www.namb.net

Your Baptist State Convention

Available from your pastor or church office or from the SBC Web site, *www.sbc.net* (click on SBC Search and then State Convention Directory)

Your Baptist Association

Available from your pastor or church office, from your state convention's Web site, or from the SBC Web site, *www.sbc.net* (click on SBC Search and then State Convention Directory, which also lists Baptist associations)

Woman's Missionary Union

Highway 280, East
100 Missionary Ridge
P.O. Box 830010
Birmingham, AL 35283-0010
(205) 991-8100
Customer service, (800) 968-7301
www.wmu.com

LifeWay Christian Resources

One LifeWay Plaza
Nashville, TN 37234
(615) 251-2000
Customer service, (800) 458-2772
www.lifeway.com

The Southern Baptist Convention

901 Commerce Street
Nashville, TN 37203-3699
(615) 244-2355
www.sbc.net

Leading a Group Study

This section contains suggestions for preparing to lead a group study of *The Acts 1:8 Challenge: Empowering the Church to Be on Mission*. Step-by-step suggestions for conducting each group session are included at the bottom of each page in chapters 1–6 of this book. Resources you will need for the study are provided on the pages following this introduction (pp. 146–76).

Advance Planning

1. Schedule the study for a time that allows as many people as possible to attend. A minimum of six 1½-hour sessions will be needed to complete this study.
2. Promote the study through your various church media.
3. Enlist five members to present dramatic monologues during sessions 1, 2, 3, 4, and 6. Make copies of the five monologues on pages 147–51 in this guide and give them to the enlisted members several weeks in advance. Ask them to read their monologues several times and to pray that God will help them capture the personalities of the missionaries and will speak to the heart of every group member.
4. No dramatic monologue is planned for session 5. Instead, consider enlisting your associational director of missions to speak for 15 to 20 minutes near the end of the session, covering these areas:
   - *The work of the association*. How many churches are in the association? What size churches compose the association? What ethnic congregations are represented in the association? What does an association of churches do? What are some ways churches work together in an association? What are some challenges the association faces?
   - *His work as a director of missions*. What is his background? How did he sense a call to be a director of missions? What is his typical weekly schedule?
   You will need to abbreviate the group activities in session 5 to give the director of missions ample time near the end of the session. If possible, arrange for your church to give him an honorarium to thank him for his work and for his participation in the session.

Gather Resources

The following checklists will help you gather resources. The session plans at the bottoms of the pages in chapters 1–6 provide instructions for using the resources.

Resources for All Sessions

☐ *Member books*. Obtain a copy of *The Acts 1:8 Challenge* (item 0-6331-9613-4, available from LifeWay Church Resources Customer Service or a LifeWay Christian Store) for each participant. Try to conduct registration and distribute books before the first session. Encourage members to read chapter 1 and to complete the learning activities before group session 1.

☐ *Media and supplies*. Obtain an overhead projector, a projection screen, large sheets of paper or a marker board, markers for the board and for the cels, felt-tip pens and large sheets of paper for small-group work, adding-machine tape for making sentence strips, poster board for making placards, three-by-five-inch cards, and tape.

☐ *Overhead cels*. The 18 cel masters in this guide (pp. 152–69) provide visual presentations of important points. Cels can be made from the masters on a copy machine, or you may prefer to build a computer presentation from the information on the masters.

☐ *Study sheets*. The five study-sheet masters in this guide (pp. 170–74) can be used to make copies for participants. The study sheets involve members in various activities that help them achieve the learning goals.

☐ *Teaching posters*. Sixty-six poster ideas are provided in this guide (pp. 175–76), 11 for each group session. Posters can be made on a computer or by copying the statements on poster board or large sheets of paper with a marker. An excellent poster size is 11 by 17 inches. Teaching posters create an attractive room environment, allow learning to begin as soon as the first person arrives, reinforce learning, and provide review. Mount the teaching posters in random order and at various angles around the room to attract learners' attention.

Resource for Sessions 2–5

❏ *Acts 1:8 visual.* You will need to create a large visual patterned on the chart on page 104. Select an 8-by-10-foot area on the front wall that can serve as a focal point for each session. Trim large sheets of paper to make the horizontal and vertical headings. Use 20 sheets of 11-by-17-inch lightweight paper to make the principles. Use the same color for all calling principles, another color for all cultures principles, and so on. The color coding will help reinforce learning. At the beginning of session 2, the visual should be blank except for the vertical headings along the left side and the horizontal headings across the top. The chart will be developed incrementally in sessions 2–5. For example, in session 2 you will add the principles that complete the ends-of-the-earth column, in session 3 you will add the principles that complete the Samaria column, and so on. As you prepare for sessions 2–5, consider photocopying page 104, cutting the chart apart, and practicing adding to the visual as you will construct it on the wall during the sessions.

Resources for Session 1

❏ Cels 1–6
❏ Teaching posters (p. 175)
❏ One copy of William Carey monologue (p. 147)
❏ Copies of your church bulletin or newsletter (p. 9)
❏ "The Creation" by James Weldon Johnson (p. 12)
❏ A 25-foot cord, clothespins or tape, and placards (p. 17)
❏ A long strip of colored cloth or paper (p. 22)

Resources for Session 2

❏ Cels 7–9
❏ Copies of study sheet 1, "How Can They Hear?" for all members
❏ Copies of study sheet 2, "Evangelism and Missions," for all members
❏ Teaching posters (p. 175)
❏ One copy of Adoniram Judson monologue (p. 148)

Resources for Session 3

❏ A large map of the holy land in the time of Christ (p. 55)
❏ A supply of newspapers and a variety of magazines for three small groups (p. 71)
❏ Cel 10
❏ Three copies of study sheet 3, "Living Water"
❏ Teaching posters (p. 175)
❏ One copy of Annie Armstrong monologue (p. 149)

Resources for Session 4

❏ A large map of your state (p. 77)
❏ Cels 11–12
❏ Teaching posters (p. 176)
❏ One copy of David Brainerd monologue (p. 150)

Resources for Session 5

❏ Cel 13
❏ Copies of study sheet 4, "Agree or Disagree?" for all members
❏ Teaching posters (p. 176)

Resources for Session 6

❏ Posters made from the quotations on page 146
❏ Detailed information about your church's giving to missions—how much money your church gives to missions each year through the Cooperative Program, associational missions, the Lottie Moon Christmas Offering® for international missions, the Annie Armstrong Easter Offering® for North American missions, the state missions offering, and other offerings such as gifts for mission trips and designated missions giving. Be prepared to show the total amount of missions giving as a percentage of the total church receipts for the year (p. 133).
❏ Cels 14–18
❏ Copies of study sheet 5, "Acts 1:8 Commitment," for all members
❏ Teaching posters (p. 176)
❏ One copy of Lottie Moon monologue (p. 151)

Preparing for Each Session

1. Review the chapter and the teaching suggestions at the bottoms of the pages in each chapter of this book. Make additional notes as needed. The teaching suggestions may require more time than the session allows. Select the activities that best meet the needs of your group.
2. Obtain and prepare the materials and resources you will need for the session activities.
3. Arrange the meeting room to create an atmosphere conducive to learning.
4. Pray for each group session and for each participant.
5. Evaluate each session afterward and identify ways to improve learning in the next session.

Teaching Tips

1. There is no substitute for prayerful, intensive study and preparation. Reading the entire book several times will give you a good foundation on which to build your teaching. Read all of the Scripture references in the book and complete the learning activities. Teaching ideas will come to you as you read; jot them down.

2. Arrive early to greet participants as they arrive. Start and stop on time.

3. Strongly encourage members not only to read each chapter but also to complete the learning activities. Completing these activities will reinforce learning and will help members apply what they study.

4. Try to create an atmosphere that helps everyone feel a sense of belonging. Be an encourager.

5. Be sensitive to the needs of the group. Be willing to adapt your teaching plans. Be flexible, but do not allow the discussion to wander. Keep the focus on the subject at hand.

6. Involve participants. Do not talk too much and do not be afraid of silence. Encourage members to share their insights, experiences, questions, and feelings.

7. Magnify the Bible as our source of authority. As directed in the leader plans for sessions 1–5, encourage members to memorize the five Great Commission passages during this study:

   Session 1: Acts 1:8   Session 4: Luke 24:47
   Session 2: Matthew 28:19-20   Session 5: John 20:21
   Session 3: Mark 16:15

8. Remember to open and close each session with prayer.

Answers to Study Sheet 4

You and the group may disagree with our responses that follow, and that's OK. Some of the statements are open to interpretation, and valid cases can be made for both positions.

1. *Disagree.* A church should give priority to fulfilling all of Jesus' Acts 1:8 command. A careful study of the Book of Acts shows that Jesus' followers were to implement His command simultaneously rather than sequentially.

2. *Disagree.* Of course, sometimes the statement could be true, but often it is just as difficult to reach people nearby as it is to reach people far away.

3. *Disagree.* Both are important, and one should not be put above the other.

4. *Disagree.* Both are important.

5. This is a tough one. We tend to *disagree* with the statement. Although a great deal of cooperation is in evidence (the Lottie Moon Christmas Offering® for international missions is a good example), there is also evidence of competition among churches.

6. *Disagree.* It is true that churches should seek to start new congregations, but to say that every church should start a new church in its community is not realistic.

7. This is another tough one. We tend to *agree* with the statement. As a general rule, a congregation for each language and culture group can reach more people, and the worship can be more indigenous. On the other hand, a congregation composed of different language and culture groups is a wonderful expression of Revelation 7:9-10.

8. *Disagree.* The Holy Spirit will help every church reach its community.

9. *Agree.* Amen and amen!

10. *Disagree.* For too long Christians have compartmentalized their lives.

11. *Agree.* Churches should focus on every person who needs to hear the gospel.

12. *Disagree.* This country needs many new churches. Serious commitment to the Great Commission will result in the creation of many new congregations.

Posters for Session 6

The following posters will be used to enhance session 6. Prepare the posters in advance and have members hold them up as directed in the group-study suggestions for session 6. Because the group-study suggestions refer to the posters by number, you will need to number each poster as indicated below.

1. "You are called into a partnership with Christ the King. In this partnership, you will become involved in His mission to reconcile a lost world to God." —Henry Blackaby and Avery Willis[1]

2. "The yearning of our Master's heart is that the world may know God."—Baker James Cauthen[2]

3. "Expect great things from God; attempt great things for God."—William Carey[3]

4. "The most glorious works of grace that have ever taken place have been in answer to prayer." —William Carey[4]

5. "Through prayer a church can span the barriers of distance, time, and spiritual opposition." —Nate Adams[5]

6. "Let us give ourselves to prayer till He ignites us with the flame of His love and scatters us as firebrands throughout the darkness of a lost world." —Robertson McQuilkin[6]

7. "If Jesus Christ be God and died for me, then no sacrifice can be too great for me to make for Him."—C. T. Studd[7]

8. "You belong to God. Your life, with every talent you possess, is His."—Baker James Cauthen[8]

9. "We have but one life to invest for God." —J. Christie Wilson Jr.[9]

10. "He is no fool who gives what he cannot keep to gain what he cannot lose."—Jim Elliot[10]

11. "May we announce, not only to North America but to every single nation on the face of the earth, that Jesus is Lord to the glory of God the Father." —Walter C. Kaiser Jr.[11]

12. "No generation has less excuse than ours if we do not do as He asks."—Ralph D. Winter[12]

13. "We need to become global Christians with a global vision, for we have a global God." —John R. W. Stott[13]

14. "Please pray that I'll be kept from useless side tracks."—Nate Saint[14]

15. "The unbreakable promise of the Lord Jesus to be with His servants to the end of the age is our unfailing source of strength." —Baker James Cauthen[15]

[1]Henry T. Blackaby and Avery T. Willis Jr., "On Mission with God," in Ralph D. Winter and Steven C. Hawthorne, eds., *Perspectives on the World Christian Movement* (Pasadena, CA: William Carey Library, 1999), 58.

[2]Jesse C. Fletcher, *Baker James Cauthen: A Man for All Nations* (Nashville: Broadman Press, 1977), 177.

[3]Timothy George, *Faithful Witness: The Life and Mission of William Carey* (Birmingham, AL: New Hope, 1991), 32.

[4]Ibid., E.53.

[5]Nate Adams, *The Acts 1:8 Challenge: Empowering the Church to Be on Mission* (Nashville: LifeWay Press, 2004), 132.

[6]Robertson McQuilkin, *The Great Omission: A Biblical Basis for World Evangelism* (Waynesboro, GA: Gabriel Publishing, 1984), 80.

[7]Norman Grubb, *C. T. Studd: Cricketer and Pioneer* (Fort Washington, PA: Christian Literature Crusade, 1933), 132.

[8]Baker James Cauthen, *Beyond Call,* comp. Genevieve Greer (Nashville: Broadman Press, 1973), 35.

[9]Paul Borthwick, *A Mind for Missions: 10 Ways to Build Your World Vision* (Colorado Springs: NavPress, 1987), 11.

[10]Elisabeth Elliot, *Shadow of the Almighty: The Life and Testament of Jim Elliot* (San Francisco: Harper, 1958), 247.

[11]Walter C. Kaiser Jr., "Israel's Missionary Call," in Winter and Hawthorne, *Perspectives,* 16.

[12]Ralph D. Winter, "Four Men, Three Eras, Two Transitions: Modern Missions," ibid., 261.

[13]John R. W. Stott, "The Living God Is a Missionary God," ibid., 9.

[14]Russell T. Hitt, *Jungle Pilot* (Grand Rapids: Discovery House Publishers, 1997), 77.

[15]Fletcher, *Baker James Cauthen,* 203.

William Carey

I am William Carey. I've never been one to talk about myself. My preference has always been to talk about my Savior and His great faithfulness. But I've been asked to share about my life.

When I was growing up in Paulerspury, England, my father was a teacher. Therefore, I learned to read at an early age and read the Scriptures from my earliest years. I also loved books of adventure, science, and history.

When I was 14, my parents assigned me as an apprentice to a shoemaker. Although I had been brought up in the Church of England, I did not have a personal relationship with Jesus Christ. Through the persistent witness of a fellow apprentice, I trusted Christ and was genuinely converted at age 18. I immediately began witnessing to my family and other acquaintances.

When I was 21, I became a bivocational pastor. A year later, I was baptized by immersion and became a Baptist. I thank God for the wonderful Baptist pastors who took me in and mentored me, helping me grow in the faith. During the next 10 years I continued to work as a cobbler while teaching night school in my home for village children and preaching on Sundays. I had married just before my 20th birthday, and times were hard for our growing family. We never had much money, and sometimes we had little food. I never went beyond elementary school myself, but I taught myself Latin, Greek, Hebrew, Italian, French, and Dutch.

I kept a map of the world before me in my shoe shop and a stack of books beside me. Reading *The Journal of Captain Cook's Last Voyage* had a profound influence on me; I wanted people everywhere to know Christ as Savior. *The Life and Diary of David Brainerd* by Jonathan Edwards also moved me very deeply. I also read of the missionary work of the Moravians. Once I stood at a ministers' meeting and proposed that we discuss the topic "The Duty of Christians to Attempt the Spread of the Gospel Among Heathen Nations." One of the senior ministers loudly proclaimed to me: "Young man, sit down. When God pleases to convert the heathen, He will do it without your aid or mine!" But I could not be stopped. The more

I studied and prayed, the more I knew that God wanted me to do something. I began to write my thoughts and convictions, which grew into a book to which I gave a very long title, but for you I will just call it "An Enquiry." The book articulated my conviction that the Great Commission is just as binding today as it was for the early churches. Unfortunately, many pastors and churches did not share my conviction.

During the spring meeting of our association in 1792, I was appointed to preach in a morning service. Realizing that God could use this moment to involve our churches in missions, I chose as my text Isaiah 54:2-3, which speaks of lengthening the cords and strengthening the stakes. Applying God's message for ancient Israel to the churches of my day, I poured my heart into the message and summarized by saying: "Expect great things from God; attempt great things for God." The next day our association of churches began making plans to form a Baptist society for propagating the gospel. I was thrilled!

One year after the formation of our mission society, I set sail for India with my wife and four children, along with two associates. The beginnings of our work in that vast country were plagued by difficulties and setbacks. Our five-year-old-son, Peter, died not long after we arrived, and two other children died later. My wife, Dorothy, grew depressed and sank into a severe mental condition. A tragic fire destroyed much of my translation work, and I had to start over. It took us seven years to win the first Hindu to faith in Christ.

But there were successes. God blessed our work. My colleagues and I translated the Bible into more than 30 Asian languages and compiled dictionaries of several languages. We started Serampore College to train church planters and evangelists. We formed more than 100 rural schools, 18 mission stations, and many churches.

I am now 73, and my life is drawing to a close. Whatever you may read or hear about me, please know that it is not what I have done; it is what Christ has done. "If I ever get to heaven, it must be owing to divine grace from first to last."

Based on Timothy George, *Faithful Witness: The Life and Mission of William Carey* (Birmingham, AL: New Hope, 1991).

Adoniram Judson

Good day. My name is Adoniram[1] Judson. I served as a missionary in Burma, now called Myanmar, a country near India. I was one of the first American missionaries overseas, the first one to Burma—a pioneer, you might say, and the first Baptist missionary from America.

I was born in Massachusetts, the first son of an American Congregationalist pastor. My parents provided a good learning environment for me, my brother, and my sister. My mother taught me to read when I was only three. I became an avid learner, and my father was very proud of my ability to learn. He instilled in me the ambition to be a great man. I pursued this goal as a young man, following worldly ambitions, to the grief of my parents. Now I realize that by *great man,* my father meant a great man for God to use. Although it took time for me to understand the difference, I whole-heartedly surrendered my life to God.

I studied to become the best preacher I could be. One day while reading an old sermon at the seminary, I was impressed by the statement that Christians are to go and tell the good news afar. Disturbed, I pondered the assertion for a long time. During a solitary walk in the woods, meditating and praying, feeling half inclined to forget about it, I clearly and powerfully heard Christ's command in my heart and mind: "Go into all the world and preach the gospel to the whole creation."[2]

Since then, in spite of discouragement, I endeavored to obey. My conviction was so strong that it motivated fellow students to embrace missions and the American Congregationalists to organize in support of foreign missions. Many churches joined in their effort. The first four ordained American missionaries and our wives sailed to India in 1812. God had called us to forsake all and follow Him.

After a long, long journey we arrived at Calcutta, India, where fellow missionaries received us. But soon after our arrival the authorities issued an order for us to return home. Missionaries were no longer welcome in India. Several times we had to change plans, separate, move, and even hide to remain in the country.

During that time some of us became convicted that infant baptism is not scriptural. Our conviction led us to be baptized by immersion, embracing Baptist doctrine. By forsaking our former creed, we forfeited our support as Congregational missionaries. We hoped that Baptists in America would decide to support their first missionaries abroad even though they had not sent us, and they indeed began supporting us in time.

With no place to go and persecuted by the authorities, my wife and I took the only boat available to Burma. The city was a place few outsiders dared to go. Its ruler was a very cruel man who did not like foreigners. Unjust imprisonment, torture, and death were common under his rule, but because 17 million people were lost in darkness without God's Word to guide them, I knew God had sent me there.

We took time to get acquainted with the people and learn the language. When the time was right, my work to translate the Bible into Burmese began.

After six years teaching from a *zayat,* a small, three-walled house for teachers to teach or preach, we had our first convert. However, as soon as portions of the Bible were translated, we gave copies to the people, and they started to come, asking to hear more about Jesus.

We suffered persecution, illness, imprisonment, and physical and emotional strain. We fought discouragement, deprivation, frustration, and loss, but it was worthwhile. After 39 years the entire Bible had been translated into Burmese. More than seven thousand Burmese were Christians, thanks to the power of God's Word and the sustenance of our great and mighty God.

Missions is a matter of the heart. It starts in the heart of God, from which His love pours to all people. Don't forget that, my friends!

---

[1]Pronounced *add-uh-NIGH-rum.*

[2]Mark 16:15.

Based on Courtney Anderson, *To the Golden Shore* (Boston: Little, Brown, & Company, 1956).

Annie Armstrong

Thank you so much for inviting me to visit with you. I am delighted to know of your interest in missions. You see, missions has been the passion of my life.

My name is Annie Walker Armstrong. For a long time I served as the correspondent secretary of Woman's Missionary Union, Auxiliary to the Southern Baptist Convention. For years I had to answer the question that many people asked: Why is North American missions needed when there are so many people in other nations who have never heard the gospel? Well, there are two ways to do missions: you go, or God brings people to you. We must not focus on one and neglect the other. In my case, God gave me a heart for those around me.

I was born in 1850 to a privileged Baltimore family. Because my siblings and I lost our father when I was two, our mother reared us. She was a strong Christian woman of prayer who was very involved in church and charity work. We attended a church that loved missions and encouraged women's work at a time when not all churches did, so I became acquainted with missions very early. Baltimore was an ideal place for missions, for the city was the open door to hundreds of immigrants who came to our shores, as well as the home to many African-Americans who had been freed from slavery.

I became a believer at 20. Before, I had been a free spirit who wanted nothing to tie me down. When I became a believer who tasted true freedom, I began to search for God's purpose for my life. I needed to get busy. I rejoiced when my church appointed me as a Sunday School teacher for infants, when I became involved in the women's missionary group at church, and when I started helping at a nearby orphanage. I was interested in every avenue of service.

When I heard about the pressing needs and conditions of Native Americans, I was moved. I was touched by the needs of immigrants and African-Americans who had no money, no work, and no acquaintances. Efforts to help were sporadic and unorganized. God gave me a vision of the results we could achieve if we organized and combined resources. We could start with the churches in Baltimore, then Maryland, and then all southern states. All Southern Baptists should be involved! We started with the churches in our area, organizing into groups to pray for North American missions and to give money for its support.

In 1882 the Woman's Baptist Home Mission Society of Maryland was organized, and I was appointed as its first president. Soon we organized Mission Rooms in Baltimore to create and distribute information about missions. We created and published literature, publications, and periodicals. Eventually, we were filling orders to Canada and 31 states and territories.

In 1888, with 32 representatives of 10 states, Woman's Missionary Union (WMU) was organized, and I was appointed as its first corresponding secretary. Giving equal emphasis and support to North American and international missions, WMU helped the Southern Baptist Convention's missions agencies by praying for missions, giving to support missions, and learning about missions work. The mission boards distributed the money that WMU encouraged church members to give.

Before I go, I have to mention my favorite projects. First, we organized a week of self-denial for prayer and giving in the spring, which we later called the Easter week of prayer and offering for home missions. Second, a Christmas week of prayer and offering for international missions was suggested by Lottie Moon. I suggested that we call it the Lottie Moon Christmas Offering®, in honor of the great pioneer missionary in China. Third, I was always writing to stimulate giving, to encourage missionaries and their families, and to stir women to support Southern Baptist missions work.

I believe Malachi 3:10. God will open the stores of blessings from heaven to pour on His children when we give from love. Love in our hearts is the fuel to tell everyone that Jesus loves us so much.

Based on Bobbie Sorrill, *Annie Armstrong: Dreamer in Action* (Nashville: Broadman Press, 1984).

David Brainerd

I am most unworthy to speak about my life, but I will attempt to share with you God's works of grace.

There were 12 of us at home in Connecticut during my early years. My father died when I was 9, and my mother died when I was 14. When I was 21, I was gloriously saved, and I dedicated my life to serving God. Two months later I entered Yale University, but school was difficult for me, for I found little spirituality there. The next year I became ill and had to go home. I returned to Yale in the fall of 1740 and found it a different place altogether. George Whitefield, the great preacher from England, had been there, and a spiritual awakening had ignited the campus. But to my dismay I found that the faculty and staff discouraged revival and prayer meetings. When I remarked about one of the teachers, "He has no more grace than this chair," I was expelled and was never allowed to finish school.

Praying about what to do with my life, I became burdened for the Native Americans of my home state and the surrounding states. They were precious souls for whom Christ died, but no one was telling them about His great love and salvation. Sponsored by a society in Scotland, I became a missionary to the Native Americans.

I preached to the Native Americans in New York near the border of Massachusetts and spent one year with them, but I saw few results. Next I labored with the Native Americans in Pennsylvania for a year, again with few results. Then I moved to New Jersey and began my ministry there. Oh, how God blessed! Within a year there were 130 believers, adults as well as children. But my weary body would not sustain me. Growing very weak and ill, I had to say good-bye to my Native American brothers and sisters.

Most of my life I have been weak and scarcely able to do much at all. But oh, the sweetness and comfort I find in prayer. I treasure the time I spend alone with God and then recording in my diary the thoughts of my heart. I long to "spend and be spent for God."

Based on Jonathan Edwards, *The Life and Diary of David Brainerd* (Grand Rapids: Baker Book House, 1989).

Lottie Moon

The ship is sailing off the coast of my beloved China, the home of my heart for 39 years. My life is almost spent, and I am left with the indescribable peace of having given it to my Savior and Lord. My only regret is having only one life to place at His feet.

My name is Charlotte Digges Moon, but people call me Lottie. I was born in 1840 to a Virginia family of privilege. For 39 years I have been a missionary to China. As a child and young woman, I was blessed to receive the best education, far beyond most women of my time.

It took me a while to become a Christian. In my youth I was skeptical, even sarcastic, about the claims of Christianity. One day a revival for students was held in the city where I was studying. I did not know that my friends were praying for me that day, but God touched my heart, and I surrendered my life to Him.

As a new Christian I became concerned about Christ's purpose for my life. Romans 12:1 echoed in my heart. As a Sunday School teacher and an assistant to the pastor, I visited the sick and the poor, but my heart was not satisfied. When I heard about the need for missionaries in China, I wanted to go there. But at that time Southern Baptists were not appointing single women as missionaries. Discouraged, I began teaching in schools for girls and young women. But a breakthrough came in 1872, when my sister was appointed as an assistant to a missionary in China. In 1873 the Foreign Mission Board appointed me as a missionary to China.

After weathering a fierce storm on the way, we arrived at Tungchow in northern China. The missionary work in China was difficult. My sister and I had to adjust to unclean living quarters while enduring the hardships of a primitive, dangerous place that was not fond of strangers. I started to work right away, learning the language and the culture; accompanying the missionaries to villages, streets, and homes; and sharing the gospel with everyone who would listen. Curious people, especially women and children, gathered around us everywhere. When I learned the language well enough, we started schools. During the day we taught at the schools; after school we continued our missionary work. Every day we worked to exhaustion. Many Chinese women came to hear about Jesus until late at night, and I could not turn them away.

In 1885 I left Tungchow and went inland to Pingtu, a highly populated region where no foreigner had ever been. When my fellow missionary got sick and could not work anymore, I remained and worked alone. I adopted the Chinese way of dressing, eating, and sleeping in mud beds, which helped me get closer to the people. I learned to respect the Chinese culture and people and to love them deeply. Jesus died for them too.

We needed more missionaries, but none were available. Missionaries in Pingtu were constantly exposed to extreme weather, fatigue, contagious diseases, and mob attacks. I saw many of them, including my sister, break under the physical and psychological strain. In spite of the hard work and suffering, it was wonderful to see many churches planted in Pingtu and, in time, to see them led by native pastors and leaders. When my age prevented me from traveling from village to village, I returned to Tungchow to run the schools and to teach the Chinese women who gathered at my home. Some traveled a long distance to hear about Jesus.

I constantly wrote to the Foreign Mission Board, pleading for it to send more missionaries to China. I suggested that the Woman's Missionary Union set aside Christmas week for sacrificial giving to international missions so that more missionaries could be sent.

In 1912 war broke out. The revolution, the destruction of crops, and economic inflation were followed by severe famine. My heart broke for the Chinese. Their suffering was great, and I could not refuse the ones who came to my door for food and shelter. My heart's passion still burned inside me like the burning bush in the desert. "Present your bodies as a living sacrifice"[1] still echoed in my heart. Isn't that what Christ called us to do, just as He did?

O Lord, remember me! I will be among the crowd of those who greet you in Chinese.

---

[1] Romans 12:1.

Based on Catherine B. Allen, *The New Lottie Moon Story* (Nashville: Broadman Press, 1980).

The Acts 1:8 Challenge

The Mission's Founder

1. Famous Last Words:
   Jesus' Acts 1:8 Challenge

The Mission's Fields

2. A New Worldview:
   Your Church's Ends of the Earth

3. The Lost Continent:
   Your Church's Samaria

4. A State of Concern:
   Your Church's Judea

5. The World Next Door:
   Your Church's Jerusalem

The Mission's Followers

6. Embrace the Challenge:
   Your Church on Mission

Jesus Issues the Challenge

"You will receive power when the Holy Spirit has come upon you, and you will be My witnesses in Jerusalem, in all Judea and Samaria, and to the ends of the earth."

Acts 1:8

Goals for Our Study

- To understand Jesus' Acts 1:8 challenge to share the good news with the world

- To learn ways the early churches reached their ends of the earth, Samaria, Judea, and Jerusalem

- To identify spiritual needs in our modern-day ends of the earth, Samaria, Judea, and Jerusalem

- To develop a missions strategy for reaching our ends of the earth, Samaria, Judea, and Jerusalem

- To become more involved, as individuals and as a church, in God's worldwide redemptive mission

Dear God, please help us see the world as You see it and to love it as You love it. Use this study to challenge us, to motivate us, and to involve us in your redemptive mission. In Jesus' name. Amen.

Jesus' Last Words Continue God's Old Testament Purpose

- God's Glory Radiating

- God's Creation Reflecting

- God's People Rebelling

- God's Love Reaching

- God's People Revealing

- God's People Resisting

Jesus' Last Words Communicate God's New Testament Purpose

- God's Son Restoring

- God's Church Receiving

- God's Church Radiating

- God's Redeemed Responding

Are You a Missionary?

A missionary is someone who, in response to God's call and gifting, leaves his or her comfort zone and crosses cultural, geographic, or other barriers to proclaim the gospel and live out a Christian witness in obedience to the Great Commission.

The Holy Spirit Directs and Empowers Churches

- The Holy Spirit calls out missionaries.

- The Holy Spirit communicates God's heart.

- The Holy Spirit leads churches where He is already at work.

- The Holy Spirit carries out God's plan.

Mission Concepts

- Calling
- Cultures
- Church Planting
- Cooperation
- Challenges

Jesus' Great Commission in Matthew

"Go, therefore, and make disciples of all nations, baptizing them in the name of the Father and of the Son and of the Holy Spirit, teaching them to observe everything I have commanded you. And remember, I am with you always, to the end of the age."

Matthew 28:19-20

Jesus' Great Commission in Mark

"Go into all the world and preach the gospel to the whole creation."

Mark 16:15

Jesus' Great Commission in Luke

"Repentance for forgiveness of sins would be proclaimed in His name to all the nations, beginning at Jerusalem."

Luke 24:47

Barriers in the Judea Mission Field

- Self-Serving Religion
- False Security
- Cultural Christianity

Jesus' Great Commission in John

"As the Father has sent Me, I also send you."

John 20:21

Mission

Making Jesus Christ known
among all peoples

Vision

Leading Southern Baptists
to be on mission with God to bring
all the peoples of the world to
a saving faith in Jesus Christ

NORTH AMERICAN MISSION BOARD

Mission

The North American Mission Board exists to proclaim the gospel of Jesus Christ, start New Testament congregations, minister to persons in the name of Christ, and assist churches in the United States and Canada in effectively performing these functions.

Your Church's Response to the Acts 1:8 Challenge

- Prepare
- Learn
- Pray
- Give
- Go
- Tell
- Send
- Multiply

Praying for Missions

- Pray for a kingdom perspective.

- Pray for unevangelized peoples.

- Pray for missionaries.

- Pray for workers for the harvest.

- Pray for boldness and opportunities to share the gospel.

- Pray in the contexts of your church's ends of the earth, Samaria, Judea, and Jerusalem.

A Prayer for the Mission

O loving Father,
"This is eternal life:
that they may know You,
the only true God,
and the One You have sent—Jesus Christ."

John 17:3

Use us, we pray, to make Thee known, to tell the gospel story by life and word, each one of us in just that place where needed most.

And help us send the good news on beyond us with all our energies, until the very last person on earth has a chance to hear—even now in our own day.

Let this be our passion, we pray in Jesus' name.
Amen.

Winston Crawley, *Global Mission: A Story to Tell: An Interpretation of Southern Baptist Foreign Missions* (Nashville: Broadman Press, 1985), 354.

How Can They Hear?

Nations will come to your light,
and kings to the brightness
of your radiance.

As the Father has sent Me, I also send you.

There is no Jew or Greek, slave or free, male or female; for you are all
one in Christ Jesus.

Everyone who calls on the name of the Lord will be saved.

But how can they call on Him in whom they have not believed?

And how can they believe without hearing about Him?

And how can they hear without a preacher? And how can they preach
unless they are sent?

**Now everything is from God, who reconciled us to Himself through
Christ and gave us the ministry of reconciliation: that is, in Christ, God
was reconciling the world to Himself, not counting their trespasses
against them, and He has committed the message of reconciliation to us.**

Therefore, we are ambassadors for Christ; certain that God is appealing
through us, we plead on Christ's behalf, "Be reconciled to God."

Isaiah 60:3; John 20:21; Galatians 3:28; Romans 10:13-15; 2 Corinthians 5:18-20

Evangelism and Missions

Read the following statement from "The Baptist Faith and Message" and respond to the questions.

It is the duty and privilege of every follower of Christ and of every church of the Lord Jesus Christ to endeavor to make disciples of all nations. The new birth of man's spirit by God's Holy Spirit means the birth of love for others. Missionary effort on the part of all rests thus upon a spiritual necessity of the regenerate life, and is expressly and repeatedly commanded in the teachings of Christ. The Lord Jesus Christ has commanded the preaching of the gospel to all nations. It is the duty of every child of God to seek constantly to win the lost to Christ by verbal witness undergirded by a Christian lifestyle, and by other methods in harmony with the gospel of Christ.[1]

1. What is the difference between evangelism and missions? _____

_____

2. How would you answer someone who says that it is arrogant and antagonistic to impose the gospel of Christ on other peoples who already have religions?

_____

3. What can one follower of Christ realistically expect to do in discipling all nations? _____

_____

4. What are some examples from the New Testament in which the new birth resulted in the birth of love for others?

_____

5. What is the relationship between a verbal witness and a Christian lifestyle? _____

_____

6. What are some other methods that can be used to win the lost to Christ? _____

_____

_____
[1]*The Baptist Faith and Message* (Nashville: LifeWay Christian Resources of the Southern Baptist Convention, 2000), 16.

Living Water

Narrator: Jesus left Judea and went again to Galilee. He had to travel through Samaria, so He came to a town of Samaria called Sychar near the property that Jacob had given his son Joseph. Jacob's well was there, and Jesus, worn out from His journey, sat down at the well. It was about six in the evening. A woman of Samaria came to draw water.

Jesus: Give Me a drink.

Woman: How is it that You, a Jew, ask for a drink from me, a Samaritan woman?

Jesus: If you knew the gift of God, and who is saying to you, "Give Me a drink," you would ask Him, and He would give you living water.

Woman: Sir, You don't even have a bucket, and the well is deep. So where do you get this "living water"? You aren't greater than our father Jacob, are you? He gave us the well and drank from it himself, as did his sons and livestock.

Jesus: Everyone who drinks from this water will get thirsty again. But whoever drinks from the water that I will give him will never get thirsty again—ever! In fact, the water I will give him will become a well of water springing up within him for eternal life.

Woman: Sir, give me this water so I won't get thirsty and come here to draw water.

Jesus: Go call your husband and come back here.

Woman: I don't have a husband.

Jesus: You have correctly said, "I don't have a husband," for you've had five husbands, and the man you now have is not your husband. What you have said is true.

Woman: Sir, I see that You are a prophet. Our fathers worshiped on this mountain, yet you Jews say that the place to worship is in Jerusalem.

Jesus: Believe Me, woman, an hour is coming when you will worship the Father neither on this mountain nor in Jerusalem. You Samaritans worship what you do not know. We worship what we do know, because salvation is from the Jews. But an hour is coming, and is now here, when the true worshipers will worship the Father in spirit and truth. Yes, the Father wants such people to worship Him. God is spirit, and those who worship Him must worship in spirit and truth.

Woman: I know that Messiah is coming. When He comes, He will explain everything to us.

Jesus: I am He, the One speaking to you.

Narrator: Just then His disciples arrived, and they were amazed that He was talking with a woman. Yet no one said, "What do You want?" or "Why are You talking with her?" Then the woman left her water jar, went into town, and told the men, "Come, see a man who told me everything I ever did! Could this be the Messiah?" They left the town and made their way to Him. In the meantime the disciples kept urging Jesus to eat something.

Jesus: I have food to eat that you don't know about. My food is to do the will of Him who sent Me and to finish His work. Don't you say, "There are still four more months, then comes the harvest"? Listen to what I'm telling you: Open your eyes and look at the fields, for they are ready for harvest. The reaper is already receiving pay and gathering fruit for eternal life, so the sower and reaper can rejoice together. For in this case the saying is true: "One sows and another reaps." I sent you to reap what you didn't labor for; others have labored, and you have benefited from their labor.

Narrator: Now many Samaritans from that town believed in Him because of what the woman said when she testified, "He told me everything I ever did." Therefore, when the Samaritans came to Him, they asked Him to stay with them, and He stayed there two days. Many more believed because of what He said. And they told the woman, "We no longer believe because of what you said, for we have heard for ourselves and know that this really is the Savior of the world."

John 4:1–42

Agree or Disagree?

Indicate whether you agree or disagree with each statement by marking it A (agree) or D (disagree).

____ 1. A church should give priority to reaching its own community for Christ rather than places far away.

____ 2. It is easier to reach our own community for Christ than to reach a place far away.

____ 3. The church gathered in worship is more important than the church scattered throughout the community sharing Christ.

____ 4. Evangelism is more important than discipleship.

____ 5. Churches today are characterized more by cooperation than by competition.

____ 6. Every church should seek to start a new church in its community to reach the lost.

____ 7. A church should not try to assimilate believers from different language groups and cultures but should begin separate congregations for them.

____ 8. A large church can reach its community more effectively than a small church can.

____ 9. Participating in God's mission is not just an occasional activity but is 24 hours a day, 7 days a week.

____ 10. Christians should compartmentalize their lives into sacred and secular and not mix the two.

____ 11. A church should focus on people who may never enter the church building.

____ 12. Most communities in this country are overchurched.

Acts 1:8 Commitment

Check each statement that represents a commitment you are willing to make.
Keep this sheet in your Bible to remind you of your commitment.

I commit to carry out Jesus' Acts 1:8 challenge
by taking one or more of the following actions.

❑ I will pray regularly for the lost people at the ends of the earth.

❑ I will pray regularly for the lost people in North America.

❑ I will pray regularly for the lost people in my state.

❑ I will pray regularly for the lost people in my community.

❑ I will pray for missionaries in the four Acts 1:8 mission fields.

❑ I will tell others about Jesus.

❑ I will go on mission to one or more of the Acts 1:8 mission fields.

❑ I yield my life to God for Him to use in any way He desires.
My prayer is "Here I am. Send me" (Isa. 6:8).

Signed _____ Date _____

Teaching–Poster Ideas

Chapter 1

We need to see in terms of eternity.

God is a seeking, loving God.

"The Son of Man has come to seek and to save the lost" (Luke 19:10).

Worshiping God means acknowledging His great worth.

God's love for lost people is active and relentless.

Jesus is the center of God's redemptive plan.

Everything we do should be for God's glory.

The Great Commission is given to every follower of Jesus.

Every church has a Jerusalem, Judea, Samaria, and world responsibility.

God has committed the message of reconciliation to us.

In today's world many lost people still wait to hear the message.

Chapter 2

The Great Commission is a supernatural task and requires supernatural power.

The Holy Spirit still calls out missionaries.

The Holy Spirit directed the missionary activity of the early churches.

Redeeming the lost peoples of the world is God's mission.

God calls us to join Him in His redemptive mission.

Every people group deserves the opportunity to hear the gospel in its own language.

God deserves the praise of every tribe, tongue, and people.

The Holy Spirit's main work is to make disciples of Jesus.

First-century churches gave sacrificially.

No place and no people group are beyond the reach of Jesus' Great Commission.

The Holy Spirit continues to speak to the church today.

Chapter 3

The families of our Samaria are thirsty for the gospel.

God doesn't show favoritism.

Our Samaria is the North American continent.

Even nearby people can be far away from the gospel.

The church must bridge racial, ethnic, religious, and socioeconomic barriers.

North America is a melting pot of religious practices and secular options.

Missions education encourages missions cooperation.

Samaria is a nearby place we rarely visit.

Seven of 10 people in North America do not have a personal relationship
with Jesus Christ.

North America is becoming increasingly ethnic and multicultural.

Does our church see its Samaria as Jesus sees it?

Chapter 4

Judea represents our state or region.

Works and goodness do not earn God's acceptance.

The Holy Spirit uses short-term mission trips to cultivate lifelong missions commitment.

People in our Judea are in many ways like us.

Christianity is a life-giving relationship with God, not a legalistic religion.

Much of our Judea mission field is unreached.

One Canadian Southern Baptist church exists for every 151,338 people.

Compassionate ministry can earn credibility to share the gospel.

The more churches impact their Judea mission field with the gospel, the more
they can expect opposition.

Sometimes our Judea is surrounded by the thick walls of false religious security.

Our mission to Judea is often a mission within the same culture.

Chapter 5

Our Jerusalem mission field is the community where we live.

Our Jerusalem calls for us to continually reach out with the good news.

Who in our community does not know Jesus?

What will be required to communicate the gospel to the lost people in our Jerusalem?

Churches must work cooperatively to evangelize their Jerusalem.

Reaching our Jerusalem requires as much intentionality as the mission fields of
Judea, Samaria, and the ends of the earth.

Most of us travel through our Jerusalem every day.

Our Jerusalem mission field serves as a training ground.

Our Jerusalem needs acts of sacrificial service.

Participation in God's mission is daily and local.

A church that is intent on reaching its Jerusalem focuses on people who may
never enter the church building.

Chapter 6

Every church should be a worldwide missions center.

A church's primary, most urgent mission is beyond the walls of its building.

God is calling us to leave our comfort zones and help take the gospel to the world.

The Holy Spirit gives us all we need to overcome any challenge.

God deserves nothing less than the praise and adoration of every nation, tribe,
people, and language.

Fulfilling God's mission to the world is the frontline of battle in spiritual warfare.

Jesus' Acts 1:8 challenge is a biblical way to express God's love for the world.

Churches need an ongoing awareness about God's redemptive activity in the
world's mission fields today.

Through prayer Christians can be involved anywhere in God's mission.

Churches combine their resources to spread the gospel.

The marketplace is a key mission field.